350-3
6

Also by Staughton Lynd

Labor Law for the Rank & Filer, Revised edition, 1982, Singlejack
Books

Rank and File: Personal Histories by Working-Class Organizers,
Edited with Alice Lynd, Second edition, 1981, Princeton University Press

Intellectual Origins of American Radicalism, Second edition, 1982,
Harvard University Press

The Fight Against Shutdowns

Youngstown's Steel Mill Closings

Staughton Lynd

Singlejack Books
San Pedro • 1982

The author gratefully acknowledges permission to reproduce:
Quotations reprinted from *Business Week*, Jan. 9 and Dec. 18, 1978, by special permission, © 1982 by McGraw-Hill, Inc., New York, NY 10020. All rights reserved.
The map on page xiii, and a portion of the article by Thomas J. Brazaitis, Mar. 30, 1979, from *The Cleveland Plain Dealer*.
Text and Table from *The New York Times*, Apr. 15, 1978, Jan. 2, 1981, and Aug. 17, 1981, © 1978/81 by The New York Times Company. Reprinted by permission.
Quotations from the issues of July 24, 1972, June 5, and Dec. 31, 1979, July 22, 1980, and May 5, 1981, reprinted by permission of *The Wall Street Journal*, © Dow Jones & Co., Inc., 1972, 1979, 1980, 1981. All rights reserved.
Portions of the Open Letter to President Carter from *The Washington Post*, Sept. 15, 1978.

John Barbero at the rally of 17 March 1979.
Photo by Greg Klink.

This book is dedicated to the memory of
JOHN BARBERO
1924–1981

CONTENTS

Acknowledgments

Bob Miles and Stan Weir, founders of Singlejack Books, were the first of several persons to suggest that this story deserved its history. Stan wrote to me in February 1978: "A journal should be kept starting now, even if only for one half hour a day, so that a legitimate history can be written."

The pictures in this book were taken by two professional photographers, Rob Engelhart and Steve Ilko of the *Warren Tribune*, and three steelworkers, Greg Klink, Steve Clancy, and Sam Myers. All made their photographs available free of charge.

Carol Greenwald and Dorie Krauss are making a documentary film on the steel mill shutdowns in the Mahoning Valley to be called *Shout Youngstown!* They generously provided transcripts of a number of tape recorded interviews.

The editors of *Democracy* and *Radical America* published draft versions of the Conclusion, and in the process, helped me to state the ideas of that part of the book more clearly.

A number of persons read the manuscript in various drafts. The following offered particularly detailed and incisive criticism: Ken Doran, formerly of Local 1462, United Steelworkers of America (Brier Hill Works); Bob Clyde and Jim Callen, fellow attorneys at Northeast Ohio Legal Services; Reverends Ed Weisheimer and Chuck Rawlings of the Ecumenical Coalition; Carol Greenwald; Ann Markusen of the Department of City and Regional Planning, University of California at Berkeley; Roger Hickey of the National Center for Economic Alternatives; Laurien Alexandre; Agis Salpukas of the *New York Times*; John Greenman of the *Warren Tribune*; and my son Lee.

As the footnotes seek to make clear, much that is set forth in the following pages is based on the persistent investigative reporting of three local journalists: Dale Peskin, first at the *Youngstown Vindicator* and later at the *Warren Tribune*; and John Greenman and Greg Garland at the *Warren Tribune*.

Thus this book owes a great deal to many persons, and is to some degree a collective product. At the same time, I alone am responsible for the facts and interpretations presented.

During the fifteen months in which I was writing *Shutdown* I came to have a deeper understanding of what is described in the text as "brown-field" development. My mother Helen Lynd was no longer able to live alone in New York City. My wife Alice and I struggled to make it possible for my mother to live with us in Niles. At the same time that I was writing about the desirability of modernizing industry in sites where it already exists, I was trying to find a way for three generations of my own family to live, and mutually support one another, in the same place. I should like to thank my wife and mother, not only for their helpful reactions to the manuscript as it was read aloud at our kitchen table, but more profoundly for being part of the search for community which this book is about.

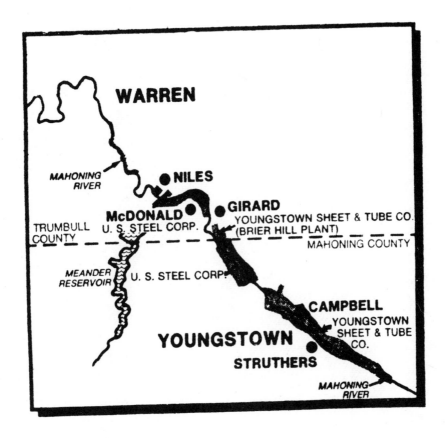

The Mahoning Valley

Cast of Characters

GORDON ALLEN. Superintendent of Jones & Laughlin Steel operations in the Mahoning Valley

GAR ALPEROVITZ. Economist and head of the National Center for Economic Alternatives, author of the principal feasibility study on reopening the Campbell Works

LEN BALLUCK. Grievance committeeman for the open hearths at the Campbell Works, and co-chairperson of Steelworkers United for Employment

JOHN BARBERO. Vice president of Local 1462, United Steelworkers of America, representing production and maintenance workers at the Brier Hill Works

RUSS BAXTER. President of Local 2163, United Steelworkers of America, representing production and maintenance workers at the steelmaking end of the Campbell Works

GRIFFIN BELL. Attorney General of the United States, who permitted the merger of the Lykes and LTV conglomerates without attaching conditions

RENO DEPIETRO. President of Local 1307, United Steelworkers of America, representing production and maintenance workers at the McDonald Works

GERALD DICKEY. Recording secretary of Local 1462, United Steelworkers of America, representing production and maintenance workers at the Brier Hill Works

KEN DORAN. Active rank and file member of Local 1462, employed in the test lab at the Brier Hill Works

THOMAS GRAHAM. Chief executive officer of Jones & Laughlin Steel

ROBERT HALL. Head of the Economic Development Administration of the United States Department of Commerce

DUANE IRVING. Vice president of Local 1418, United Steelworkers of America, representing production and maintenance workers at the finishing end of the Campbell Works

WILLIAM KIRWAN. Superintendent of United States Steel's Youngstown Works

THOMAS LAMBROS. Judge of the United States District Court for the Northern District of Ohio

FRANK LESEGANICH. District Director of District 26, United Steelworkers of America

JAMES MALONE. Bishop of the Youngstown Diocese of the Roman Catholic Church

ED MANN. President of Local 1462, United Steelworkers of America, representing production and maintenance workers at the Brier Hill Works

PAUL MARSHALL. Steel analyst

LLOYD MCBRIDE. President of the United Steelworkers of America

CHUCK RAWLINGS. Presbyterian minister employed by the Episcopal Diocese of Ohio, principal organizer of the Ecumenical Coalition of the Mahoning Valley

DAVID RODERICK. Chairman of the board of United States Steel

WILLIAM ROESCH. Chief executive officer of United States Steel

JAMES SMITH. Assistant to Lloyd McBride

BOB VASQUEZ. President of Local 1330, United Steelworkers of America, representing production and maintenance workers at the Ohio Works, and chairman of the board, Community Steel

JACK WATSON. Assistant to President of the United States Jimmy Carter

Glossary of Terms

BEETLE STUDY. First feasibility study on reopening the Campbell Works by economist George Beetle

BOP SHOP. Steelmaking facility in which steel is made by the Basic Oxygen Process

BRIER HILL WORKS. Steel mill in Youngstown and Girard, Ohio, owned by Youngstown Sheet & Tube and then by Jones & Laughlin Steel

BROWNFIELD. An existing steelmaking community; thus, "brownfield modernization" is modernization in a community where steel is already being made

CAMPBELL WORKS. Steel mill in Campbell and Struthers, Ohio, owned by Youngstown Sheet & Tube and then by Jones & Laughlin Steel

CAPITAL COST. The cost of building a facility, in contrast to the cost of operating it

CAPITAL-INTENSIVE. Requiring large amounts of expensive machinery in comparison to the cost of labor

COMMON STOCK. Stock of a corporation which entitles the owner to vote at annual stockholders meetings

CONGLOMERATE. A corporation which owns or controls operating companies in several different fields of economic activity

CONNEAUT, Ohio. Town on the shore of Lake Erie where United States Steel proposes to build a huge new steel mill

CONSENT DECREE. A court order, agreed to by the parties in a law suit and approved by the court

CONTINUOUS CASTER. A modern device for taking the hot steel as it comes out of the furnace and semi-finishing it in a single process

DEBT-EQUITY RATIO. The relation of a company's borrowed capital to the capital raised by stock investment

DISINVESTMENT. When a company invests in a new line of business rather than modernizing the business it is already in

ECUMENICAL COALITION OF THE MAHONING VALLEY. Coalition of religious organizations in the Youngstown area which tried to reopen the Campbell Works

EDA. Economic Development Administration of the United States Department of Commerce, administrator of the steel industry loan guarantee fund

ELECTRIC FURNACES. Method of making steel which involves melting metal scrap

EMPLOYEE–COMMUNITY OWNERSHIP. Plan for operating a company the main feature of which is that both workers and community residents own common stock of the company and are represented on its board of directors

ENA. Experimental Negotiating Agreement, whereby the major steel companies and the United Steelworkers of America have agreed since 1973 that any impasse in the negotiation of the Basic Steel Contract will be resolved by arbitration

EPA. United States Environmental Protection Agency

EQUITY. Common stock

ESOP. Employee Stock Ownership Plan

FEASIBILITY STUDY. Study of whether a particular proposed activity would be profitable

FIXED COSTS (OR EXPENSES). Costs which a plant has to pay whatever the level of its operations, such as rent, taxes, vacation pay

GOVERNMENT PROCUREMENT. Government purchase of a company's product

GREENFIELD. A community where steel has not previously been made, usually a rural area (hence, "green field")

HUD. The United States Department of Housing and Urban Development, administrator of Urban Development Action Grants

INJUNCTION. A court order forbidding or requiring an act

INTEGRATED STEEL PLANT. A steel plant which carries on the entire steel-making process from preparation of the iron ore (coke ovens, blast furnaces) to steelmaking (open hearths, electric furnaces, or BOP shop) to semi-finishing (blooming mills or continuous casters) to finished product (rolling mills)

INTERNATIONAL UNION. A national union with Canadian members

INVESTMENT DECISIONS. Decisions about the basic nature of a business, such as what products to make, where to locate plants, whether to close plants, and how to allocate profits

J & L. Jones & Laughlin Steel

LEHMAN BROTHERS KUHN LOEB. Investment banking house which recommended closing the Campbell Works

LOAN GUARANTEE. A legally enforcible promise to repay all or most of a loan should the borrower default

LTV. Ling Temco Vought, the conglomerate which owns Jones & Laughlin Steel

LYKES. The conglomerate which owned Youngstown Sheet & Tube until it merged with Ling Temco Vought

MANAGEMENT PREROGATIVES (OR RIGHTS) CLAUSE. The clause in a typical collective bargaining agreement which gives management the right to make investment decisions, and to hire and fire

MCDONALD WORKS. Steel mill in McDonald, Ohio, owned by United States Steel

MERGER. The legal unification of two or more previously independent businesses

MINI-MILL. A mill where steel is made by an electric furnace and production is limited to one finished item (see p. 182)

MVEDC. Mahoning Valley Economic Development Committee

NCEA. National Center for Economic Alternatives, the organization headed by Gar Alperovitz which did the principal feasibility study on reopening the Campbell Works

NLRB. National Labor Relations Board, federal agency which administers the National Labor Relations (Wagner) Act

NATIONALIZATION. Ownership of a business by the national government

NO-STRIKE CLAUSE. The clause in a typical collective bargaining agreement which prohibits strikes and other interruptions of production during the life of the agreement

OHIO WORKS. Steel mill in Youngstown, Ohio, owned by United States Steel

OPEN HEARTH. Furnace for making steel

OPERATING COST. The cost of operating a facility, in contrast to the cost of building it

OPIC. Ohio Public Interest Campaign

OPTION. A legally enforcible right to make a choice, for instance, to buy a certain piece of property

PREFERRED STOCK. Stock of a corporation which does not entitle the owner to vote at annual stockholders meetings

PRODUCTIVITY CLAUSE. The clause in the Basic Steel Contract of 1971 creating joint labor-management teams to increase productivity

REINDUSTRIALIZATION. Modernization of basic industries such as steel

ROUNDOUT. Modernization in brownfield sites by improving some but not all parts of an industrial complex

SAVE OUR VALLEY CAMPAIGN. The campaign by means of which unions, churches, and individuals deposited money in special savings accounts with the understanding that the money would be invested in common stock of Community Steel if the Campbell Works reopened

SOUTH BEND LATHE. Worker-owned company in South Bend, Indiana

STANDING. Legal term for having enough connection with a controversy to become a party in a law suit about the problem

SUE. Steelworkers United for Employment, an organization of unemployed steelworkers who supported the reopening of the Campbell Works

TRI-STATE CONFERENCE ON THE IMPACT OF STEEL. An organization of religious personalities and steelworkers in Youngstown and Pittsburgh, successor to the Ecumenical Coalition

TRUNDLE CONSULTANTS. Company which studied the feasibility of reopening the Ohio and McDonald Works under employee-community ownership

TVA. Tennessee Valley Authority, a public corporation created by Congress in the 1930s for the purpose of flood control and electrification in the valley of the Tennessee River

UDAG. Urban Development Action Grant, administered by the United States Department of Housing and Urban Development

WREDA. Western Reserve Economic Development Agency

YOUNGSTOWN WORKS. Collective term for the Ohio Works and McDonald Works of United States Steel

Introduction

According to a local newspaper, Youngstown, Ohio has scored a number of firsts:

> the first strike by nurses in the country, and the first strike by teachers; the first school system in the nation to close due to a lack of money; during the 1950s, number one in gangland car bombings, and today, first in the number of unsolved gangland murders; and the largest plant closing in the nation's history. . . .[1]

This book tells the story of that plant closing, of the two additional steel mill shutdowns which followed in 1979–1980, and of the resistance to the shutdowns by steelworkers and the community.

A shutdown is a devastating experience for the victims. Most of us have come to feel that factories are permanent fixtures. Our jobs in them create a kind of conservatism which has now been attacked at the root. As one Youngstown steelworker put it to me, "You felt as if the mill would always be there." Because steelworkers felt this way they put up with boredom, and danger, and humiliating harassment from supervisors every day, trading off these indignities for the fringe benefits which would come to them from long service at a particular plant. Now that bargain has been broken, and workers in Youngstown and elsewhere are beginning to ask: Why is the company allowed to make a shutdown decision unilaterally? Since the decision affects my life so much, why can't I have a voice in the decision?

The communities in which shutdowns occur are starting to ask the same questions. A plant closing affects more than the workers at the

3

plant. City income from industrial property taxes goes down, schools start to deteriorate and public services of all kinds are affected. Lay-offs occur in businesses which supplied raw materials for the shut-down plant and in businesses which processed the product, retail sales fall off. All the signs of family strain—alcoholism, divorce, child and spouse abuse, suicide—increase. Why may a corporation unilaterally decide to destroy the livelihood of an entire community? Why should it be allowed to come into a community, dirty its air, foul its water, make use of the energies of its young people for gener-ations, and then throw the place away like an orange peel and walk off?

Youngstown experienced shutdowns three times in close succession. As a result we were subjected to a short course in the analysis of shut-downs, and the strategy and tactics of resisting them. Each successive struggle was more militant and successful than the one before. Similarly, other communities should be able to begin where our ex-perience ended rather than having to relive our experience from scratch. A corporation which closes plants in several places learns from its experience. By the third or fourth closing the company acts with sophisticated precision. In each of the affected communities, however, rank and file workers are confronting a shutdown for the first time. So in this book I try to even up the odds a little by telling the Youngstown story to help others.

Let me first explain *where* this story took place; *what* happened and *when*; and *who* were the people who took part in the struggle.

Where

Youngstown is located halfway between Cleveland and Pittsburgh, just west of the Ohio-Pennsylvania state line.

In the 1980 census the city of Youngstown numbered approximately 115,000 persons, about 45,000 of them members of minority groups. The Youngstown-Warren metropolitan statistical area contains more than 500,000 inhabitants.

Manufacturing employment represents close to half of the employ-ment in the Youngstown-Warren area, compared to about one quarter in the United States as a whole. Steel has been the dominant industry. Even after the closing of the steel mills described in this book, steel remained strong in the area. The new General Motors plant in Lordstown now accounts for about one third of regional industrial employment. Steel and steel fabricating make up a second third, and trucking and other industries the remainder.

The region is a melting pot. Youngstown was a part of the "Western Reserve" once claimed by the state of Connecticut and there is a strong White Anglo-Saxon Protestant influence. The hymn "The Old Rugged Cross" was written in the Youngstown area. So were the McGuffey Readers with which 19th century American children learned to read. William McKinley, the conservative Republican elected president of the United States in 1896, grew up in nearby Niles.

The other major population group is from Eastern Europe. Poles and Italians are the most numerous nationalities. The Eastern European community is heavily represented in the Roman Catholic Church, the most important church in the area. It has produced such folk heroes as Frank Sinkwich, who won the Heisman trophy as a running back for the University of Georgia football team in the 1940s.

The area has also produced a number of rebels. The abolitionist John Brown lived in this part of Ohio for a time, and the "underground railroad" which helped fugitive slaves to escape had many stations. Clarence Darrow was born in nearby Kinsman and admitted to the bar in Youngstown. This is a strong union town. Part of East Youngstown was burned to the ground during a strike at the time of World War I. Some of the most bitter clashes of the Little Steel Strike of 1937 took place in Youngstown and surrounding cities. More recently the region has been an occasional stronghold of rebel truckdrivers in FASH (the Fraternal Association of Steel Haulers) and TDU (Teamsters for a Democratic Union).

The Mahoning River runs through the area, providing water for the steel mills. The commonly used term for the region encompassing all the mills is the Mahoning Valley. A signpost on the Ohio turnpike south of Youngstown declares:

> The Mahoning Valley is the heartland of America's steel industry, a complex of roaring furnaces and tall smoke stacks lining the Mahoning River for a stretch of 25 miles. As the industry prospers so do the people of the Valley. Many times, at night, the skies north of the service plaza reflect the fires in the

mill furnaces of such steel centers as Youngstown, Niles, Warren and Girard.

Youngstown in 1976, when my family and I moved to the area, was a place in which the American Dream seemed to have come true for many working-class families. Houses to rent were hard to find: most people owned their homes, and were to be seen mowing their neat lawns, painting, or adding a patio. A few miles from our house was Eastwood Mall, one of several huge shopping malls on the outskirts of Youngstown. At the same time, Old World tradition lived on strongly, as in the widespread passion for gardening. Often three generations of a family worked in the same mill and lived close to each other in the same neighborhood. Graduation from high school was the occasion for a party, hosted by proud parents for relatives and friends. Communities united behind their football and basketball teams. Roller rinks and bowling leagues flourished. So did theatrical groups. The A & P was open twenty-four hours a day for the convenience of all three shifts, and the hardware store sold building and plumbing supplies on Sunday. It was a way of life that did not exist before the 1930s.

There was a sense that this way of life—with its materialism and false security, as well as with its dignity—was created by the union. My friend and neighbor John Barbero once reflected: "It was a wonder, the difference the [Little Steel] strike made in our house. . . . A whole town achieved dignity."[2]

What and When

Each fall from 1977 to 1979 a major steel mill in the Mahoning Valley announced its intention to close. The mills that closed, who owned them, and when they shut down, are shown in Table 1.

The number of workers permanently laid off at the three mills was about 10,000: 5,000 at the Campbell Works; 1,500 at the Brier Hill Works; and 3,500 at the Youngstown Works.

The sequence of events is especially hard to follow between September 1977 and December 1978. During most of this period the stories of all three mills were developing at the same time. The chronology in Table 2 may help the reader to keep track of the main dates.

Table 1

Steel Mill	Steel Company That Owned the Mill	Conglomerate That Owned the Steel Company	Date Shutdown Announced
Campbell Works	Youngstown Sheet & Tube	Lykes	September 1977
Brier Hill Works	Jones & Laughlin (Brier Hill belonged to Youngstown Sheet & Tube until it merged with J & L in 1978 as a result of the merger of their parent conglomerates)	Ling Temco Vought (LTV)	October–December 1978
Youngstown Works (Ohio Works and McDonald Works)	United States Steel	none	November 1979

Table 2

Date		Campbell Works	Brier Hill Works	Youngstown Works
1977	Sept.	Permanent closing of most of Works announced Sept. 19.		Company promises to keep Works open if they can be made profitable.
	Oct.	Ecumenical Coalition formed.		
	Nov.	Coalition issues Pastoral Letter.	Lykes and LTV announce intent to merge.	
	Dec.	Beetle Study released.		
1978	Jan.			
	Feb.	Save Our Valley campaign begins.		Wm. Kirwan made superintendent.

Table 2 (cont.)

Date	Campbell Works	Brier Hill Works	Youngstown Works
1978 Mar.			
Apr.	Alperovitz releases preliminary report.		
May			
June	Attorney General Bell permits LTV and Lykes to merge without attaching conditions.		
July			
Aug.			
Sept.	Alperovitz releases final report. Coalition meets with Jack		
Oct.	Watson. Government reserves $100 mil. in loan guarantees.	Lykes-LTV prospectus states intent to close Brier Hill.	
Nov.	J & L gives the Coalition an exclusive option to buy at a definite price until June 1979.		
Dec.		Lykes and LTV merge. Local 1462 pickets.	
1979 Jan.	UDAG application submitted.	Meeting with company Jan. 19. Confrontation with Gordon Allen Jan. 22.	
Feb.			
Mar.	Revised UDAG application submitted. Loan guarantees denied by EDA.	Poor turnout at Mar. 17 rally. Agreement with company for orderly shutdown.	

Date	Campbell Works	Brier Hill Works	Youngstown Works
1979 Apr.			David Roderick becomes chairman of the board.
May			
Oct.			
Nov.			Permanent closing of Works announced Nov. 27. Temporary occupation of USS Pittsburgh headquarters Nov. 30.
Dec.		Mill closes.	Law suit filed.

Who

A group of friends—steelworkers, ministers, lawyers, and others—lived through the Youngstown struggle together. Some of the steelworkers whom the reader will meet again and again in this book are:

DUANE IRVING. Irving's grandfather and father worked at steel mills in the Youngstown area. A star athlete in high school, he started working at the Campbell Works in the summer time as a carpenter and never went back to school. During the events described in this book, Irving was first a grievance committeeman, and then vice president, of Local 1418, representing production and maintenance workers in the finishing end of the Campbell Works.

ED MANN.[3] Born in Toledo, Mann served in the Marines and then went to work in the Brier Hill Works open hearth soon after World War II. Together with his friend John Barbero he was active in a national rank-and-file caucus in the Steelworkers union, the Rank and File Team (RAFT). In 1973, Mann was elected president of Local 1462, representing production and maintenance workers at the Brier Hill Works. He continued in this position throughout the shutdown struggle.

When the Brier Hill Works closed one small department (cold drawn wire) remained open, and Mann continued as president of his now-tiny local until he retired in spring 1981.

JOHN BARBERO. Barbero was born in Campbell, where his father was active in organizing his plant for the CIO. He volunteered for World War II, but became deeply committed to the peace movement as a result of his wartime experiences. When the war ended he worked in Japan for two years, visited Hiroshima, and married Miyo Homma. Barbero once told a peace meeting that with an Italian father, a Czech mother, and a Japanese wife, in any forseeable war he'd have a cousin on the other side.

Barbero came back to Youngstown with his wife Miyo and, like Ed Mann, went to work in the open hearth at Brier Hill. He was vice president of Local 1462 from 1973 to 1979, and thereafter grievance committeeman for the open hearth. He was a fierce rank and filer. He died on July 4, 1981, when he fell from a scaffold while painting his house.

GERALD DICKEY. A rigger, Dickey was recording secretary of Local 1462 from 1976 to 1979, and vice president of the local union thereafter. He also edited the *Brier Hill Unionist*. Dickey and his friend Duane Irving both took partial leaves of absence from the mill to help the Ecumenical Coalition in its effort to reopen the Campbell Works. After the Brier Hill Works closed, he had opportunities to move to New York or Washington as editor of a labor newspaper, or to work as a reporter for the *Warren Tribune*. Dickey chose instead to take a job in the coke department at Republic Steel in Warren.

BOB VASQUEZ. Bob's mother's father worked in the coal mines in Pennsylvania. His father is a molder. His uncle worked in United States Steel's tin mill in New Castle, Pa. until it was closed in the 1930s, and then went to work for United States Steel in Youngstown. Vasquez's cousins (his uncle's sons), his brother, and he all worked at the Youngstown Works. Vasquez was elected president of Local 1330, representing production and maintenance workers at the Ohio Works, in 1979. He lives with his German-born wife and son in New Castle, just across the state line, and is an ardent gardener. After the Works closed, and the fight to reopen the mills was lost, he became a staff man for the international union.

During the shutdown events, Mann and Barbero were about fifty years old, Irving, Dickey, and Vasquez about thirty.

You should also know something about the teller of the story: myself. I was a participant in each of the shutdown battles described. I was general counsel (overall attorney) for the Ecumenical Coalition of the Mahoning Valley, which tried to reopen the first mill to close. I represented the local union at the second mill shut down. And when the shutdown of the third mill was announced, I became lead counsel in a law suit filed in Federal court by the local Congressman, six local unions, sixty-five unemployed steelworkers, and a religious group, which tried to prevent the mill from being closed, or to require the company to offer the property to the workers so that they could run it. This work gave me a good chance to see what was happening.

I was a historian before I became a lawyer. After our struggle ended, it was natural to think of telling the story as best I could.

I am acutely aware that there is no such thing as "the history" of what happened in Youngstown. Each major participant would tell the story somewhat differently. There is a natural tendency to give most attention to events in which one was personally involved, and about which one can testify at first hand. I have sought to go beyond my own biases by asking more than a dozen other participants to read and correct the manuscript, as well as by drawing extensively on documents obtained through Freedom of Information Act litigation to view the unfolding drama through the eyes of corporate and government decisionmakers. At the risk of burdening the text with footnotes I have documented my assertions in the usual scholarly manner.

I have deliberately placed rank-and-file steelworkers in the center of the narrative. I think that they belong there. It was a steelworker, John Barbero, who first talked in Youngstown about the importance of modernizing mills in existing steelmaking communities ("brown-field" modernization) rather than building new mills in rural sites. It was a steelworker, Gerald Dickey, who heard someone suggest at a mass meeting, "Why don't we buy the damn place?," and first proposed employee-community ownership of the mills. It was steelworkers, Ed Mann and Bob Vasquez, who led hundreds of friends and fellow workers to occupy the administration building of U.S. Steel. It was a Pittsburgh steelworker, Frank O'Brien, who while serving as a Pennsylvania state legislator developed the idea of a "Monongahela Valley Authority" which could buy and operate steel mills that private companies no longer wish to run.

Part I. The Ecumenical Coalition's Campaign to Reopen the Campbell Works

Chapter One. Rumors

The Youngstown Sheet & Tube company was created early in the twentieth century in Youngstown, by Youngstown investors. The company headquarters was a palatial structure on Market Street in Boardman (south Youngstown). Originally the company possessed only the Campbell Works. In the 1920s it bought out the Brier Hill steel company and added the Brier Hill Works in Youngstown and Girard. Hot iron was made in blast furnaces at the Campbell Works, shipped several miles north to the Brier Hill Works to be made into steel in the Brier Hill open hearths and semi-finished into components of seamless pipe known as "rounds." The rounds were then shipped back to the Campbell Works for finishing. In addition, some of the hot iron made at the Campbell Works was sent directly to the Campbell Works' open hearths, to be made into steel, semi-finished in the blooming mill, and rolled into coils of sheet steel in the Works' hot and cold strip mills.

Later, Youngstown Sheet & Tube added a third facility at East Chicago, Indiana, just west of Gary. Thereafter most of the company's new investment was in the Indiana Harbor Works.

The Campbell Works employed more than 5,000 men and women, the Brier Hill Works about 1,500. Production and maintenance workers at the two Works were represented by local unions 2163 (Campbell Works steelmaking), 1418 (Campbell Works finishing), and 1462 (Brier Hill Works), United Steelworkers of America.

The Need for Modernization

There was never any question that the steel mills of the Mahoning Valley were old, were technologically obsolete, and needed to be modernized. A study in 1976 by Booz, Allen & Hamilton, management consultants, concluded: "The integrated steel plants in the Mahoning River Valley of Ohio (Youngstown/Warren area) are considered to be among the least economically viable in the domestic steel industry."[1] At United States Steel's plants in the Valley, maintenance rather than modernization expenditures had had priority for many years, the report found. The Ohio Works' 4 blast furnaces and 14 open hearths were smaller than units at other U.S. Steel plants. The newest finishing mill at the McDonald Works (the 18 mill) was 40 years old.

Youngstown Sheet & Tube's area facilities were more modern, according to the consultant. From 1958 to 1974 the company had invested over $224 million in major capital projects. The 79 inch hot strip mill at the Campbell Works was completely rebuilt about 1960.

But area steelworkers knew that the Campbell and Brier Hill Works, like the Ohio Works of United States Steel, made steel in obsolete open hearths. An open hearth takes 9 to 10 hours to make a batch or "heat" of steel from iron, limestone, and other ingredients. A basic oxygen furnace (often referred to as a BOP, or Basic Oxygen Process, shop) can do the same work, with less labor, in 45 minutes. In 1974, Youngstown Sheet & Tube authorized a new basic oxygen shop for the Campbell Works.[2] It was estimated to cost $90 million and to require 36 to 42 months to construct and place in operation.[3] Then in 1976 the company announced that "because of the 1975 recession's impact on internally generated funds" the timetable for construction of the Campbell Works BOP shop had been extended.[4]

Would Modernization Have Been Profitable?

Before as after the shutdowns, some argued that it would not pay to modernize the Mahoning Valley mills because of their location. According to this view the market for steel had moved westward, giving facilities in Chicago, Texas, and the West Coast a competitive edge over mills in Youngstown or Pittsburgh. Furthermore, it was argued, plants had originally been located in Youngstown and Pittsburgh because of proximity to coal and iron deposits, but in modern times iron ore came from Minnesota, Canada or Venezuela, and was most cheaply transported by water and most cheaply processed in a facility at the water's edge.

The best answer to this argument that modernization in Youngstown was prohibited by geography is that many steel mills in the Youngstown area or nearby did *not* shut down and are making a profit. Three economists employed by the Federal Reserve Bank have found that steel companies, all of whose plants are in northeastern Ohio or western Pennsylvania, have rates of profit above the national average for the industry.[5]

Table 3

Company	Employment	Location	Profitability
Copperweld Steel Co.	2,500	Warren	5.53%
Sharon Steel Corp.	6,000	Hubbard	5.09%
Total Iron & Steel			4.74%
Total Manufacturing			7.67%

Moreover, although published data do not permit one to break out the profitability of Republic Steel's Warren plant from the company's profitability nationwide, Republic Steel has committed itself to modernizing the Warren facilities.

The key to successful modernization of steelmaking in the Mahoning Valley appears to be the use of electric furnaces rather than basic oxygen furnaces. A basic oxygen furnace makes steel from immense quantities of coal, iron ore, and limestone. There seems to be no dispute that these are most cheaply transported by water and most cheaply processed in facilities at the water's edge as in Chicago, Gary, Cleveland, and Lackawanna, New York. But the BOP shop is not the only alternative to the antiquated open hearth. Steel can also be made cheaply and efficiently in electric furnaces. In this process, rather than making the steel from basic raw materials it is made from scrap, abundantly available in inland locations such as Youngstown and Pittsburgh. The geographical advantage of a waterside location disappears when steel is made in electric furnaces. Not surprisingly, the companies which have modernized and survived in the Youngstown area emphasize electric furnace steelmaking. Moreover, in each of the abandoned mills—the Campbell Works, the Brier Hill Works, and the Youngstown Works—small reopenings have occurred, in every case involving the use of electric furnaces.[6] The evidence is persuasive that the mills which closed could have been profitably modernized had their owners opted to install electric furnaces. Instead, U.S. Steel, which used electric furnaces in its newest plant at Baytown, Texas in the early 1970s, rejected electric furnace modernization when proposed by the superintendent of its Youngstown Works, as will be described in Part III.

False Assurances

When Youngstown Sheet & Tube decided in the spring of 1976 to postpone the installation of a BOP shop at the Campbell Works, rumors began to circulate. Two months later, in June 1976, Frank Nemec, chairman and chief executive officer of Sheet & Tube, resigned, and a *Wall Street Journal* article speculated that the company might have to eliminate its Brier Hill Works in order to solve its financial problems.[7]

Rumors continued in 1977. Early in August, Youngstown Sheet & Tube laid off some office personnel, and local union officers inquired with concern whether the company's plants were in trouble. Bill Sferra, president of Local 1418, United Steelworkers of America, at the Campbell Works, stated under oath to the National Labor Relations Board that Sheet & Tube executives Towns and Lambeth told him on August 11 and 25, "We'll make it."[8] Ed Mann, president of Local 1462 at the Brier Hill Works, told the NLRB that Lambeth said, "It was tough but they were going to make it." There was no hint of a shutdown of facilities, according to Mann. He felt no need to ask to bargain about a shutdown decision because everything was going to be all right. Gerald Dickey, Local 1462 recording secretary, recalled an encounter with Towns at still a third meeting on August 17 between Towns and the officers of Local 1462. Dickey stated under oath that the following exchange occurred:

DICKEY: Do you anticipate cutbacks?

TOWNS: No cutbacks. Order book good 6–9 mos. We should have normal production.

The most dramatic testimony is from Russ Baxter, president of Local 2163, another Campbell Works local. Local 2163 had its regular monthly meeting on September 13, 1977. A member said there was a rumor of a shutdown early the next week. Baxter left the podium and telephoned John Stone, a vice president of Sheet & Tube. He asked if there was any truth to the rumor of closing. Stone replied, according to Baxter: "No truth to it." Baxter then returned to the meeting and repeated what Stone had said.

According to his statement to the NLRB, Baxter called Stone again on Friday, September 16 to ask when a certain bridge at the Campbell Works would be repaired. Stone bet him a bottle of whiskey it would be finished by Thanksgiving.

Chapter Two. Shutdown

For Russ Baxter, Frank Gidaro, Bill Sferra, and Ed Mann, Monday, September 19, 1977 began between 7:30 and 8 in the morning when each received a phone call from Gary Wuslich, in charge of labor relations for Youngstown Sheet & Tube in the Mahoning Valley. The men were the presidents of the four local unions representing production and maintenance workers at the Campbell Works and Brier Hill Works.

Wuslich told the four men that there would be an important meeting at the Industrial Relations office at 10 A.M. Wuslich did not tell Sferra what the meeting was about, and Sferra didn't ask. Ed Mann asked, "Is it good news or bad news?," and Wuslich said, "Bad." To Baxter, Wuslich volunteered "I have bad news." Baxter tried to find out what the bad news was but Wuslich wouldn't say.

After the presidents gathered at Wuslich's office they were asked to cross the street to the office of the general superintendent, Scott. Scott was not there. The company spokesman was Ronald Towns, the district manager. In addition to Gidaro, Sferra, and Mann, the union people present were Bob Dill (representing Russ Baxter); Charles Hinchcliffe, staff representative for the production and maintenance workers; and Ann Hudak, staff representative for the office and technical workers.

Towns handed the union people copies of a statement that he said was simultaneously being released to the international union and to the media. Towns read aloud the statement which began:

> Youngstown Sheet and Tube Company, a subsidiary of Lykes Corporation, announced today that it is implementing steps im-

mediately to concentrate a major portion of its steel production at the Indiana Harbor Works near Chicago.

The statement went on to say:

> The Company now employs 22,000 people. The production cut-back at the Campbell Works will require the lay-off or termination of approximately 5,000 employees in the Youngstown area.

At this point Mann interrupted and said: "Are you cutting the cord? Are they done?" Towns said: "Yes."

Gidaro recalls that somebody said: "What can we do about it? Can there be negotiations?" Wuslich responded: "At this time I cannot make a comment."

Towns said he had to go to another meeting. Sferra remembers asking: "Is there any opportunity to save the plant?" Towns didn't answer and walked out.

The Impact

For about a year Monday, September 19, was known as "Black Monday." A national ABC documentary on the shutdown used the same term. Finally the black community made its feelings known, and the phrase was dropped.

The *Brier Hill Unionist* compared the impact of the shutdown announcement to the impact of Pearl Harbor. (Later, when U.S. Steel closed its Youngstown Works, Joe Gavini who had worked there for forty years made the same comparison. He told filmmakers Carol Greenwald and Dorie Krauss: "The only thing I can compare it with is Pearl Harbor.") Duane Irving recalls: "Most people couldn't believe it. It was so huge and had operated so long and so many people depended on it for their livelihood."[9] Frank Leseganich, highest-ranking representative of the Steelworkers union in the area, stated:

> There was no advance notice. This bombshell was dropped on us suddenly. In fact we met with the company a few weeks ago and company officials assured us that nothing like this would happen. This is the exact reverse of what I thought would occur.[10]

On the shop floor at the Campbell Works, as later at the Brier Hill and Youngstown Works, the shutdown announcement created frustration, fear, hope, and humor which hung in the air like a thick fog. Frustration was felt mainly by younger workers, who did not have the 10 years' service required under Federal law to acquire a secure ("vested") pension, or the 20 years which triggered additional benefits under the contract. Older workers, close to retirement, feared that something (including resistance to the shutdown) might cause their pension benefits to be lost. Hope flourished in an atmosphere of rumor and counter-rumor. It was fed by supervisors, often themselves in the dark, who spread the word that "they're going to open back up," or that no other mill in the company could match the quality of the Campbell (or Brier Hill, or Youngstown) Works. The jokes had an edge. One day at Brier Hill, Ken Doran noticed that a water main had burst and that a fork lift was dislodging several sections of sidewalk to repair the damage. Doran sarcastically spread the word that "they're taking the sidewalks to Aliquippa."

There was also anger. On the Friday which ended the week beginning with September 19, the first group of terminated men left the Campbell Works for the last time. As they crossed the Mahoning River on the footbridge which led to the clockhouse many threw into the river the hard hats and metatarsal shoes of their trade.

Petition Campaign

The first response to the shutdown was planned at a meeting called by Director Leseganich which took place at 6 P.M. on September 19. The local union presidents who had met with Towns and Wuslich that morning were there, as was Gerald Dickey, recording secretary of Local 1462. Dickey recalls:

> We're sitting around this conference table, everybody just knocked down. Especially [Russ] Baxter [president of the local union most affected, Local 2163]. I'll never forget the guy. I sat right next to him at the end of the table. Baxter's an ex-boxer. He was like down for the count. The man's a big man and he was breathing heavy, his whole thing wiped out: five terms as president, you know.
>
> Nobody knew what to do. There we were. You still didn't want to believe it. People were still asking, "Is it really true?"
>
> We kicked it around. My only contribution was to talk about nationalization. That's all I could think of that first day. I put it,

"I think it's coming anyway. Five, ten years down the road. Like the railroads: when you finally milk it to the point that you can't get any more, you give it to the government." I said, "Well hell, let's go get it now."

I remember Frank Leseganich, when I talked about five or ten years, said: "Yeah, you might be right, but what about today?" He sort of brushed it aside. And he was the District Director.

So we went around the table, and Swierz, the president of the property protection local, kept saying, "Let's get petitions." Finally, he said it enough, and everybody said, "O.K. we'll get petitions."[11]

Swierz wrote up the petition. In Gerald Dickey's view, "Roderick [chairman of the board of U.S. Steel] . . . could have written that petition."

The petition stated:

SAVE THE MAHONING VALLEY
We Need Jobs, Not Welfare

We, the undersigned, petition the President of the United States, the Honorable Jimmy Carter, and the Congress to give immediate Relief to the American Steel Industry by Imposing Emergency Import Quotas, Relaxing the E.P.A. Standards, and Allowing the Steel Industry to EARN A FAIR PROFIT.

110,000 signatures were collected on this petition between Tuesday noon, when they were delivered by the printer, and the end of the day Thursday.

Five buses carrying 250 workers took the petitions to Washington on Friday, September 23, the same day that the first wave of terminated workers left work for the last time.

One of the riders later recalled:

We arrived in Washington at 12:15 p.m., and we were met by Director Frank Leseganich and other Union officials. We assembled and began to march around the . . . White House . . . carrying our protest signs. [The signs said: "Steel Town to Ghost Town," "Save The Steel Valley."] After one trip around the block, we stopped at the gate to present the petitions to President Carter, or at least one of his aides. After a heavy discussion between our leaders and the White House guards, we were turned away. We could not present our petitions. . . .[12]

It was the first of many futile journeys to Washington.

Second Thoughts

Returning to Youngstown, moreover, even those most active in promoting the petition began to wonder if they had deceived themselves. The petition's demands were directed exclusively to the government. Yet it was not the government of the United States, and still less the government of Japan, that had decided to close the Campbell Works. The program carried to Washington by the petitioners was the steel industry's program: stop imports, relax environmental restrictions, permit steel prices to be raised. We had allowed our anger to be deflected away from the conglomerate which purchased the Youngstown Sheet & Tube Company in 1969 only to close its second-largest plant less than a decade later. People began probing the Lykes Corporation.

The Role of the Lykes Corporation

The Lykes Corporation, we learned, was a holding company controlled by a Florida family of that name. Before absorbing Youngstown Sheet & Tube in 1969, Lykes got 85 per cent of its income from steamship interests. Although Sheet & Tube was merged into Lykes, before the merger Lykes had annual sales of only $100 million compared to $8-900 million for Sheet & Tube.[13] Thus, as a result of the merger, a relatively small company acquired a cash flow eight or nine times larger than it previously enjoyed.

The most serious analysis of the effect on Sheet & Tube of its acquisition by Lykes was made by the Ohio Public Interest Campaign (OPIC). OPIC charged irresponsible management by Lykes. The merger, OPIC said, made a healthy company part of a sick conglomerate. OPIC showed that:

1. After taking over Sheet & Tube in 1969, *Lykes failed to modernize*, investing an average of only $27 million annually between 1970 and 1973.

2. *Lykes had the cash to invest* in the early 1970s when its cash flow earnings were high even in periods when its reported net income was not.

3. Instead of returning this income to its steel division, *Lykes made other investments*. Lykes acquired Coastal Plains Life Insurance Co. (1969), W. R. Grace Company's half of a steamship

company jointly owned by Lykes and Grace (1971), Ramseyer and Miller, Inc. (1973), and Great Western Steel Company (1975).

4. *Lykes took on too much debt.* Lykes borrowed $150 million from a group of banks to purchase a minority interest in Sheet & Tube, and as part of the takeover arrangement, issued $191 million in bonds.

5. *Lykes could not fully benefit from steel boom periods*, such as 1974, because of its previous failure to modernize.[14]

The OPIC charges were confirmed in a dramatic way in November. I discovered that the Department of Justice had predicted, prior to the merger of Lykes with Sheet & Tube, that Lykes would use Sheet & Tube as a source of cash for conglomerate acquisitions and fail to make the necessary investment in modernization. An investigative report for the Anti-Trust Division of the Department in 1969[15] stated that the merger then pending

> jeopardizes Youngstown's competitive viability, in terms of finances required for technological improvements and innovations in its steel production facilities.

The report found that Youngstown Sheet & Tube was slated to become an appendage of Lykes, "even though this is a case of the tail wagging the dog." In sum, the report concluded,

> after providing for interest on long-term debts and debentures and for preferred dividends of LYC [Lykes Youngstown Corporation], the yearly funds available for modernizing Youngstown will decrease; and the new top management, without tradition in steel making and not committed to the old management's "Facilities Plan" and "Opportunities Survey," is much less likely to modernize Youngstown along the lines planned by the old management and found necessary by the industry experts to keep Youngstown competitive. . . .[16]

Less than a month after the September 19 announcement, the gist of the foregoing analysis had become common currency in the Valley. People did not blame the closing on the steel industry generally, or on the capitalist system. The finger of blame was pointed at the Lykes Corporation. The general feeling was that Lykes was a bad company, a group of outsiders not really interested in steel, who had pushed aside the "real steel men" in control of Youngstown Sheet & Tube and run Sheet & Tube into the ground.

The question remained, was there anything that could be done about it?

Chapter Three. *"Why Don't We Buy The Damn Place?"*

Meantime the strategy behind which the community was to unite also took form. Suggested at a public meeting on September 25, energetically propagated by Gerald Dickey, the idea of employee-community ownership became Youngstown's contribution to the national debate on shutdowns.

The September 25 meeting was one of several that took place in the affected communities of Campbell and Struthers immediately following the shutdown announcement. I attended one such meeting in the Struthers high school gymnasium. It began as any high school assembly would have begun, with patriotic observances. The colors were honored. "The Star Spangled Banner" was played. Then a succession of political figures made brief speeches. By and large the speakers echoed the demands of the September 23 petition: stop imports and relax EPA requirements. An aide to Senator Glenn said there had been no fish in the Mahoning River since the Civil War, so why start to be worried about it now? A Chamber of Commerce representative stated that no one had ever died of dust in the air. [17]

The bleachers were full of worried steelworkers, wearing the neat but casual clothes of working-class America off the job. Their wives had come with them. As politician followed politician, these quiet couples, sitting where they had often sat to watch their children play basketball, didn't respond much. They seemed to be waiting for something which never materialized.

Another such meeting took place in the Campbell city council chambers on Sunday, September 25. "Before the people behind the fence . . . could speak," Dickey recalls,

26

they let every politician in the room speak. [Congressman] Carney got up, [State Senator] Meshel, they said: "Don't worry, the schools are going to be open." Then they'd go around to every council member, every union president, every board of education guy. And Attorney Phil Creno [a member of the Board of Education] said, "Why don't we all put up five thousand bucks and buy the damn place?"

Then later on, after the people behind the bar could talk, a grocery store owner took the floor, and said the same thing.[18]

This was the first public proposal in Youngstown for what came to be called "employee-community ownership." The idea was simply that a closed plant could be reopened if *both* the employees who used to work there *and* other residents of the community put up money to buy the plant from the people who shut it down.

The idea was mentioned again a few days later at a press conference called by the local unions. Dickey was there. He tried to get one of the presidents to endorse the idea. "They wouldn't touch it. They didn't want to say No, and they didn't want to call me a jackass to my face, so they said: You say it." So Dickey did. He recalls the reporter for the *Vindicator* laughing and shaking his head. But the paper carried the story that the purchase plan had been suggested again.

Selling the Idea of Employee-Community Ownership

Dickey then began a one-man search for allies in the community. He talked to Mayor Jack Hunter of Youngstown. He talked to investment banker David Tod, descendant of a family which had helped to create Youngstown Sheet & Tube with local capital. (Tod advised him to buy Wisconsin Steel in Chicago, which went bankrupt a few years later.) He talked to District Director Leseganich, to his fellow-officers at Local 1462. The people he talked to talked to others.

I recall laying the idea on the organizer in Youngstown for the Ohio Public Interest Campaign over lunch in the kitchen of the law office where I then worked, and bringing it up at the first breakfast meeting of what was to become the Ecumenical Coalition, as well as with Gar Alperovitz in Washington.

One of the ways Dickey tried to sell the idea was as follows. "There were certain examples out there," he recalls. "A guy like

Onassis. He went to Argentina with two hundred bucks, and ends up owning all the ships in Greece. He never limited himself in what he thought he could do. I kept saying, a hundred million dollars wouldn't bother Onassis, would it? Just think like Onassis. We'll get it. It's there. Keep going."

Industry Week picked up the story, and it was read by a man who worked for the South Bend Lathe Company in Indiana who called Dickey. Bill Sullivan of the Western Reserve Economic Development Agency arranged for the president of South Bend Lathe to fly to Youngstown, and to meet with Dickey, Sferra and Mann. It was explained that after a conglomerate closed the South Bend Lathe plant, the plant reopened with the help of stock purchases by workers through an Employee Stock Ownership Plan (ESOP). It was *not* explained that the new company considered these stock holdings a substitute for a pension so that the workers had no pension plan.

Dickey was encouraged by a meeting with Tom Cleary, a Lykes director and longtime Sheet & Tube manager in the Mahoning Valley.[19] The meeting was set up by Bill Sferra. Dickey recalls:

> We went out to the Boardman office. It's classic. Six guys with empty pockets went out to that building. They had teakwood on the walls.
>
> Cleary said, "Well, Bill, what have you got on your mind?" And Sferra turned to me and said, "You can explain it better." So I said what I had been thinking. I wanted to buy the whole district, Brier Hill, Campbell, everything. And I even told Cleary, "I know the Ohio Works and McDonald Works are going down eventually. We'll take that, too."
>
> His response was, "They've got good iron at the Ohio Works." It didn't bother that guy. We asked whether it was for sale. His answer was, "I don't know." We asked about a purchase price, and about access to raw materials.
>
> We also asked whether if the whole of the Campbell Works was not for sale we could run the shutdown part. He had one of his aides bring aerial photographs. He showed us how you could put up a fence. He said the way you would work it was for one company to own, say, the shops, and lease to the other.
>
> The man was not negative. He didn't say anything discouraging. He closed that meeting by saying, "If anybody could do this, I know you guys could. But I want to tell you, you've got to move and move fast. You've got to have your sales group in

place. You've got to have your management team." And I think
the third thing was, we had to be ready to take over by the first
of the year. I don't know if he knew there was going to be a
merger and was trying to tip us off.

Why the Idea Began to Catch On

The idea of employee ownership made headway not so much because of these episodes as because no one had an alternative. I remember a meeting of steelworkers in my basement about this time.[20]
Those present included Marvin Weinstock, who had run for national
office in the Steelworkers union; Joe Sims, an experienced committeeman from the Campbell Works; Ed Mann and John Barbero;
and Gerald Dickey. The topic was, "what should we do about the
shutdown?" Nobody had anything to suggest except Dickey.

There was general agreement that the labor movement had had
some bad experiences with producers' cooperatives. Very often
workers are no more able than the former owners to make the business a success, and the cooperative fails. Another common experience
is that the cooperative succeeds but only by ceasing to be a cooperative, and coming to resemble the capitalist enterprise it replaced.

Everybody agreed, but still, Dickey was the only person who had
any notion about something to do. Things broke up on that note.

The growing interest in worker-community ownership is suggested
by an anonymous editorial which Dickey wrote for the *Brier Hill
Unionist*. Entitled "A Possible Alternative—Employee Ownership,"
the editorial said:

> In the aftermath of the shocking announcement by the Lykes
> Corp. to close facilities and eliminate 5,000 jobs, some strange
> ideas were discussed in the community.
>
> Perhaps the strangest idea of all was to pool the resources of
> the community and purchase the mill. At first, most people did
> not pay any serious attention to the purchase suggestion.
>
> The biggest handicap to community acceptance of the idea
> was that very few people were aware that a community/employee
> owned business had ever been operated anywhere successfully.
>
> There are, however, a few employee owned companies in the
> U.S., most notably the South Bend Lathe company in Indiana.

When news arrived of this successfully operated company, people wanted to know more details.

The background of South Bend Lathe was similar to Youngstown Sheet & Tube. The company was owned by a conglomerate that decided to close the business. More than 400 employees faced the loss of their jobs and the closing would have severely hurt the community.

The company president, with the help of local bankers, arranged an employee buy-out for the price of $10 million. The employees did not have to put up one cent, it was all borrowed money. Half of the loan was backed by the government, and the other half came from commercial banks. The deal went through, the company is operating successfully and the employees have been receiving pay increases and bonuses for the past 2½ years.

Dickey then pointed to the major problem for employee-community ownership of the Campbell Works.

> While South Bend Lathe is a success story, an employee buy-out of any Sheet & Tube facilities is different. The project would be at least 10 times bigger and it has never been accomplished on such a scale. . . .
>
> . . . Bill Sferra, president of L.U. 1418, commented on the project. "This is a long shot at best, but we owe it to our membership to study every possibility, no matter how long these odds might be."
>
> Local 1462 president Ed Mann was quick to caution, "We are not trying to raise false hopes and I think optimism on anyone's part is premature. Our chances of success are very slim. There would be no precedent for an employee ownership program this large anywhere in the country."[21]

The caution expressed by Sferra and Mann reflected substantial skepticism toward the idea of worker ownership. The business community and news media such as the *Youngstown Vindicator* warned of raising "false hopes." Down in the plant, too, many workers thought employee-community ownership ridiculous, and some, especially older workers, feared that it would imperil their benefits. Gerald Dickey's strongest supporters could not help noticing that he had advocated nationalization, then import restrictions, and then worker ownership, all in the space of a few weeks. Ken Doran recalls that one day in the fall of 1977 he, Dickey, and John Barbero were talking at the Brier Hill Works, and Barbero commented: "We are like a bunch of chickens running around with our heads cut off, and Gerald is the head chicken."

Thus, from the very beginning, advocates of the idea of worker-community ownership faced the challenge of persuading not only Washington but Youngstown as well, and struggled with the dilemma that it is hard to sell people on the possibility of a long shot.

This became the task of the Ecumenical Coalition.

Chapter Four. The "Save Our Valley" Campaign

"That is ecumenical," according to my dictionary, "which belongs to all the world, or is world-wide in its breadth and inclusiveness." An "ecumenical" activity is one which brings together members of different churches.

The Ecumenical Coalition of the Mahoning Valley was initially the creation of a Roman Catholic bishop, an Episcopal bishop, and a Presbyterian minister. James W. Malone, bishop of the Roman Catholic Diocese of Youngstown, became the Coalition's chairperson. The associate chairperson was John H. Burt, bishop of the Episcopal Diocese of Ohio. Burt was living in Cleveland in September 1977, but he had previously served in Youngstown, where he and Malone became friends and worked together on behalf of racial integration. Reverend Charles ("Chuck") Rawlings, a Presbyterian minister, was working in September 1977 for the Church and Society department of the Episcopal Diocese and was freed by it to devote most of his very considerable energy to Youngstown during the next two years.

These three men functioned throughout the Youngstown struggle under a variety of pressures, especially from businessmen in the Episcopal Church. Each in his own way took a principled stand against the political attacks which predictably followed the Coalition's endorsement of employee-community ownership of a steel mill. Together with their associates in the Coalition they redeemed the Church in the eyes of working people in Youngstown. At one point in the ensuing struggle a poll determined that less than 20 per cent of the people in the Valley had confidence in President Jimmy Carter, but more than 80 per cent trusted the leadership of the Coalition.

As the result of many telephone calls by Chuck Rawlings, an interfaith breakfast was held at the rectory of St. Columba Cathedral in Youngstown on September 26, just one week after the shutdown announcement. Richard Barnet of the Institute for Policy Studies in Washington had been working closely with the Episcopal bishops on urban problems, and was invited to be present. So was I. The principal decision of the meeting was to hold a conference. A press release struck the characteristic note of future Coalition pronouncements: "As religious leaders we are committed to studying the moral dimensions of this problem. What is the responsibility of an industry to the citizens of the community in which it is located?"

Founding Conference of the Ecumenical Coalition

A month later, on October 28 and 29, 1977, the Coalition (then calling itself the "Youngstown Religious Coalition") held a founding conference at the First Presbyterian Church. The letter of invitation was co-signed by Bishop Malone and Reverend Richard Speicher, executive director of the Mahoning Valley Association of Churches and a member of the Church of the Brethren. Among the faiths represented were the United Methodist, Christian Church, United Church of Christ, Jewish, Baptist, and Eastern Orthodox. A number of national religious personalities and economic experts also attended. The conference program listed "Mr. Gerald Dickey, Economic Adviser."

The evening before the conference began, there was a dramatic meeting at St. Johns Episcopal Church between certain of the visiting religious dignitaries and Youngstown steelworkers.[22] Len Balluck, grievance committeeman for the Campbell Works open hearth, spoke of the bitterness of his fellow workers who on July 4 and July 8 had broken all previous production records. He described foremen saying good-bye to the men they had worked with; grown men crying; and steelworkers leaving the mill for the last time throwing their work clothes into the Mahoning River. Len said he wanted to see the Campbell Works reopened. Sam Myers, recording secretary for Local 1418 at the Campbell Works, said that the conference should not limit its attention to Lykes because other steel companies had the same problems.

At the conference, Mark Raskin of the Institute for Policy Studies made a speech pointing to the assumption that labor should follow capital. This assumption led capitalists to permit their equipment in particular locations to run down until wholly depreciated and then move elsewhere, Raskin said. He called for the alternative of capital coming to labor, or as we were beginning to put it, of "brownfield" development.

The most important speech at the conference was by Gar Alperovitz, historian, economist, former fellow of the Institute for Policy Studies, and director of the National Center for Economic Alternatives. The speech followed closely an extraordinary memorandum by Alperovitz dated October 9, 1977, entitled "Preliminary Observations: Youngstown, Ohio." The memorandum began with the flat statement: "At this stage, I believe virtually all of the significant issues in Youngstown are moral and political, not economic."

Private investors were unlikely to put up money to reopen the mill, Alperovitz continued. The only other potential source of capital on the scale required was the Federal government, and only an "unusual political mobilization" could get the government to do this. Thus, precisely to meet the economic need for large amounts of capital it was necessary to mount "a dramatic local and national moral campaign."

Alperovitz argued that a local campaign to "Save Our Community" should ask citizens to put up money to reopen the mill. This suggestion became the germ of the "Save Our Valley" campaign. Nationally, he proposed, the religious denominations should commit themselves as they had in the 1960s to efforts such as "Mississippi Summer."

Reflecting as well as helping to create the spirit which was being born in the Mahoning Valley, Alperovitz ended with a quotation from Acts 4:31-35 which said in part:

> 32 And the multitude of them that believed were of one heart and of one soul: neither said any of them that aught of the things which he possessed was his own; but that they had all things common.

> 34 Neither was there any among them that lacked: for as many as were possessors of land or houses sold them, and brought the prices of the things that were sold,

> 35 And laid them down at the apostles' feet: and distribution was made unto every man according as he had need.

Throughout the campaign which followed, Alperovitz remained faithful to this visionary call for a program which would work because of its capacity to excite people. The government, instead of offering Youngstown welfare programs, should identify a specific set of manufacturing needs such as for mass transit and sponsor a

"TVA-type development corporation" to help provide money and technical assistance. He said:

> Another question that might be raised is that if the Federal Government took responsibility for helping put the unemployed back to work in Youngstown, wouldn't it have the moral responsibility to do so for the growing number of suffering communities and unemployed people throughout the nation? A good question. The answer is yes.[23]

Instead of generalized averages of unemployment, which concealed the difference between Oklahoma City (3.2 per cent) and Johnstown, Pa. (12.9 per cent), Alperovitz suggested the concept of full employment in each community. The nation should establish a floor beneath which local unemployment would not be allowed to fall. Workers would still be free to move from Detroit to Phoenix should they so desire. But government policy would ensure that workers could stay in a Detroit or Youngstown by programs which would bring "jobs to the people." These programs might include locational tax incentives to encourage business to invest in particular areas and geographical targeting of public procurement.[24]

At the close of the Ecumenical Coalition's founding conference, a statement was issued by the newly-formed Coalition executive committee: Bishops Malone and Burt; Bishop James Thomas of the Methodist Church; and the Reverend John Sharick, executive presbyter of the Eastminster Presbytery. The statement tentatively endorsed the idea of employee-community ownership proposed by Gerald Dickey. The Coalition pledged itself to "examine the possibility of sponsoring a feasibility study on the acquisition and operation of the Campbell facility by a community/worker group or the conversion of the property to some other use."

"Brownfield" or "Greenfield" Modernization?

The Coalition's statement also adopted as the policy of the organization the "brownfield" objective of retaining "basic steel and associated jobs in communities steelworkers live in." This concept also had first been proposed in Youngstown by a steelworker, John Barbero. Shortly before the shutdown announcement at the Campbell Works on September 19, Barbero read an article reporting a speech given in northern Ohio by Stewart Udall, Secretary of the

Interior from 1961 to 1969. The article stated that Udall was opposing U.S. Steel's plan to build a giant new steel mill at Conneaut, Ohio, about 60 miles north of Youngstown on the shore of Lake Erie. Udall termed this proposed facility "greenfield" because it would be built in a hitherto unspoiled, rural area. He contrasted the concept of "brownfield" modernization in a traditional steelmaking community where homes, schools, roads, sewers, and other elements of social "infrastructure" already existed, and where unemployed steel-workers were looking for work. I can recall John Barbero, sitting at his kitchen table with the newspaper in front of him, saying: "*This* should be our program. Bring the technology to the people, rather than the other way around."

Soon after Barbero began to push the idea in print. He wrote in the *Brier Hill Unionist* for October-November 1977 "that not only should the steel industry be saved but the steel towns must be saved too. . . . [M]odernization [should] take place in the steel towns where the steelworkers already are."

The Coalition's Pastoral Letter

One of the most important outcomes of the Ecumenical Coalition's founding conference, proposed by Mark Raskin of the Institute for Policy Studies, was the drafting of a "pastoral letter" on the Mahoning Valley steel crisis. The first draft was written by John Carr of the United States Catholic Conference in Washington, D.C. Members of the Coalition executive and steering committees together with close coworkers then amended the draft. The document was completed in time to be released at Thanksgiving, 1977, signed by 185 religious leaders from Mahoning and Trumbull counties.

"Our community was wounded on September 19," the letter opened. "This blow to our community has generated shock, anger, and genuine fear. . . . This decision raises profound issues of cor-porate responsibility and justice."

What exactly were the issues presented by the closing of the Camp-bell Works? The pastoral letter identified these issues among others:

> "[There is a] way of doing business in this country that too often fails to take into account the human dimension of eco-nomic action";
> "The purpose of economic life is to serve the common good

and the needs of the people. . . . Economic institutions, although they have their own purposes and methods, still must serve the common good and are subject to moral judgment. We are convinced, in short, that corporations have social and moral responsibilities";

"[I]ndustrial investment decisions ought to take into account the needs and desires of employees and the community at large. In its refusal to invest in new equipment or necessary maintenance, the Lykes Corporation failed to do this. Human beings and community life are higher values than corporate profits";

"[E]conomic decisions ought not to be left to the judgment of a few persons with economic power, but should be shared with the larger community which is affected by the decisions."

The pastoral letter expressly rejected the idea that the decision to close the Campbell Works was "a private, purely economic judgment which is the exclusive prerogative of the Lykes Corporation." It affirmed that the decision "is a matter of public concern since it profoundly affects the lives of so many people as well as the future of Youngstown and the Mahoning Valley."

As to the *cause* for the closing, the pastoral letter was unclear.

Some say that a conglomerate in deep financial trouble, faced with large capital costs for modernization and environmental protection, shut down an unprofitable steel mill. Others say that poor management, declining product quality, inadequate investment and absentee ownership resulted in a decision to close the mill. Still others believe that the steel industry has embarked on a strategy of concentration and reducing productive capacity in order to take full economic advantage of steel needs in the future and make the industry more profitable. . . . We suspect that each of these explanations contains some elements of truth.

What the letter was absolutely clear about was that a corporation making such a decision must be responsible for the *consequences*. Moreover, there was a duty to speak this truth to corporate power.

Our God is a God of justice. "The Lord, Who does what is right, is always on the side of the oppressed." (Ps. 103:6). His message is very direct: "Cease to do evil. Learn to do good. Search for justice. Help the oppressed." (Isaiah 1:16–17). For those who are Christians, the life and ministry of Jesus lead us to similar concerns. Jesus came "to bring good news to the poor, to proclaim liberty to captives and new sight to the blind and to set the downtrodden free." (Luke 4:18). He very clearly identifies Himself with the poor and the victims of injustice. "Whenever you did it for one of these, the least of my brothers, you did it for me." (Matt. 25).

Passing to the question of what was to be done, the pastoral letter called on other major employers in the Valley, "especially other steel companies, to pledge publicly, community and employee consultation in future economic and investment decisions affecting economic and community life." Further, the letter called on Lykes to respond generously to efforts "to reopen the mill under community, worker or public ownership," for instance in setting a selling price for the purchase of the mill.

The pastoral letter of the Ecumenical Coalition ended with these words of the prophet Isaiah:

> Look, you do business on your fastdays,
> you oppress all your workmen and strike
> the poor man with your fist,
> let the oppressed go free,
> and break every yoke,
> share your bread with the hungry
> and shelter the homeless poor,
> clothe the man you see to be naked
> and not turn from your own kin?
> Then will your light shine like the dawn
> and your wound be quickly healed over. . . .
> If you do away with the yoke,
> the clenched fist, the wicked word,
> if you give your bread to the hungry,
> and relief to the oppressed,
> your light will rise in the darkness,
> and your shadows become like noon.
> You will rebuild the ancient ruins,
> build up on the old foundations.
> You will be called "Conciliator,"
> "restorer of households."
>
> (Isaiah 58)

Getting Organized

In November, December, and then January of 1978, the Coalition began serious organizing. The executive committee was expanded to include Rabbi Sidney Berkowitz and William Laurie, the Conference

Minister of the Ohio Conference of the United Church of Christ, together with Malone (Roman Catholic), Burt (Episcopal), Thomas (Methodist), and Sharick (Presbyterian). Richard Speicher of the Mahoning Valley Association of Churches became treasurer. These denominational executives met every two weeks to set policy. From day to day the affairs of the Coalition were coordinated by a "steering committee" also composed of representatives of the major participating churches: Father Ed Stanton (Roman Catholic), Chuck Rawlings (Episcopal), Don Walton (Methodist), and Bert Campbell (Presbyterian). Over the succeeding months the steering committee added Dianne Kenney, chaplain at Youngstown State University; Ed Weisheimer, pastor of the Central Christian Church of the Disciples of Christ; Reverend David Stone, a Baptist minister; myself as the Coalition's general counsel; and others.

In December, the Coalition hired Reverend Dick Fernandez, formerly organizer of Clergy and Laity Concerned about the Vietnam War, to help the community mobilize the funds needed to buy the plant. (Because of the huge sums required, the actual aim was to show the Federal government that the community was doing all that it could.) A plan was developed so that individuals and groups could open special "Save Our Valley" accounts at local banks. The idea was that, in the event an employee-community corporation came into being, "Save Our Valley" accounts could be converted into shares of common stock.

The "Save Our Valley" campaign was kicked off on February 16, 1978, at an evening service at the Boardman Methodist Church. Years later steelworkers remembered the occasion with awe. The Sheet and Tube Chorus sang the "Ave Maria" and the "Battle Hymn of the Republic." The New Bethel Baptist Church Trio sang "Nobody Knows The Trouble I've Seen." Individual unemployed steelworkers rose to testify. Rabbi Berkowitz welcomed the attenders; Reverend Sharick and Bishop Burt shared lessons from Jeremiah and Hebrews; Reverend Norman Crewson of the host church led us in invocation:

> Leader: Unless the Lord builds our city,
> People: They labor in vain who build it.
> Leader: Unless the Lord guards our city,
> People: The watchman waits in vain.
> Leader: O Lord, hear our cry;
> People: Renew the life of our valley.
> Leader: O Lord, make haste to help us!
> People: O Lord, make speed to save us!

A Four Million Dollar Vote of Confidence

As of November 1978, 4,138 Save Our Valley accounts had been opened, totalling $4,014,927.26. Nineteen banks (or savings and loan institutions) cooperated in opening the accounts. Depositors included 45 Mahoning Valley churches, with deposits typically of $5,000 or $10,000, and the following state and national denominations among others:

National Division of the Board of Global Ministries of the United Methodist Church	$160,000
Vermont Conference of the United Church of Christ	2,000
Board of Pensions, United Presbyterian Church of the USA	200,000
Domestic and Foreign Missionary Society of the Protestant Episcopal Church in the USA	60,000
National Ministries—American Baptist Churches USA	25,000
US Missionary Society (Disciples of Christ)	20,000
United Presbyterian Foundation	300,000
National and Women's Division, United Methodist Church	200,000
Riverside Church, NYC	100,000

These deposits were in addition to an ultimate total of close to half a million dollars provided by church groups to the Ecumenical Coalition in outright grants for its organizing work.

Chapter Five. Alternative Ownership Plans

Following its founding conference in October 1977, the Ecumenical Coalition turned more and more to the question of whether an employee-community corporation might be able to reopen and run the Campbell Works.

Other Experiments with Employee Ownership

There was nothing particularly new about the idea of worker ownership. During the period October 1977-March 1979 when the Coalition was formulating its proposal, the following more or less worker-owned or worker-managed enterprises were in the news:

an asbestos mine in northern Vermont;

Rushton Mining Company's underground mine in central Pennsylvania;

the Indianapolis Rubber Company;

18 plywood plants in the Pacific Northwest;

International Group Plans, a Washington, D.C. insurance company;

the Bates Manufacturing Company in Lewiston, Maine;

a library furniture factory in Herkimer, New York;

a knitting mill in Saratoga Springs, New York;

and, of course, the South Bend Lathe Company which had inspired Gerald Dickey in the first place.[25]

Moreover, on March 1, 1978, Congressmen Kostmayer, Lundine, and McHugh introduced the Voluntary Job Preservation and Community Stabilization Act which sought to provide funds to assist employee "buyouts."[26]

What was new in the Youngstown venture was the notion that workers and community residents could own and operate a *steel mill*. Steel is self-evidently a basic industry. If employee-community ownership could be made to work in steel, it could be made to work anywhere. There is all the difference in the world between an experiment on the margins of the system, and an experiment at its heart. Worker or worker-community ownership of a relatively small enterprise—say, an enterprise with less than 200 workers, requiring less than $5 million to purchase and begin to operate—can be dismissed precisely for the reason that the enterprise is small. Employee-community ownership of the Campbell Works would have challenged the capitalist system on the terrain of the large-scale enterprises in basic industries.

Feasibility Studies

Because what we were proposing was in this sense new, and required so much capital investment, there was all the more reason to be sure that what was proposed was feasible. We could not reopen any of these monster mills without amounts of capital that only the government could provide, and the government wanted feasibility studies. Moreover, both the Coalition itself, composed as it was of clergy men and women all of whose congregations included businessmen, and the Youngstown community, for so many decades a company town of Youngstown Sheet & Tube, needed an outside expert to tell them that the idea of reopening the Campbell Works made sense.

The Coalition sponsored two feasibility studies, initially providing $12,500 for each. The first, by the Western Reserve Economic Development Agency (WREDA), was a 30-day assessment by a respected economist using data provided by Youngstown Sheet & Tube. It was confined to the economic and financial feasibility of reopening the closed plant facilities. Necessarily, because of the speed with which it was prepared, it was confined to "a relatively general level of detail."[27] The second study, ultimately funded by the Department of Housing and Urban Development (HUD) with grants of over $300,000, was administered by Gar Alperovitz of the National Center for Economic Alternatives. The initial focus of the Center's study was the structure of employee-community ownership under which the reopening might be carried out. But the government also required the Center to explore in depth the conclusions reached by WREDA with regard to economic feasibility, a task contracted to one of the nation's leading steel analysts, Paul Marshall of Putnam, Hayes & Bartlett.

Later, critics of the Alperovitz study charged that his desire to see worker ownership put into practice led him to endorse a plan for re-opening the Campbell Works which was economically unsound. This criticism overlooked the fact that the WREDA analyst, a consulting engineer from Philadelphia named George Beetle, also concluded that the Campbell Works could be reopened profitably.

Both Alperovitz and Beetle recommended that the Campbell Works replace its antiquated open hearths with electric furnaces.[28] Both Alperovitz and Beetle assumed sales of about 1.4 million tons a year.[29] Both Alperovitz and Beetle assumed a modest increase in pro-ductivity due to employee involvement in the new firm.[30] Both Alperovitz and Beetle estimated that purchase and modernization of the Campbell Works would require a capital investment of about $500 million,[31] and both men concluded that, nevertheless, the ven-ture could be earning a profit after about five years.[32]

The Alperovitz Model: Employee-Community Ownership

The real genius of the work of the National Center for Economic Alternatives, as of Gar Alperovitz's initial strategy, was its grasp of the explosive potentiality of employee-community ownership.

This was manifest at Alperovitz's first meeting with Youngstown steelworkers, at St. Johns Episcopal Church in the weeks after the Coalition's founding conference.

There were perhaps three dozen steelworkers in the room. They were local union officers, grievance committeemen, and active rank-and-file members. I do not recall a single staff representative or repre-sentative of the District office.

"What would we do if the plant was ours to run?," Alperovitz asked, and the discussion never stopped. One important conclusion, shared by every person there who expressed himself, was that neither workers nor community representatives should alone be in charge. Workers would too often be short-sighted and make decisions which might be in their personal interests, but not in the public welfare, these steel-workers felt. On the other hand, the last thing they wanted was to trust a reopened Campbell Works to the community politicians who were thought to have offered little leadership in the crisis. It was because of this meeting that from then on the awkward phrase "employee-community ownership" was always used to talk about what we had in mind. This was the ownership model that the workers themselves chose.

Yet what exactly did the model mean? Were we talking about a corporation, with a board of directors? If so, who should be the directors, and how could they be made more responsible than the Lykes directors who met on September 18, 1977 and decided to close the Campbell Works? What about the union? Assuming (as we all did) that the shop would be unionized, how would a union function in a plant where workers were part owners? How could the same union representatives sit on both sides of the table, as management and union spokespersons at the same time?

A first cut at answering these questions was taken by Brad Dewan, a lawyer associated with the National Economic Development Law Project in Berkeley, and Karl Frieden, a Boston attorney, on contract from the Alperovitz study.[33] They began by listing several criteria by which an ownership model for the Campbell Works should be judged, principally (1) local control, to avoid a repetition of the shutdown of the Campbell Works; (2) union recognition; and (3) ability to attract capable management and sufficient financing. They then presented a "recommended model" for ownership, as well as (more briefly) other possible models, such as a workers' cooperative.

Employee Stock Ownership Plans (ESOPs)

The recommended model was a private, for-profit corporation, in which stock would be held by three kinds of owners: workers, holding stock through an Employee Stock Ownership Plan (ESOP); the community, which would acquire stock to be held by a separate nonprofit community development corporation; and ordinary common shareholders, hopefully from the local community.

The recommended model reflected the different pressures a new company would experience. It was desperately important to raise as much equity capital as possible. The capital needs anticipated were so great that Alperovitz and Marshall were projecting a 9:1 ratio of capital raised by borrowing (debt) to capital raised by investment in stocks (equity). Equity capital is more desirable, because dividends on stock are optional, but interest on loans must be paid. The "Save

Our Valley" campaign was directed to the mobilization of equity, and implicitly assumed that the new corporation would offer stock for sale. For this reason a conventional for-profit corporation recommended itself, in contrast to, for example, a workers' cooperative.

But how would a conventional corporation assure a workers' voice in investment decisions? Dewan and Frieden wrote that "employees will be able to have *some input* into the direction and operations of the operating company by their ability to elect one third of the board of directors. . . . The employees *likely will be permitted* to direct the trustee [of the ESOP] on how to vote the unallocated shares. . . ." (Emphasis added.)[34] These seemed dangerously weak expressions.

A typical ESOP is set up as follows: A trust fund is created, which lends money to an operating company. (The money may be loaned to the trust by the government.) The company deposits a block of its common stock with the trust as collateral for the loan. The company pays back its loan to the trust with operating income which it is not required to report for tax purposes. (This is why businessmen like ESOPs.) As the loan is repaid, a corresponding amount of the stock held by the trust is allocated to the accounts of individual employees, who receive it when they leave the employ of the company.

Especially in the early years of the ESOP, therefore, the trust holds many shares of stock not yet allocated to individual workers. In the typical ESOP these unallocated shares are managed by a conventional trustee, such as a bank. Workers who participate in such an ESOP have little control. They are merely employee-shareholders, receiving dividends from shares which are voted by a bank.

Moreover, the so-called community corporation recommended by Dewan and Frieden did not inspire workers' confidence, either. This entity reflected the fact that the entire project would be dependent on grants, loans, and loan guarantees from Washington. The community corporation would serve merely as a conduit for these Federal funds, yet would receive stock of the company corresponding to these funds. Thus it would acquire a one-third voice in management without making any contribution of its own. Nor was it encouraging to learn that "[t]he board of directors of this community corporation will be composed of recognized community leaders. . . . [I]t may be desirable for the board of directors to be composed of locally elected officials or their appointees. . . ."[35] Youngstown had had its fill of these "recognized" leaders. Locally elected officials and their appointees were felt to have failed in the crisis caused by the Campbell

Works closing. The Ecumenical Coalition was perceived as a breath of fresh air, an organization without an axe to grind which could rise above the squabbling of locally elected officials.

Finally, Dewan and Friedan declined to restrict purchase of stock to local residents, for the understandable reason that "[a] significant equity investment from all sources may be critical for the success of the operating company."[36] They sought to solicit outside capital without destroying local control by envisioning a class of non-voting preferred stock which would be "offered primarily to individuals and organizations residing or operating outside the immediate geographical area."[37]

These matters were debated in lively meetings at the First Presbyterian Church in Youngstown on July 26 and 27, 1978. Dewan and Frieden explained their recommended model and asked for comment and criticism. The concern for worker input in investment decisions was fully aired. James Bennett, a lawyer for a local law firm, suggested that this concern could be allayed if workers were given a veto over certain kinds of decisions, such as a decision to close a plant. This became a permanent element in our thinking. By offering ordinary stockholders the possibility of control of the corporation one could attract investment, but by assuring workers a veto over decisions which especially concerned them one could safeguard their interest, too.

What Part Would a Union Play?

Meantime the question of what part a union would play in the new structure was thrashed out among steelworkers. At a meeting in the Local 1462 (Brier Hill Works) union hall, Gerald Dickey stood at the blackboard and wrote down the suggestions of a dozen or so of the steelworkers most active in the Coalition. It was agreed without much discussion that full-time union representatives should not simultaneously serve as members of the board of directors. To do so would create an impossible conflict of interest for them. Yet there was warm response to the idea that workers should serve on the board, so as to safeguard workers' interests and be present when investment decisions were made. To accomplish this, those present turned to an organization they knew well: the credit union for Youngstown Sheet & Tube employees. The credit union included members of more than one local union, just as Community Steel probably would. Members of the credit union board of directors were nominated and elected in the various mills, and so it could be with worker directors of Community Steel. There was sentiment that each area or department should elect a board member, just as they elected a grievance committeeman. It was felt that the local union presidents, who could not themselves be Community Steel directors, should nominate others for that office. But it was also felt that rank-and-file members should be able to nominate by petition, lest local union officers get too much control of the situation.

How "Community Steel" was to be Governed

Community Steel, as the proposed corporation came to be known, was never actually incorporated during the struggle to reopen the Campbell Works. (However, it was incorporated during the later effort to reopen mills belonging to U.S. Steel.) As of December 1978, discussion among the Coalition and its supporters had refined the model as follows:[38]

1. *The 6-6-3 Ratio.* Common stockholders would elect 6 directors. Employees would elect 6 directors. A community corporation would elect 3 directors.

2. *Nomination of Employee Directors.* Employee directors would be nominated in two ways: (a) by a nominating committee made up of the presidents of USWA locals, members of which work in the mill, (b) by petition. Full-time union representatives would not be permitted to serve as employee directors, so as to avoid putting the union on both sides of the bargaining table. Employee directors would not have to be employed [in the mill].

3. *Fundamental Changes.* As suggested by Attorney James Bennett this past summer, fundamental changes would have to be approved by 80 per cent of each group of stockholders (common stockholders, employees, community corporation). There could be no corporate action resulting in the layoff of more than 10 per cent of the employees without such approval.

4. *Community Corporation and Economic Development.* It is hoped that EDA will loan money to the community corporation which in turn will be loaned to the ESOP trust for purchase of stock. The moneys repaid to the community corporation would

be used as a revolving fund for general economic development of the community. For this to be possible, the community corporation must be created by a government entity.

Thinking through this structure in dialogue with Brad Dewan and Karl Frieden was perhaps the most creative concrete act of the Coalition. We still think the structure would have worked.

Chapter Six. The Role of the International Union

Alperovitz calculated that reopening and modernizing the Campbell Works would require about $500 million. He estimated that actually buying the plant would cost less than a tenth of that amount. It was hoped that the Federal government would make an outright *grant* of the money needed to buy the plant, in the form of a UDAG (Urban Development Action Grant) from the Department of Housing and Urban Development, and an ESOP (Employee Stock Ownership Plan) grant from the Economic Development Administration. As for the much larger sum required to modernize the mill after it was purchased, Alperovitz suggested that the Federal government *guarantee private loans* in this amount from a special steel industry loan guarantee fund created in the fall of 1977 and administered by the Economic Development Administration (EDA) of the Department of Commerce.

In a project requiring millions of dollars in Federal grants, and hundreds of millions of dollars in Federal loan guarantees, the national Steelworkers union (known as "the international," because it includes Canadian members) would inevitably play a key role. There was no hope of amassing the clout required to bring so unusual a plan to fruition without support from the international. Even neutrality on the part of the international union would assure the defeat of Community Steel.

In September 1977, the international union was headed by Lloyd McBride, victor over insurgent Ed Sadlowski the previous winter. McBride's first response to the closing of the Campbell Works did not inspire hope. On September 20, the day following Lykes' shut-down announcement, McBride testified before a House Ways and Means subcommittee and blamed the wave of steel industry shut-downs on imported steel.[39] This was the same position being taken by the companies,[40] and by the petition brought to Washington at the end of that week by steelworkers from Youngstown. When the bus-loads from Youngstown arrived in Washington on September 23, 1977, several rank and filers succeeded in seeing McBride, who had remained in the city for a union legislative conference. He told them, as they reported his remarks, that the closing of a steel mill was like the closing of a corner grocery and that there was nothing to be done about it. McBride did not even visit Youngstown, about 75 miles from the international union headquarters in downtown Pittsburgh, for more than six months.

"The Foreign Competition Hoax"

The international union's passivity when confronted with the ter-mination of 5,000 of its members at the Campbell Works was the end product of a slow process of change in union attitudes. In 1959, the year of the last national steel strike in the United States, the USWA published a pamphlet entitled "The Foreign Competition Hoax" which charged that foreign steel was finding customers in the United States "BECAUSE AMERICAN PRICES AND PROFITS ARE UNJUSTIFIABLY HIGH."[41] The pamphlet showed that American companies were limiting production, charging high prices, and making high profits. Thus in 1958, according to the pamphlet, U.S. Steel had operated at only 59.2 per cent of capacity yet had made more than $300 million in profits, an amount exceeded only three times in the corporation's history. The American industry had actually raised prices in the summer of 1958 when over one-third of American steelworkers were either laid off or working part-time. In 1977, the same analysis was adopted by dissident union members in District 31 (Chicago-Gary), who charged that the real purpose of the companies' campaign against imported steel was "to sell steel on the American market at artificially inflated fixed monopoly prices," and called on the international union "to withdraw its support from the import restrictions campaign."[42] By 1977, however, the international union had long since abandoned its position that agitation against imports was a "hoax" and had adopted an analysis of the American steel industry's problems indistinguishable from the analysis of the companies.

Giving Up the Right to Strike: A History of the Experimental Negotiating Agreement

The critical change in the position of the United Steelworkers of America came in 1973, when the union gave up the right to strike. More than 90 per cent of the collective bargaining agreements in force in the United States contain a clause which unconditionally surrenders the right to strike *during the life of the contract*. What was new in the Experimental Negotiating Agreement (ENA) of 1973 was that it also gave up the right to strike at the *expiration* of the three-year Basic Steel Contract. The ENA was negotiated under the leadership of McBride's predecessor I. W. Abel. The reason Abel gave for what he did was imported steel. Here is what happened.[43]

I. W. Abel had been elected as president of the Steelworkers union as a reform candidate. He stated in his inaugural address on June 1, 1965:[44]

> While we are sure Steelworkers never welcome strike action, we are equally confident they know that there are times when the alternatives are worse. And under the ground rules of freedom, American workers revere and uphold the precious right to lay down their tools when it becomes necessary. We shall always seek the orderly, harmonious solution through peaceful negotiations; *but we will never surrender our inherent right to withhold our labor* when the events of time justify such action. (Applause.)

Nevertheless, almost from the moment he took office Abel began the secret negotiations which resulted eight years later in ENA.

On October 11, 1967, Abel presented to the union's International Executive Board a proposal he had worked out with R. Conrad Cooper of United States Steel, chief bargainer for the steel industry. The proposal called for the Steelworkers to commit themselves in advance of the expiration of the Basic Steel Contract to submit any unresolved issues in the next contract to arbitration. The proposal was opposed by Joseph Germano, director of District 31 (Chicago-Gary), and James Griffin, director of District 26 (Youngstown). "In an all-day debate, the dissenters voiced fears that the union would cripple itself by giving up the right to strike.''[45] Cooper publicly urged the union to reconsider. The International Executive Board met again on December 2, 1967, at which time it adopted a statement describing the exploration which had occurred, rejecting the no-strike proposal for the time being, and stating unequivocally

> that no agreement of this type could possibly be reached, under any circumstances, without prior approval from all policy-making bodies within our union, including the International Wage Policy Committee, the newly-established Basic Steel Industry Conference of local unions *and a poll of the membership directly involved.*[46]

Joint Productivity Committees. Creation of joint labor-management productivity committees in the 1971 contract led to revival of the no-strike proposal. An industry spokesman explained why the companies liked the productivity committees:

> This is a very subtle thing. It's a forum of communication we've never had before. If union members through these committees learn to appreciate some of our problems so that we may be able to end our crisis bargaining every three years, it would mean a hell of a lot more to us than a couple extra percentage points in productivity.[47]

A small group of union and industry representatives, including Bernard Kleiman, General Counsel of the Steelworkers, began to work on a no-strike proposal. The ENA was negotiated by a "Top Committee" consisting of the three top officers and two top lawyers of the union, two representatives from U.S. Steel, and one each from Bethlehem and Republic. A first draft of the agreement was submitted by company representatives on the Top Committee on June 19, 1972. Between that date and March 1973 the Top Committee met twenty times to work on the agreement, all without informing the members of the union that talks were going on.[48]

"Where's Joe?" The first hint to the membership that something was in the wind came in the form of a movie called "Where's Joe?" The film was financed jointly by the international union and the steel companies,[49] and was shown on company time to all employees in basic steel. The argument of the movie is that loss of jobs in the steel industry is caused by imports. This is so, according to "Where's

Joe?," because imports increase every three years at the end of the Basic Steel Contract, when steel consumers hedge against the possibility of a strike by buying large quantities of foreign steel. Edwin H. Gott, then chairman of the board of U.S. Steel, tells viewers that unless this hedge-buying can be stopped there will be more "Joes" missing from American mills. And I. W. Abel states, "In my judgment, we must find a way to bargain out our contractual differences peacefully and satisfactorily."

The international union and the companies signed the ENA on March 29, 1973. The International Executive Board first saw the agreement the day before. The presidents of local unions in basic steel were summoned to vote on the agreement without knowing the reason for the meeting, and directed to cast their votes without an opportunity to ask instructions from their members. The membership had no opportunity to vote on ENA.

In the ENA, the union agreed not to strike at the end of the Basic Steel Contract. Any issues unresolved as of April 15, 1974, were to be submitted to binding arbitration. In return, the companies promised a bonus of $150 to every union member in basic steel.

Grassroots Reaction to the ENA. Rank-and-file reaction was strong and immediate. In the Chicago area, where I was living at the time, rank-and-file groups in every major local put out leaflets showing I. W. Abel in bed with United States Steel and denouncing the $150 bribe. Resolutions condemning the ENA were passed at Locals 65 (United States Steel South Works) and 6787 (Bethlehem Steel Burns Harbor Works), and would probably have been passed elsewhere had a vote been allowed. A District 31 Defend the Right to Strike Committee was formed, put out a booklet entitled "Where's I. W. Abel?," consulted attorneys about going to court, and began to circulate petitions.

Willie Aikens, Red Thompson, and others, helped to collect 1,700 signatures on the petition at mill gates in the Youngstown area in August and September 1973. Ed Mann recalls:

> It was amazing the people who would walk up and say, "The only thing that makes a union is the right to strike. Without it, what do we need a union for?"[50]

On September 17, Bill Litch, together with George Edwards of Local 1104 (United States Steel Lorain Works) and Bill Ross of Local 65

(United States Steel South Works), attempted to deliver petitions to I. W. Abel at the union's headquarters in Pittsburgh. They were told that Abel had another commitment and could not meet with them. Two days later Litch, Barbero, Ken Doran, and Bob Lewis, all of Local 1462, tried to present the petitions to the director of District 26 in Youngstown. They, too, received only a receipt. When the international union issued a press release characterizing the protesters as a small minority of the union, Litch and Barbero challenged the international to open up the pages of *Steel Labor* to debate on the question and to hold a membership referendum. By this time the controversy had made the front page of the *New York Times*.[51]

As the research arm of the protest, I collected figures showing that imports of foreign steel had *decreased* from 1971 to 1973, while in the same period 40,000 jobs had been lost in basic steel, presumably for other reasons. We also tried to prove that giving up the strike weapon had hurt steelworkers' wages. Bureau of Labor Statistics figures showed that in 1958, the year before the last national strike in the steel industry, the average hourly earnings of steelworkers were higher than the earnings of auto, rubber, oil, and mine workers, whereas by 1969 steelworkers' earnings were lower than the earnings of all four other groups.[52] Friends at the New School of Social Research demonstrated that the average annual percentage increase in real hourly earnings of steelworkers was 3.76% a year from 1949 to 1960 (the "strike period") and only 0.44% a year from 1961 to 1970 (the "no-strike period").

Important fact finding was also done by steelworkers themselves. In October 1973 an internal U.S. Steel memorandum "fell off a truck" at the company's South Works in Chicago. Dated October 15, 1973, the memorandum was from Bruce Johnston, United States Steel Vice President of Labor Relations, to R. O. Hawkenson, United States Steel Vice President of Public Relations, with copies to R. Heath Larry, chief negotiator for the industry (succeeding Cooper), and others. The memo asked that a United States Steel advertisement placed in many national magazines that month which featured Steelworkers president Abel should *not* be displayed on bulletin boards in company mills. The reason offered was:

> We have all feared overexposure of I. W. Abel on this whole ENA-Productivity question, and we have recognized the risk of setting him up for his political opposition by too much identity with us. He has trusted us not to do this.

The Sadlowski Campaign. The ENA struggle left behind it a deep distrust of the national Steelworkers union. Opposition to the ENA, support for a change in the Steelworkers constitution to require a membership vote on contracts, became the platform of rank and filers everywhere. Thus, when Mann, Barbero and Litch ran for election as delegates to the 1976 Steelworkers convention, their literature called for abolishing the ENA:

> The E.N.A., like the joint company and Union productivity efforts, promised job security. Ask any young steelworker who has been on the street the last two years, *"Where is it?"* Over 100,000 were laid off; in the meanwhile, conditions in the plants become less safe and filthier. If you were an industry owner, wouldn't you cut jobs and let working conditions go to pot, if you knew that your employees couldn't strike from 3 to 6 years in advance? *We steelworkers must not allow the E.N.A. to become a pattern as our leadership suggests and let's end it in Basic Steel now!*[53]

These were also the ideas on which Ed Sadlowski ran for president of the Steelworkers union in the winter of 1976–1977. As a candidate for district director of District 31 in 1973 and 1974 Sadlowski had refused to take a public position against ENA. By 1976 a majority of union members in Basic Steel had come to feel that ENA offered no solution to the problem of job security, and Sadlowski concurred. Speaking in Warren, Ohio during the campaign, Sadlowski said that ENA had "deprived the union of its masculinity," opposed productivity clauses, predicted that the time would come when jobs were guaranteed for the duration of a contract, and supported the concept of bargaining over investment decisions.[54] The steelworkers who later led the fight against mill shutdowns were all Sadlowski supporters. Sadlowski's ideas won wide support in the Youngstown area, as in all Basic Steel. He lost the election because only 300,000 of the Steelworkers' one million members work in steel plants. Sadlowski's majority among steelworkers was not large enough to offset the margin of his opponent Lloyd McBride among non-steelworkers in the union.

Fear of shutdowns played a direct part in Sadlowski's defeat by his opponent Lloyd McBride. In an interview that appeared in the January 1977 issue of *Penthouse* magazine, during the closing weeks of the campaign, Sadlowski said that it might be a good thing to reduce the number of jobs in Basic Steel to 100,000 *if* the men and women displaced were retrained at company expense to do cleaner and more interesting work as professionals. Working forty hours a week in a mill drains the lifeblood of a man, Sadlowski said in the interview. There are "workers . . . who are full of poems" and doctors who are operating cranes. The ultimate goal of organized labor should be that no man should have to work at a blast furnace. The labor force in steel, Sadlowski went on, had been reduced from 520,000 to 400,000 in fifteen years. "Let's reduce them to 100,000." Let the steel industry subsidize the education, as carpet layers, doctors, plumbers, of the steel workers displaced.

McBride's people promptly put out the word that Sadlowski wanted to take away steelworkers' jobs. John Barbero, Sadlowski's campaign manager in the Youngstown area, believes that this was when "the Sadlowski stickers came off the hardhats."*

Youngstown-area steelworkers lost doubly when Sadlowski was beaten. In the opinion of rank-and-file observers, Marvin Weinstock, an able staff representative with a background in Left politics, would have defeated incumbent District 26 director Frank Leseganich had Weinstock not decided to withdraw from the local race to become vice presidential candidate on Sadlowski's slate. Weinstock's withdrawal left rank-and-file groups demoralized and divided. The insurgent vote was split among several last-minute candidates. Leseganich was reelected as district director. The result was considered by many to be weak union leadership in the shutdown crisis.

The Union and the Campbell Works

Lloyd McBride, president of the international union, inherited the attitudes of his predecessor I. W. Abel. Rather than blaming the companies for restricting output and raising prices for the sake of

---

*History repeats itself. Local 1397, USWA, representing production and maintenance workers at the historic Homestead Works near Pittsburgh, elected an insurgent slate to local union office in 1979. Thereafter it led the fight against steel mill shutdowns in the Pittsburgh area, staging demonstrations both at company and international union headquarters, publicly criticizing the McBride administration, and sponsoring legal actions in the Federal courts. On February 22, 1982, U.S. Steel announced that it might shut down the Homestead Works blast furnaces and open hearths. Two days later, international union vice president Joseph Odorich blamed the shutdowns in both Youngstown and Homestead on "a very militant element" in the local unions.[55]

profits, as it had in 1959, the international union joined the companies in trying to restrict imports. Instead of insisting that the American steel industry modernize so as to be able to compete effectively with steelmakers in Japan and Europe, the international union stood by passively while the companies closed plants.

Inevitably the vibrations from Pittsburgh were reproduced by the District 26 leadership in Youngstown, headed by District Director Frank Leseganich, a McBride supporter.

Ad Hoc Steelworker Meetings. Later it would seem that steelworkers had taken almost no part in the Coalition effort, and the question arose: Why are clergymen, rather than steelworkers, leading this effort? And why are steelworkers supporting "employee-community ownership" rather than seeking to run the mills themselves?

Criticisms along these lines overlook the difficulty of developing mass worker participation in the face of opposition by both regional and national union leadership. In October 1977, before the Ecumenical Coalition organized, Gerald Dickey, recording secretary of Local 1462, USWA, brought together active members of Sheet & Tube locals in the Valley to take common steps. For a variety of reasons, the local union leadership at the Campbell Works had not developed as aggressively or imaginatively as its counterparts at the Brier Hill Works and Youngstown Works. Dickey, however, got around this problem by forming an ad hoc group which included several local union presidents but surrounded them with lesser local officers and grievance committeemen. The group held at least three meetings at the Local 1418 hall.

The ad hoc group was not given the time to develop a strategy. At its last meeting, the group endorsed a suggestion that it consider a stockholders' suit against the Lykes board of directors. Many Sheet & Tube workers owned stock in the company. Indeed the company promoted stock ownership by awarding shares of common stock to outstanding workers designated as "Pros of the Month." The idea of the suit was that these steelworker stockholders would sue the board of directors of Lykes for actions harmful to the company. To this end, a letter to the Board was drafted detailing the mismanagement of Lykes from 1969 to 1977 and demanding:

1. Layoffs must stop at once;
2. Idle facilities should be "mothballed" for eventual reopening;

3. If the decision to close facilities is irrevocable, Lykes should open negotiations "to give or sell them to an employee-community consortium which would operate them itself";

4. Plans to transfer corporate offices from Youngstown to Indiana should be abandoned.

Who knows whether this proposed litigation would have been any more or less effective than any of the other bricks we threw at corporate tanks during the following three years? It was a first step which we had decided to take together. The letter itself, which denounced the shutdown decision as an "inhuman" action violating "the trust of investors and employees," touched a deep nerve. It was read aloud, and I recall that when the reading finished the grievance committeeman of the Campbell open hearth said, "Let me sign that." Eventually the letter was signed by hundreds of employee-stockholders, including several "Pros of the Month" and four presidents of local unions.

The Union's District Director Intervenes. Leseganich then intervened. He directed the Sheet & Tube local union presidents henceforth to meet only with himself, at meetings that were to include no other local union officers, and a different attorney. The press was told that District 26 was considering legal action.[56] The Sheet & Tube local union presidents were asked to collect the names of possible shareholder plaintiffs.[57] I was instructed to discontinue my representation of the locals.[58] And then . . . nothing happened. The momentary threat to the authority of the District leadership having been brought under control, the Director resumed his policy of doing nothing. No law suit was ever filed.

Opposition from the International. Meantime the feasibility studies on the possibility of reopening the Campbell Works began to appear. The international union made its first comment in a paper prepared by McBride aide James W. Smith.

Smith's paper cited a number of "opinions which are widely held in the Mahoning Valley." He agreed with some of them: that Mahoning Valley steelworkers are among the best in the world; that Campbell Works and Brier Hill have always made profits for Y. S. & T., but too much of the profits were spent at Indiana Harbor instead of being used to modernize the Mahoning Valley plants; that Lykes' management drained profits out of the Youngstown District, and furthermore made serious judgmental errors in managing the Mahoning Valley plants. Then he listed two more:

4) That suppliers, customers, employees, and other interested persons can invest enough money to buy the closed facilities.

5) That the Federal government will grant, or guarantee loans, for most of the money needed to modernize the Works.

Smith concluded that very few people outside the Mahoning Valley agreed with these last two opinions.[59]

Early in April 1978 the Alperovitz task force released its preliminary findings. Alperovitz and Paul Marshall came to Youngstown, and presented their results to a morning meeting of the Ecumenical Coalition, and an afternoon meeting of the Mahoning Valley Economic Development Committee, held in the chambers of the Youngstown City Council. The plan was to make a similar presentation to the United Steelworkers of America at a dinner to be held in the Mahoning Country Club. The occasion was the more important in that Lloyd McBride was making his first visit to Youngstown since the closing of the Campbell Works and was to be at the dinner.

The evening began cordially. I recall meeting Mr. McBride during the cocktail hour, and sitting at dinner next to Russ Gibbons, editor of the international union newspaper, *Steel Labor*. McBride was introduced, made a few remarks, and called for questions. Duane Irving stood up. In an altogether matter-of-fact and unthreatening manner, he referred to the projected U.S. Steel mill at Conneaut and asked what the union could do to prevent further shutdowns when Conneaut came on line. Then, as Irving recounts it:

He flew, he really flew into a rage. He said that somebody had put me up to that question and he didn't give me an answer. I thought it was amazing. If I were going to Youngstown and there had just been a giant plant shutdown I would have had some type of plan to announce to people. But he didn't have any.[60]

After Irving's question it was time for Alperovitz to be introduced and to share the results of his feasibility study. Just at this moment, McBride led the assembled union brass out of the room, leaving Alperovitz to address local union officers and rank and filers.

What may have lain behind this behavior is suggested by a memo-

randum which Smith wrote a few weeks later.[61] Addressed to Leseganich and copied to other union associates, this document contained the following main points:

1. According to Smith, Alperovitz made three key, unrealistic
assumptions about *financing*. First, financing was assumed to be on
a 9:1 ratio of debt to equity capital. Smith felt this would burden the
new company with an excessive load of fixed interest payments.
Second, it was proposed to raise $50–70 million in equity capital for a
company one-third of the directors of which would be elected by
employees. "I do not believe that the people who have or control that
kind of money will gamble that much in a company structured in
such a way," Smith wrote. Finally, the sources envisioned for proposed loans of $450 to 600 million would not be willing to make that
much available, Smith thought.

2. More fundamentally, Smith criticized the *basic concept* of the
proposed Coalition venture. He suggested that it was a throwback to
the producers' cooperatives sought by the Knights of Labor in the
period 1870 to 1895. Most of these ventures failed, he noted. In the
few that succeeded the workers became capitalists, and eventually
dropped out of the Knights. "Eventually the Knights itself folded,
for various reasons, one of which was the depletion of its treasury by
investments in worker ownership." The United Mine Workers rejected the Knights' approach and decided to concentrate on collective
bargaining. The UMWA affiliated with the AFL in the 1890s and
helped to found the CIO in the 1930s. In each federation its philosophy
on this subject became widespread.

Smith's conclusion, intended only for the eyes of other top USWA
personnel, candidly expressed the international union's basic concerns:

> The time may come when organized labor should take a new
> look at this whole subject. However, when and if we do, that
> action will have to be taken by the decision-making bodies of the
> Union, and not by individuals.
>
> In the meantime, I would not recommend that the Interna-
> tional Union engage in the promotion of such schemes. If Local
> Unions wish to do so, or if our members wish to do so, I do not
> believe that President McBride or the other Officers would be
> inclined to interfere, but it is a very different thing for the Inter-
> national Union to place its stamp of approval on such ventures.
>
> The NCEA [National Center for Economic Alternatives] paper
> calls upon our International Union to invest in and promote its

plan of community/worker ownership. The writers of the paper are either ignorant of American labor's bad experiences with such schemes, or they know perfectly well what the situation is and are simply seeking to discredit the Union in the eyes of those members who wish to see the Campbell Works reopened. I strongly suspect that the latter is the case.

Coalition representatives met with Smith to discuss this disturbing memorandum. Brandishing a small book written by Alperovitz and myself on approaches to a new American socialism,[62] Smith reportedly Red-baited the two of us in no uncertain terms.

The elected local leadership of the Youngstown steelworkers rejected Smith's attack on the Coalition proposal, Alperovitz, and myself. They had asked us in on the basis of our record in fights for rank-and-file causes, and resented any effort to undercut local control of the campaign.

Conflict at the 1978 Convention. The conflict between the international union and the Youngstown rank and file came to a head at the national Steelworkers convention in September 1978. On September 19, 1978, one year to the day from the shutdown announcement at the Campbell Works, Ed Mann, president of Local 1462, approached the floor mike at the convention to speak on a resolution concerning plant shutdowns. Like all resolutions offered at USWA conventions on behalf of the top officialdom, this one had been prepared by a hand-picked Resolutions Committee and was reported to the floor under by-laws which prohibited amendments. The resolution called for a government-sponsored steel research center in Youngstown, a pet project of former District 26 director James Griffin. The resolution said not one word about the Coalition proposal then being brought before the nation in full-page newspaper ads. Mann wanted to say that the research center would create only 200 jobs at a cost of $750 million to $1 billion, whereas a reopened Campbell Works would employ 3,500 workers and cost less. Unable to amend the resolution on the floor, he wanted to ask the delegates to reject it and to put in its place a resolution supporting the Coalition effort which had been endorsed by Local 1462, the District 26 conference, and the Ohio AFL-CIO.[63]

> . . . [International union] vice president Joe Odorcich was in the chair. . . . Local Union president Ed Mann and the entire

Local 1462 delegation, along with many delegates from the Campbell Works were lined up at the microphone waiting to speak. Odorcich called on a delegate from District 31. It was Charles Hobbs from Local 1011, Indiana Harbor. Hobbs simply stated that Ed Mann was waiting to speak on mike 12 and requested that he be given the chance, because "he's got a lot to say."

Mann addressed the delegates. . . . He received a nice round of applause.

Odorcich called for a vote. The "yes" vote was rather weak. It was the kind of vote that you automatically expect to hear at conventions from delegates supporting the chair, but having little interest in the issue.

The "no" vote was strong across the hall, overwhelming in District 26. Nobody heard Odorcich rule on the resolution. Did it pass or fail? Nobody could say.

District 26 delegates were on their feet. They were waving their hands and shouting, "Point of order!" Odorcich either didn't hear them or he chose to ignore them because he simply went on to the next resolution. Confusion prevailed. Russ Baxter, president of Local 2163, was furious. "I wanted to speak," he said. "I lost 2,100 members and I wanted to ask him what he was going to do about it."[64]

The next day President McBride held a press conference and was asked about Youngstown. He declined to support any existing proposal (including, of course, the Coalition's) and intimated "that there was another proposal that would bring back slightly more than 3,500 jobs, but . . . refused to go into details."[65] For a few days the workers and press[66] of the Mahoning Valley held their breaths. Once again . . . nothing happened. The "McBride Plan" had as little reality as the law suit Director Leseganich had hinted at a year earlier. Persons present at the press conference believe that McBride was confused about what to say and made up the notion of another proposal on the spot.

Six months later, in March 1979, McBride endorsed the Coalition proposal and Smith worked with Coalition consultants to refine the labor cost portion of the plan. By then it was too late.

Chapter Seven. No Help from the White House

The summer of 1978 was a period of uncertainty and reassessment for the Ecumenical Coalition. The United Steelworkers of America was not the only source of attacks on the effort. In May, a news story in the *Youngstown Vindicator* entitled "Steel Targets 3 Coalitionists" described efforts on the part of the steel companies to discredit Alperovitz, consultant Paul Marshall, and myself. "One thing's for certain," a steel industry representative was said to have told the press. "Marshall won't work for AISI [American Iron and Steel Institute] again."[67]

The *Vindicator* came to the defense of the "coalitionists" in an editorial entitled, "A Matter of Perspective."[68] But the Coalition had great difficulty in uniting the Youngstown community behind its plan. The steel industry opposed it. The international union and its district director opposed it. Many small businessmen in the Mahoning Valley were privately happy to see steel mills close because they believed it would now be possible to pay lower wages. Local politicians and media executives, closely allied with the steel industry, the international union, and small business, gave lip service to the Coalition proposal but off the record were lukewarm.

The Federal government was unlikely to endorse a project which was not supported by the entire Youngstown community, including the local Democratic Party and local businessmen. Moreover, as will be more fully described in Part II, the Federal government itself made the Coalition's task more difficult when the Department of Justice approved a proposed merger between Lykes and LTV without requiring Lykes to offer the Campbell Works for sale to the Coalition.

The Coalition's Four Requests

The upshot of this period of uncertainty was a renewed commitment to the Alperovitz strategy. To be sure, the reopening of the Campbell Works had always been a long shot from a conventional commercial point of view. But why should the government be limited to a conventional viewpoint? Why not opt to make Youngstown a national showcase of what a local community and a visionary national government could do as partners? Economically, this meant that the government would have to help not only in the initial financing of the project, but also by continuing government purchases. Politically, this meant that we would go all-out to enlist Federal support at the very highest levels. The Coalition decided to ask:

> 1. That the Vice-President or the President directly appoint someone on his staff to work with the Ecumenical Coalition to coordinate Federal efforts to achieve a "model" or "showcase" demonstration project for Youngstown. This effort would include the appointment of a Federal Task Force to include representation from HUD, DOE, EPA, Commerce, Office of Procurement, OMB, the Council on Wage and Price Stability and Ambassador Strauss' staff. . . .
>
> 2. That 400 million dollars in loan guarantee authority be placed in reserve for this project.
>
> 3. That specific programs to use federal procurement in support of the "showcase" effort be consolidated by the Federal Task Force.
>
> 4. That immediate assistance to the Ecumenical Coalition (in conjunction with the appropriate local government entity) be provided by way of a UDAG grant or other grant to purchase the facility. . . .[69]

Open Letter to President Carter

To bring about a meeting with the Vice President or President the Coalition escalated its already massive publicity efforts.[70] An Open Letter to President Carter was planned to appear in *The Washington Post* in mid-September at the same time as the release of the final report of the National Center for Economic Alternatives. Part-time organizers in Akron, Cincinnati, Cleveland, Columbus, Dayton and Toledo were hired to collect signatures for the Open Letter from clerical leaders across the state. A national conference was projected for Youngstown in late September.

The Open Letter appeared in *The Washington Post* on September 15, 1978. "Mr. President," it declared, "Youngstown Is A Moral Issue." The text began:

> Mr. President, in three months we lost 5,000 basic steel jobs in Youngstown last year. Another 5,000 steel jobs hang by a thread.

The letter continued:

> Mr. President, . . . [u]nemployment benefits are running out now in Youngstown. The thought of welfare is like a sword put to the pride and dignity of people there. Men and women whose steelmaking skills go back three generations are driven to despair and humiliated by decisions made for them by distant and unknown persons.

The letter went on to point out that $4 million had been deposited in Save Our Valley accounts in Youngstown-area banks "as a sign of our determination to help ourselves." It pointed out that the Lykes Corporation, "which brought us to this crisis, received $600 million in outright federal subsidies for its steamship operations." It observed that Attorney General Bell's decision to permit the merger of Lykes and LTV "without requiring their cooperation with the effort to reopen the mill has made our task more difficult." The letter ended:

> Mr. President, tens of thousands of human lives are involved in Youngstown. That's why it is a moral issue. If you decide to help Youngstown, we can create what your HUD Secretary calls a "new demonstration project" for self-sufficient community enterprise to save jobs, which can be an inspiration for communities in Ohio and around the nation.
>
> If you decide not to help, Youngstown will become another industrial disaster area. Ohio and national religious leaders hope to meet soon with you and the Vice President. . . .

The letter was signed by hundreds of religious personalities from Akron, Canton, Cincinnati, Cleveland, Columbus, Dayton, Toledo, and Youngstown-Warren. More than 1,000 additional names could not be printed because of lack of space.

First Use of Direct Action

On the next day, September 16, 1977, the Coalition for the first and last time engaged in some modest direct action. President Carter was scheduled to speak at the Columbus fairgrounds on September 16. Coalition spokespersons requested that he stop in Youngstown en route to Columbus. The President refused, symbolically undertaking to speak in Aliquippa, Pennsylvania at midday and then to fly over Youngstown to Columbus for his speech that night.

Bishop William Hughes of the Catholic Diocese (subbing for Bishop Malone who was in Rome), Chuck Rawlings, Dianne Kenny, Ed Weisheimer, Ed Mann, Sam Myers, and others, drove to Columbus and set up banners by the side of the road. A little further down the road were farmers, protesting low farm prices, who poured a mound of corn cobs from the back of a truck. The Coalition's banners read "Save Youngstown, Save America," and "Mr. President, Save Our Valley." Ed Mann in his yellow hard hat tried to pass leaflets to the occupants of the big black swiftly-moving limousines in which celebrities arrived for the President's speech.

Unbeknownst to the Coalition this effort was being closely watched from Washington. On September 8, 1977, Robert T. Hall, head of the Economic Development Administration which would give or deny the Coalition the loan guarantees on which our project depended, wrote a memorandum to Bruce Kirschenbaum, one of several White House liaisons on Mahoning Valley economic problems. The memo responded to information that the Coalition was planning to picket the President in Columbus on September 16 in hopes of gaining sufficient attention to bring about a meeting with Vice President Mondale. Hall wrote in part:

> The NCEA thing is so far out and unrealistic that I worry about involving the Vice President and giving further "credibility" to their effort.

Hall also wrote:

> As I indicated to you on the phone, a "constructive" effort is now forming under the leadership of the Steel Communities Coalition (SCC). Very delicate negotiations are being undertaken by the SCC which would produce alternatives to reopening the Campbell Works which would be acceptable to ECMV and its religious membership. However, the negotiations will not be completed until late September or early October.[71]

The Steel Communities Coalition was funded to a large extent by the steel companies. The delicate negotiations mentioned involved an attempt to persuade Bishop Malone to withdraw his support from the Alperovitz proposal.

$100 Million in Loan Guarantees Promised

For the moment, however, the impact of the Open Letter of September 15 and the direct action of September 16 overcame the hostility of Washington decisionmakers. The Coalition's first and last direct action produced the Coalition's first and last success in Washington.

On September 27, 1978, there took place in Washington the meeting with White House representatives so long sought by the Coalition. President Carter was not there, nor was Vice President Mondale. The meeting was chaired by Jack Watson, a White House aide. The Coalition's plan was only one of several proposals for help to the Mahoning Valley aired at the hour and a half meeting. But it was clear to participants that the Coalition proposal, now backed by the final report of the Alperovitz task force (released September 14), was the leading candidate for Federal aid.

At the meeting Watson committed the Federal government to at least $100 million in Federal loan guarantees for economic development in the Youngstown area. The money was to come from a fund of half a billion dollars set aside in 1977 to help the steel industry, and administered by the Economic Development Administration of the Department of Commerce. Since the Alperovitz study called for more than $300 million in Federal aid, Watson was asked if this doomed the plan. No, he responded. He said the government had the resources to back the Coalition effort.[72] The additional $200 million was within the capabilities of the government, he added; he had "very little doubt that we can, between the public sector and the private sector, put something together that can work."[73]

Mr. Watson, at the September 27 meeting, also indicated that the Administration would have some word for the Coalition about its proposal within three weeks. As one Washington luminary followed the other to Youngstown to campaign for Democratic Congressman Charles Carney, there was hope that one of them would prove a messenger of good news. Vice President Mondale's visit on October

14 was awaited with particular expectation. But Mondale only said, "A decision has not been made," while steelworkers at the back of the crowd held up signs saying, "Local 1418 Supports the Ecumenical Coalition," "Steel Town to Ghost Town," and "Save Our Steel Valley."[74]

A letter from Watson arrived at last, dated October 18. It stated that a decision on the Coalition proposal could not be reached "at this time," because "[t]he information on which such a decision must be based is not fully available to us." Watson asked for more studies:

First, he asked for further work in the marketing area;

Second, he asked for information as to the price at which the Campbell Works would be made available;

Third, he stated that questions had been raised about the legality and practicality of government procurement on the scale proposed by the Coalition.[75]

In retrospect, it is reasonably clear that the EDA and the Carter administration were determined to reject the Coalition proposal at the very moment Watson's letter held out some encouragement to us. Before the meeting at the White House on September 27 an EDA memorandum entitled "Briefing Paper on Youngstown/Mahoning Valley" stated of the National Conference on Economic Alternatives:

> One of NCEA's principals, Gar Alperovitz, has been extremely visible both nationally and internationally as he traveled widely in the last 6 months promoting the idea of religious groups' involvement in community ownership of basic manufacturing facilities. NCEA is less important than the other organizations [United Steelworkers of America, Western Reserve Economic Development Agency, Mahoning Valley Economic Development Committee] mentioned. It will recommend the unfeasible solution of spending vast sums of Federal dollars to reopen a facility which will never regain its market share let alone be self-sustaining. Moreover, NCEA and its ideas are strongly opposed by the Steel Workers Union and by private industry.[76]

On the same day that Jack Watson wrote his letter to the Coalition, October 18, Hal Williams of EDA wrote to his superior Robert Hall describing a discussion with Paul Thayer, chairman of the board of LTV. "Without being asked, he [Thayer] volunteered the information that the Coalition's proposal was not at all feasible," Williams stated. A day later Williams sent another memorandum to Hall, describing a conversation concerning "what else might be done, particularly with regard to the $100 million loan guarantee reservation." It seems EDA was already assuming that this money would not go to the Coalition, and was casting about for other ways to use it.

Reviewing this evidence, reporter Dale Peskin concluded that immediately before the November 1978 elections the White House sought to placate the Coalition by conditionally approving or at least not rejecting a plan it was determined to oppose. In Peskin's words, the Carter administration "deceived the Ecumenical Coalition of the Mahoning Valley for at least seven months about its proposal to re-open a local steel mill with federal loan guarantees." This deception, Peskin wrote, cost the community about $200,000 in private money and cost the Federal government $125,000 (the second HUD grant to Alperovitz).[77]

If the Carter administration's purpose was to avoid saying No to the Coalition until after the re-election of Mahoning Valley congressman Charles Carney, a Democrat, it didn't work. In the November elections voters showed what they thought of the Carter administration's response to the closing of the Campbell Works by electing the first Republican to represent the Valley since the 1930s, Lyle Williams.

Chapter Eight. Waiting for Washington

The easiest of Jack Watson's three requests to satisfy turned out to be determining the price for which the Campbell Works could be acquired.

Since early in 1978 a team of Coalition negotiators had been meeting with representatives of Lykes and LTV. The team included an acquisitions expert from the International Telephone and Telegraph company made available to the Coalition without charge through the efforts of Senator Howard Metzenbaum of Ohio.

As of August 1978 the negotiating position of the company was that: 1. the company was willing to sell only the closed portion of the Campbell Works (later the closed portion of the Brier Hill Works was added); 2. the company was prepared to hire a third party appraiser to determine the fair value of the plant; 3. the company was prepared to supply hot metal to the Campbell open hearths with price, quality, and duration of this arrangement yet to be defined; 4. the company would consider buying any steel it required in the Youngstown area from a reopened Campbell Works; 5. the company would maintain the closed facilities in mothballed condition until June 1979.[78] The company refused to name a price at which the facilities could be acquired. And it refused to provide assurance that the Coalition would be given a "first option," that is, the right to buy the facilities if it could come up with the money during a designated period of time.

The Company Offers to Sell the Plant

In November 1978 the company suddenly found itself able to name a price for the Campbell Works without first conducting an appraisal. The change came about because Lykes and LTV were on the verge of consummating a merger: the Department of Justice had approved the merger in June 1978, and shareholders' meetings of both companies to consummate the merger were scheduled for early December 1978. Senator Metzenbaum and Senator Edward Kennedy, prominent members of the Anti-Trust Subcommittee of the Senate Judiciary Committee, used the impending merger to put pressure on Lykes. On November 7, 1978, Senator Metzenbaum wrote to the Attorney General asking the Justice Department to withdraw its approval of the merger until the Coalition was given a firm price for the closed portion of the Campbell Works. Metzenbaum wrote in part: "It has now become quite obvious that the definite intent, aim and purpose of the acquiring corporation has been to stall the negotiations until such time as the merger has been finalized."[79] On November 9, 1978, Senator Kennedy wrote a strong letter to the Federal Trade Commission asking the Commission to take a fresh look at the legality of the merger.

On November 17, R. G. Allen of LTV wrote to the Coalition offering the closed facilities at the Campbell Works—principally the open hearths, blooming and billet mills, hot strip mill, and cold strip mill—for $16 million.[80] He also gave the Coalition until June 1, 1979, to come up with the money. If the Coalition could offer the named amount of money before that date the mill was ours.

The Federal government's promise to reserve at least $100 million in loan guarantees for the Mahoning Valley, together with the companies' offer of the closed facilities at a definite price, gave Coalition members the sense of having moved the ball to the opponent's five-yard line.

More Attacks

Others must have had the same impression. Attacks on the Coalition proposal escalated. Early in October the *Wall Street Journal* published an article about Youngstown entitled "Bouncing Back" which alleged that the predicted social effects of the Campbell Works shutdown had not materialized.[81] In October 1978 this conclusion had some plausibility. Workers terminated at the Campbell Works ordinarily received a substantial portion of their previous income for one year, due to unemployment compensation and Trade Readjustment Assistance, and that year for workers at the Campbell Works was just coming to a close in fall 1978. Moreover, the region's automotive industry did absorb some of the steel industry's unemployment. The ideological character of the article, however, is suggested by the fact that a year later *Fortune* published an article again called "Youngstown Bounces Back."[82] By then the phrase had become ludicrous. The Brier Hill Works was closing and U.S. Steel had just announced a decision to close the Youngstown Works. *Fortune*'s own data indicated that 35 per cent of those displaced had been forced into early retirement at half their previous earnings; another 15 per cent were still looking for work; while 10 per cent had moved to places like Houston (and in some cases, come back).

On October 24, 1978, Richard Gray, a vice president of Republic Steel, attacked the Coalition in an address to the Manufacturers' Association in Warren. His address contained phrases such as, "Outside interests have been stirring up support amongst the church groups," and, "[The National Center for Economic Alternatives is an] activist organization [that] promotes a socialistic adventure, badly conceived."[83]

Public opinion remained strongly behind the Coalition, however. An indication of this came on December 5, 1978 at the meeting of shareholders of the Lykes corporation called to approve Lykes' merger with LTV. Sister Joanna Ilgg of the School Sisters of Notre Dame presented a shareholders resolution which said in part:

> THEREFORE BE IT RESOLVED that the stockholders request the board of directors energetically to support and fully cooperate with efforts by workers, the Ecumenical Coalition of the Mahoning Valley, and other groups, to reopen the shutdown facility in Youngstown, Ohio, under workers/community ownership;
>
> BE IT FURTHER RESOLVED that the stockholders request the board of directors to prepare a report to be submitted to all stockholders within 30 days from the date of this meeting, detailing specific actions our company is prepared to take to assist in the opening of the shutdown Youngstown facilities.

The vote on this resolution was astounding: 2,484,991 for, 2,707,836 against, 3,969,058 abstain.[84]

More Feasibility Problems

The first and third concerns expressed in Jack Watson's letter had to do with sales: whether the commercial sales forecast was inflated, and whether government procurement was legally and practically sound. Very unfortunately, the further HUD grant required to enable Paul Marshall to address these questions took months to negotiate. At the same time, the decision-making cycle of the Department of Housing and Urban Development required that an application for an Urban Development Action Grant (UDAG) be filed by January 31, 1979 if a decision were to be forthcoming by April 1. The UDAG was critical, because it was from that outright grant of $17 million that the Coalition proposed to hire a management team, make a down payment to an investment banker who would "place" the necessary loans, and otherwise actually get the project on the road. Finally, LTV/Lykes was holding the closed facilities for the Coalition only until June 1. Thereafter there was no commitment as to mothballing, no commitment as to price, and no commitment that the Coalition would have a first option to buy.

The upshot of these pressures was that the initial application for a UDAG was filed at a time when the Coalition had only barely begun to rethink its proposal in response to Watson's questions 1 and 3. The first suggestion of a revised plan came from Alperovitz's associate Robert Brandwein on January 23, 1979, a week before the UDAG application was due.[85] The new plan called for a first phase in which the hot strip mill would be reopened, using purchased semi-finished slabs, and a subsequent second phase in which electric furnaces and a continuous caster would be installed. Among other advantages this phasing of the proposal brought down the loan guarantees required for Phase I to something close to the EDA target of $100 million. A second attraction of the new idea was that the needed semi-finished slabs might be obtained from Brier Hill. The merged corporation had announced that the Brier Hill Works would be closed by the end of 1979. Coalitionists hoped that if their plan for reopening the Campbell Works assigned a role to Brier Hill it might forestall the closing of this second mill. The new plan therefore called for the Brier Hill Works to continue to make steel in its ancient open hearths, and to semi-finish the steel into slabs. The slabs would then be transported to the Campbell Works and rolled into coils by the hot and cold strip mills. By the time electric furnaces were in place at the Campbell Works, so that steelmaking at Brier Hill was no longer needed, it was hoped that Brier Hill would have evolved its own modernization plan.

Thus it came about that while the Federal bureaucracies were evaluating the Alperovitz report of September 1978 and the UDAG application of January 1979 the Coalition was feverishly refining its proposal. This process culminated in an amended application, submitted on March 15, and a full-dress meeting with the EDA decisionmakers on March 21.

In those last, hectic weeks of February and March 1979 an extraordinary array of talent formed up behind the revised Coalition proposal. John Stone, former Operations Manager for Youngstown Sheet & Tube (the same John Stone who bet Russ Baxter a bottle of whiskey in September 1977 that the Campbell Works was not about to close), was one of them. Another was Frank McGough, retired Assistant to the Manager of Sheet & Tube's Indiana Harbor Division. Paul Marshall produced a set of calculations which seemed to demonstrate that the Coalition plan was viable. Tom Powers of Warburg, Paribas, Becker, a New York City investment banking firm, sketched out a commitment on the part of that house to "place" the government guaranteed loan with private lenders. Ray Sawyer of the Cleveland law firm Thompson, Hine and Flory helped with envisioning the structure of Community Steel and in a dozen tasks of drafting and oral presentation. Attorneys from another Cleveland law firm, Benesch, Friedlander, headed the continuing negotiations with J & L about acquisition of the Works.

At the very end even Lloyd McBride, Steelworkers union president, wrote to President Carter that the project had union support, and McBride aide Jim Smith endorsed the Coalition's calculations concerning labor costs.[86] This change in position was hard to understand. Had it come earlier it might have made all the difference in winning support from the Federal government. Cynics came to view a McBride/Smith endorsement in the same way as a Mafia kiss of death: when the union came out in your support, you should know you had already lost.

Steelworkers United for Employment (SUE)
and the Problem of Labor Costs

Finally, too, in this last phase of the struggle, steelworkers turned out in respectable numbers in support of the Coalition proposal.

They came together in an organization called SUE (Steelworkers United for Employment). SUE was the brainchild of Duane Irving and of Bob Clyde, director of Northeast Ohio Legal Services. Its co-chairpersons were Leonard Balluck, former greivance committeeman for the open hearth at the Campbell Works, and John McNicol, who worked as a carpenter at the Works before it closed.

SUE held a large public meeting on Monday, March 12, 1979, attended by 300–400 persons, and made a decisive contribution to the Coalition plan. By voice vote, and then by individual signatures on a written copy of the resolution, they approved the following approach to Community Steel's labor costs:

1. We support the Basic Steel Contract. If one group of steel-workers gives up part of the Basic Steel Contract, the next group of steelworkers would be asked to give up more. Even if it were in our short-term self-interest, we have an obligation to fellow union members which should prevent us from weakening the Basic Steel Contract.

2. Incentives are locally negotiated. We are open to the possibility that employees at Community Steel, Inc. would receive incentive pay tied to the firm's profits. We understand that this might mean that employees would receive reduced incentive pay during the company's early years.

3. Manning is locally negotiated. In an operating steel company, we would be hesitant to suggest reduction in manning. If it is necessary in reopening the Campbell Works to combine certain jobs for the sake of efficiency and lower costs, we are open to the possibility of doing so.

4. Vacation pay is a large cost item. We understand that in a new company employees would begin to accrue vacation time afresh, so that there would be no thirteen-week vacations during the early years of the company.

5. We are aware that at the Wheeling-Pittsburgh steel company employees were given the option of taking part of their pay in the form of stock of the company. If it were necessary in order to help the new company get off the ground, we would be open to this possibility, provided each employee was free to choose whether or not to participate.

6. It is important for a new company to hire the best possible workers. We believe that employees might participate in the hiring process to ensure that this occurs.

7. Apart from, and in addition to, all of the above, we believe that if employees are given a voice in Community Steel, Inc., productivity will increase dramatically. . . .

Jim Smith of the Steelworkers estimated that the approach represented by the SUE petition would permit labor cost savings of more than 20 per cent and ensure the success of the revised Coalition proposal. He estimated that because laid-off workers would begin as new employees, without accumulated seniority, Community Steel would be liable for 42 cents an hour for pension funding costs as compared to the 1978 industry-wide average of $1.15 an hour. (Note that this was not the same situation as at South Bend Lathe, where workers gave up their pensions in exchange for stock in a new company. Workers hired by Community Steel would not have given up their pensions. They would have received pensions corresponding to their previous years of service from Jones & Laughlin, and pensions corresponding to their years at Community Steel from the new company.) Similarly, Smith estimated, Community Steel would be liable for an average of 32.5 cents an hour for vacation costs during the first ten years as compared to the 1978 industry-wide average of 86.5 cents an hour. These two items alone (together with comparable but smaller savings on other fringe benefits) would reduce labor costs by 10 per cent, Smith estimated. It was also his opinion that Campbell Works had 5 to 10 per cent more manpower than its competitors operating similar equipment, and that if both white- and blue-collar workers were prepared to accept appropriate manning reductions the bulk of the needed increase in labor efficiency could come at the outset of operations.

Human Costs and Hopes

Balluck and McNicol were present at several of the Coalition's final meetings with government agencies. When Balluck spoke at a Coalition press conference on March 29 a Cleveland reporter described it this way:

> Len Balluck of Youngstown, a middle-aged, balding man with a thin, tired face, squirmed uncomfortably in a tie and sportcoat as he faced a room full of reporters here yesterday. . . .

The room grew stone quiet, except for the whirr and clicking of cameras, as Balluck, who had been a steelworker for 20 years until the plant closed, told his story.

"They threw 5,000 lives on a human garbage pile," Balluck said.

"When I go to downtown Youngstown, I pass two centers where people sell blood for a price," he said. "Every time I go down there, those centers are packed. I hate to think of those people who are unemployed, selling their blood."[87]

Len Balluck may have been one of the few Youngstown steelworkers who was able to convey the pain caused by the shutdowns. It was not only a question of money. Steelworkers in Youngstown tended to stay at particular mills over long periods of time because of the fringe benefits which came with seniority. This meant that they might work with certain other men and women for twenty, thirty, or even forty years. Such long-time associates became a second family.[88]

Accordingly shutdowns meant the death of many such "families." When former co-workers saw each other again after a shutdown something was missing. In place of the shared and positive experience of making a useful product, men came together to describe private misfortunes. Ed Mann, for example, looked forward to reunions of the Brier Hill open hearth. Yet when such a reunion was held in 1981, a year and a half after the mill closed, Mann had a bad time and left early. "Every one seemed to be complaining," he recalled. "I found myself starting to do the same thing."

John Barbero had a similar feeling that when he left the mill he became cut off from his "base." The people Barbero worked with were the people on whom he tried out new ideas. When he was no longer able to do this it became harder to distinguish a personal daydream from an idea that could go somewhere. Shortly before his death he told me that he thought before rank-and-file steelworkers in Youngstown could move forward again, they would need to be "healed." Another early retiree, Howard Broll, told the media that being tossed out of a job when you felt you had plenty of good years left was like being a "man without a country."[89]

John McNicol, SUE's co-chairman along with Balluck, belonged to the in-between group of steelworkers who suffered the most in the shutdowns. They were too young and had too little seniority to take early retirement. Often in their forties, married, with children in school and a home partly paid for, they were too settled to leave town. McNicol had been a carpenter at the Campbell Works. Unable to find other work in his trade, he got a job as a stock boy at Kroger's, only to be discharged just before the end of the 30-day probationary period. His distress showed; his hair fell out. In March 1979, McNicol wrote a letter to the editor, recalling another "carpenter by trade" whose purpose is remembered every Christmas. He wondered whether centuries hence people would remember the death of a steel mill and much of its community. He concluded that in Youngstown there was an opportunity few people ever experienced "to give birth to a new era and awakening of intelligence."[90]

At one SUE meeting, a millwright at the Campbell Works gave me a typed-out resume which he hoped might lead Community Steel to hire him if the mill reopened ("Nominated three different times as 'Pro' of the Quarter Award . . . U.S. Army—Feb. 1944 to Feb. 1946 —Purple Heart and Oak Leaf Cluster"). Two men from the hot strip mill told me that they had put the rolls (through which the steel is passed) "to bed," carefully packed in grease, and were the right men to get them turning again. I remembered what I had seen scrawled on the wall of the hot strip when I had visited the mill a few weeks before: the words, "We Shall Return."

Youngstown steelworkers were beginning to feel that the reopening just might happen.

The Government's Decision and What Lay Behind It

Then it all ended. On the morning of Friday, March 30, 1979 (by incredible coincidence the same day that the Brier Hill struggle ended, as will be told) Bishop Malone and Mayor Richley received a letter from the Department of Commerce, over the rubber-stamped signature of Robert T. Hall, Assistant Secretary for Economic Development and head of the EDA. According to Hall, the "overriding difficulty" in the Coalition's proposal was that in Phases I and II it would require $245 million of Federal government loan guarantees. This sum, he continued, was "well in excess of the $100 million amount which had been set as the maximum loan guarantee for any one company under the special steel program."

Bishops Malone and Burt responded in a sharply-worded telegram that same morning. Quoting Jack Watson's statements after the September 27 meeting to the effect that loan guarantees on the scale sought by the Coalition were "within the capabilities of the government," they rejected Hall's statement that $100 million had always been the maximum available. They pointed out that this had *not* been set forth as a problem in Mr. Watson's letter of October 18, which identified other problems (marketing and the availability of the plant) as needing further work. They asked why not one of the objections voiced in Hall's letter had ever been expressed to Coalition representatives, so that a consultative process could have occurred.

Much later, with the help of some Freedom of Information Act suits, we were able to see more clearly what lay behind the EDA's negative decision.

The Coalition probably lost out once it became clear that the Department of Commerce, through EDA, rather than HUD, would run the Carter administration's urban program. EDA made no loan guarantees from the steel industry loan guarantee fund larger than $100 million.[91] To have helped the Coalition, EDA would have had to view its plan as something unique which justified much greater Federal help than other applicants received. HUD had this view of the Coalition's effort, while EDA did not. All the early Federal support for the Coalition came from HUD. It was HUD which put up more than $300,000 for feasibility studies by Alperovitz. It was HUD Secretary Patricia Harris who said:

> This commendable community support is precisely the sort of local effort we are looking for in developing new Federal strategies to support areas like Youngstown that are determined to help themselves when faced with devastating plant closings.[92]

It was HUD Undersecretary Jay Janis who stated in early 1978:

> Simply put, the thing that we'd like to accomplish is that we'd like Youngstown to be a showcase. A showcase of self-help and a showcase of community involvement that somehow can be an example for the rest of the nation. . . .[93]

It was again Patricia Harris who came to Youngstown in October 1978 and told us, at a mass meeting in the Mill Creek Community Center, that the decision would not be hers alone but she was very sympathetic. EDA on the other hand was consistently negative. When the Coalition applied for an Urban Development Action Grant (UDAG) in January 1979 the application was made to HUD, which administers UDAGs. There were meetings with HUD representatives about the UDAG application both before it was filed (November 21, 1978 and January 15, 1979) and after (February 14, 1979). Yet particularly at the last of these meetings the Coalition was informed that the decision would in fact be made by EDA to whom no formal application had yet gone. Thus we were encouraged by, and we consulted with, representatives of an agency which as it turned out had no power to decide.

On February 9, 1979, Robert Embry, Assistant Secretary to HUD, sent a memorandum to Jack Watson with a copy to Hall. The memo sought to defuse the negative impact of a critique of the Alperovitz study by Dean Rosenbloom of the Harvard Business School. It said in part:

> I am concerned that we maintain momentum with respect to Youngstown. The original Coalition proposal has served to legitimately raise the level of public concern and debate. Clearly, the issues related to technological obsolescence and economic decline in older urban areas will not go away. I hope that we will continue to use the Youngstown area (and its problems) as a focus for specific economic development strategies: among them, targetted procurement, retraining and mobility options and private/public sector partnerships.

This memorandum, from a source at HUD particularly close to Alperovitz, may be considered the last gasp of the "demonstration project" idea.

On February 26, 1979, Hall sent a memorandum to Watson responding to a February 9 letter from Bishop Malone describing the Coalition's emerging three-phased reopening plan. Hall criticized the plan but warned that the Coalition would approach the White House directly to seek support for loan guarantees in excess of $100 million. Hall wrote, "we do not think it [support] should be given." And it wasn't.

There was, as there often is when battles are being lost, a series of meetings in which most Coalition participants vowed not to quit, as well as an angry follow-up meeting with Jack Watson. However, the representatives of the two key denominations—Roman Catholic and Presbyterian—made it clear that they had had enough. Bishop Malone, with characteristic candor and dignity, stated that he would not participate in street demonstrations because he could not carry his constituency with him. Presbyterian representatives Sharick, Bay and Campbell presented a resolution calling for termination of the Coalition. They said that they "intended to take this action and withdraw from Coalition activities regardless of the vote on this issue."[94]

Without the characteristic churches of Mahoning Valley workers (Roman Catholic) and managers (Presbyterian) the Coalition would have been an unrepresentative collection of particular clergy from a handful of small churches, together with out-of-town Episcopalians.

It was over. The Coalition lingered on formally for a time. Many individual Coalitionists, particularly Chuck Rawlings, continued to be active.

Rev. Chuck Rawlings

Duane Irving

Gerald Dickey at the rally of March 17, 1979

Bob Vasquez at the occupation of U.S. Steel headquarters in Pittsburgh, Nov. 30, 1979

Ed Mann at the occupation of U.S. Steel headquarters in Youngstown, Jan. 28, 1980

The picket line at Brier Hill,
Dec. 29, 1978

Rob Engelhart

Confrontation with Gordon Allen,
Jan. 22, 1979

Rob Engelhart

Brier Hill Unionist

The last day at Brier Hill

The picket line in Pittsburgh,
Nov. 30, 1979

The picket line in Pittsburgh,
Nov. 30, 1979

Kathy Centofanti

In the lobby of U.S. Steel
headquarters in Pittsburgh,
Nov. 30, 1979

On the escalator, U.S. Steel headquarters
in Pittsburgh, Nov. 30, 1979

On the escalator, U.S. Steel headquarters
in Pittsburgh, Nov. 30, 1979

Meeting at Local 1330, Jan. 28, 1980

Congressman Lyle Williams addressing the meeting at Local 1330, Jan. 28, 1980

Ed Mann addressing the meeting at Local 1330, Jan. 28, 1980

KEEP OUR MILLS OPEN

Entering U.S. Steel headquarters in Youngstown,
Jan. 28, 1980

On the roof of U.S. Steel headquarters in Youngstown, Jan. 28, 1980

U.S. Steel headquarters in Youngstown, Jan. 28, 1980

Local 1397 (Homestead Works) comments on the Youngstown struggle

Part II. The Struggle for Brier Hill

Brier Hill had what Campbell did not: a militantly democratic local union. There was no need at Brier Hill for a group of priests and ministers to substitute for steelworkers. Indeed, Local 1462, United Steelworkers of America, representing production and maintenance workers at the Brier Hill Works, was the very local which had given rise to the Rank and File Team (RAFT) and led national struggles against the productivity clause and no-strike agreement. Ed Mann of RAFT had been elected president of Local 1462 in 1973. Gerald Dickey, recording secretary of the local, had first suggested worker ownership of the Campbell Works. John Barbero was vice president and, after the spring of 1979, a grievance committeeman.

But even the most militant and democratic local union, we were to learn, faces heavy odds in a plant-closing struggle without support from the international union. If the local seeks to bargain with the company over its fate, the international can support the company in a refusal to bargain. If the local tries to involve the community in the struggle, the international can join the company in rejecting the participation of so-called outsiders.

Deprived of the support of the national Steelworkers union Local 1462 was forced to begin to explore new territory. The Brier Hill struggle led to the first direct action by Youngstown steelworkers against a shutdown. Brier Hill therefore prepared the ground for the confrontation with U.S. Steel.

Chapter One. The Merger of Lykes and LTV

The Brier Hill Works were closed as the direct result of a merger between the Lykes conglomerate, owner of the Youngstown Sheet & Tube steel company, and the Ling Temco Vought (LTV) conglomerate, owner of Jones & Laughlin (J & L) Steel. Whereas steelworkers at the Campbell Works had no warning of the shutdown announcement of September 19, 1977, at Brier Hill there was some advance notice. Local 1462's first battle was to attach conditions to the merger which would protect the jobs of workers at Brier Hill.

Lykes and LTV announced an intention to merge in November 1977, two months after the announcement of the Campbell Works shutdown, and one month after the formation of the Ecumenical Coalition. Because of a consent decree entered into by LTV at the time that it acquired J & L, in 1970, the merger had to be approved by the Anti-Trust Division of the Department of Justice.[1] The Anti-Trust Division investigated the proposed merger during the winter of 1977–78 and recommended to the Attorney General that the merger be prohibited. However, the merger was approved by Attorney General Griffin Bell, without conditions, on June 21, 1978. The Ecumenical Coalition then considered filing a suit in Federal court to stop the merger or to attach job-protecting conditions. Bishop Malone and Father Stanton took the position that such a suit would expose the Coalition to "substantial political risks in the Valley," and the idea was dropped.[2] The merger was approved by the stockholders of Lykes and LTV, and thus legally consummated, on December 5, 1978. A definitive announcement that Brier Hill would be closed came a few days later.

95

Why the Companies Wanted to Merge

Documents obtained from Lykes and LTV by the Justice Department, and viewed by steelworkers and reporters in Youngstown thanks to a suit filed under the Freedom of Information Act,[3] allow one to follow the train of thought which led each of these giant companies to a decision to merge.

Lykes' corporate planning before late 1976 had "assumed that the Company's long-term future depended largely upon its ability to fully load the Indiana Harbor facilities and to operate them efficiently. This assumption was based on the underlying premise that it was in the Company's best interests to continue as a factor in the flat rolled steel business. . . ."[4]

In November, 1976, however, the company began to consider whether "the economics of the steel business may not be attractive for other than the several largest, most diversified producers and further, [that] there may be an economically desirable way of retreating from that business." G. S. Kimmel, Lykes' Vice President—Finance, suggested selling Indiana Harbor, and continuing steel operations only in Youngstown.[5]

At the January 13, 1977, meeting of the Board of Directors, management asked for authority to prepare a preliminary evaluation of two alternatives: selling Indiana Harbor and retaining steel facilities in Youngstown, or alternatively, closing Youngstown and concentrating on expansion at Indiana Harbor.[6] A preliminary report to the executive committee of the Board in February, however, indicated that attention was directed to the first alternative, selling Indiana Harbor.[7] During the spring and summer of 1977, the First Boston Corporation, on behalf of Lykes, actively sought to market the Indiana Harbor Works at its book value of about $475 million. There was no interest on the part of Republic Steel, United States Steel, National Steel, or Inland Steel.[8] The final effort was on August 18, 1977, when First Boston representatives met with the senior officers of Inland Steel in Chicago. Lykes was not asking cash: the proposal was for Inland to assume about $300 million of Sheet & Tube's debt and to pay about $175 million in stock or notes. On August 22, Inland said No.[9]

The turning point—for the Campbell Works as well as for the Brier Hill Works—came at a meeting of the Board of Directors of the Lykes Corporation on August 29, 1977. The meeting was attended by a representative of the investment firm of Lehman Brothers Kuhn

Loeb. The Board voted to hire Lehman Brothers to prepare a plan to "stabilize" Youngstown Sheet & Tube. Further, conversations between Justice Department investigators and personnel of Lehman Brothers and the First Boston Corporation in March 1978 indicate that closing of the Campbell Works was not considered before the August 29 meeting. Before August 29, it seems, Lykes was advised principally by First Boston, and First Boston's main effort was to sell the Indiana Harbor Works.[10] Lehman Brothers "disagreed with this approach, feeling that if the company had any chance it was with IH [Indiana Harbor]."[11]

At the same time that Lykes was looking for something to sell, LTV was looking for a company to buy. In 1975, LTV/J & L was studying acquisition of a marginal steel company "with the objective of improving profitability of the resulting combination over performance possible by 'going-it-alone'." McLouth, Wheeling-Pittsburgh, and Youngstown Sheet & Tube were considered. It was recognized that steelmaking at Indiana Harbor would nicely supplement J & L's finishing facilities at Hennepin, Illinois, but the potential price of the Indiana Harbor Works was felt to be "beyond our financial capability."[12]

Even in the summer of 1977, it seems, LTV was still not thinking about acquisition of Lykes. A confidential memorandum from Lehman Brothers in August 1977 "concerning potential acquisitions" shows that one reason for this was that, because of the 1970 consent decree, LTV was convinced that acquisition of a company with assets over $100 million would be blocked by the Department of Justice as contrary to the anti-trust laws.[13] But the closing of the Campbell Works suddenly changed the equation, and made Lykes intensely desirable to LTV. Thomas Graham, president and chief executive officer of J & L, explained why to *Business Week*.

> In 1977, an ailing Lykes was seeking a buyer for various assets. First Boston Corp., its investment banker, approached Graham that summer trying to peddle Indiana Harbor. "There was no way I could consider it," recalls Graham.
>
> Despite J & L's desire for a merger with Youngstown, that, too, was ruled out, because "it couldn't pass an antitrust muster," says Graham. Antitrust aside, a merger still would have been a nonstarter because of Youngstown's antiquated Campbell Works in Youngstown, Ohio. Even in a paper-for-paper transaction, LTV could not afford to buy and then shut down the facility.

Then came the September 19 announcement.

> But in September, 1977, Youngstown closed Campbell. "That,"
> says Graham, "changed the game." The closing bore public
> witness to the depth of Youngstown's troubles and led its parent
> to argue that Youngstown—and consequently Lykes—was "a
> failing company" and thus should be exempt from the antitrust
> considerations attendant upon the merger of two significant
> competitors.
>
> In mid-September, barely a month after First Boston had
> approached Graham about Indiana Harbor, the banker called
> again, this time to talk about J & L's buying all of Youngstown.
> It found Graham eager to talk.[14]

Lehman Brothers played the part of a marriage broker. On the one
hand, Lehman had been advising LTV to buy another company since
November 1976. On the other hand, Lehman made Lykes attractive
to LTV by recommending the closing of the Campbell Works. This
removed obstacles to the merger. Legally, closing the Campbell
Works made plausible the "failing company" exception to an otherwise illegal merger. Financially, closing the ailing Works made Sheet
& Tube more attractive. In a confidential memorandum to Lykes on
October 7, 1977, Lehman Brothers endorsed a merger between Lykes
and LTV and stated that "Lehman Brothers believes that LTV would
favorably consider such a merger."[15] Lehman had reason to know
whereof it spoke.

The plot is even a little thicker. In September 1977, a management
consultant in Dallas was asked by Raymond Hay, president of LTV,
to comment on the possibility of a merger between LTV and another "second tier" steel company. In replying, the consultant suggested that "someone like Bill Roesch might be able to provide
the necessary leadership."[16] William Roesch, then between jobs with
Kaiser Steel and United States Steel, was soon after hired by First
Boston Corporation on behalf of Lykes to do a study of a potential
merger between LTV and Lykes, in which he found that there was a
"viable fit" between the facilities of the two firms.[17] Later, as president of United States Steel, Mr. Roesch also played a principal part
in the decision to close United States Steel's Youngstown Works.

Further, the Lehman Brothers representative who met with the
Lykes Board of Directors on August 29, 1977, and recommended
that instead of trying to sell its plant at Indiana Harbor the company
should close its Campbell Works, was a man named Ian McGregor.

From 1966 to 1977, McGregor was Chief Executive Officer of Amax, Inc., a major American metals and natural resources company. He is a senior partner of Lazar Freres, the investment bankers, and Chairman of the Board of Alumax Inc., Botswana RST, Bamangwato Concessions Ltd. and the Mount Newman Operating Committee (Australian iron ore mining). Subsequent to his work in facilitating the closing of the Campbell Works, and at least indirectly the merger of Lykes and LTV, McGregor became a director of LTV. On May 1, 1980, McGregor was appointed Chairman of the nationalized British Steel Corporation where he supervised the closing of a substantial part of its facilities.[18]

Thus it appears that a very few men, William Roesch and Ian McGregor among them, although wearing a variety of banking and steel company hats which suggested more competition than in fact existed, managed the "shakeout" of the American and British steel industries.

On November 4, 1977, Paul Thayer, Chairman of the Board of LTV, and Chester Ferguson, Vice Chairman of the Board of Lykes, announced that the two companies had in principle agreed to merge.

Brier Hill, the Piece of the Puzzle that Didn't "Fit"

The Justice Department's decision to approve the merger between Lykes and LTV is a case study in the politics of influence.

The Anti-Trust Division, then headed by Assistant Attorney General John Shenefield, recommended against approval of the merger. The Division did not believe that Lykes was really a "failing company."

The Wall Street attorneys for the two conglomerates then went over the head of the Anti-Trust Division to Attorney General Griffin Bell. In doing so they could make use of a Southern old boys network, fully as potent as its Ivy League counterparts. Jack Watson, the White House Assistant who was in charge of a decision about the Ecumenical Coalition's quest for Federal help, was in private practice before he came to the government with the Atlanta law firm of King and Spaulding. Griffin Bell was a prominent member of King and Spaulding before becoming a Federal judge. Stanley Rosenkranz, a partner of the Tampa law firm headed by Chester Ferguson, Vice

Chairman of the Board of Lykes, was also a former partner of King & Spaulding. Both Bell and Chester Ferguson were born in Sumter County in southwestern Georgia, as was then President Jimmy Carter. Bell's aunt Mary Frances Bell states that the Bell and Ferguson families get together about twice a year for "big blowouts." These connections among men who had practiced corporate law together in the Southeastern states were evoked by the Lykes and LTV attorneys' practice, when they wrote to the Attorney General of the United States about this merger, of addressing him as "Judge Bell."[19]

Often it is merely speculative to suggest that such personal connections influence decisionmaking. In this instance members of the Anti-Trust Division told reporter John Greenman about Bell's attitude toward their merger investigation.

> "He told us we should not treat what [the companies] tell us with suspicion as in an adversary posture," [Eric] Kaplan said. "We should put more faith in what they say to us." According to J. Robert Kramer II, a member of the staff who was absent from the lecture [by the Attorney General], "When the staff came back they said Bell told them he didn't believe respectable businessmen would shade facts." And [John] Shenefield quoted Bell to the effect that "Here you have businessmen who are in trouble. They are trying to do something. We should try to think of ourselves as their allies."[20]

Nor did LTV and Lykes rely altogether on personal connections, Greenman uncovered. Just weeks after LTV announced plans to merge with Lykes, its political action committee contributed $10,000 to the Democratic National Committee. Eight months later, after the U.S. Department of Justice approved the merger, the political committee contributed $10,000 more.[21]

As general counsel for the Ecumenical Coalition, I visited Eric Kaplan, the man in charge of the Anti-Trust Division's investigation of the proposed merger, at his office in the Old Star Building in Washington late in November 1977. The Coalition's position on the merger was that Community Steel might be a viable "alternative purchaser" of the Campbell facilities; that it would enhance competition in the steel industry if a small firm like Community Steel entered the market; and therefore, that any approval of the proposed merger should be conditioned on negotiation of an agreement between Lykes and the Coalition for reopening the Campbell Works, or at the very least, an enforceable commitment by Lykes to bargain in good faith toward that end.[22]

Local 1462 took a similar position, but with particular emphasis on the possibility that if the merger were approved the Brier Hill Works might be closed. Brier Hill, the union suggested, was the piece of the merger that didn't "fit." Gerald Dickey wrote an editorial for the *Brier Hill Unionist* with no title other than a cartoon. The cartoon showed the states of Illinois, Indiana, Ohio and Pennsylvania divided into pieces of a jigsaw puzzle. A hand labeled "J & L" is removing a piece labeled "Youngstown."

The cartoon was prompted by the rhetoric of Sheet & Tube and J & L executives throughout the year in which the LTV/Lykes merger was pending about the remarkable "fit" of the two steel companies. Thus, in their memorandum to the Anti-Trust Division of the Department of Justice, attorneys for the two companies contended that

> J & L's particular weaknesses can be alleviated without capital investment by employing Y S & T's complementary strengths. Similarly, many of Y S & T's problems can be solved through J & L's strengths.[23]

Dickey, in his editorial, quoted the more colorful comment by J & L's chief executive that the pieces fit together "as if some Soviet planner has designed it."[24]

But the Brier Hill piece did not fit. Dickey was one of the first to see it. As early as January 1978 he wrote in the local union newspaper:

> J & L's Aliquippa Works, located some 40 miles from Youngstown, has a seamless mill. Most knowledgeable people say that it is in worse shape than the one in Campbell Ohio Works. But unlike the Youngstown operation, J & L uses BOF steel to produce seamless pipe. The Union was recently notified by management that 1200 tons of rounds would be shipped from Aliquippa to be conditioned in Youngstown. . . . [T]his test and future testing could possibly result in using J & L steel, which is less costly because of the BOF process, to manufacture all or most of the seamless pipe made in Youngstown. Where does that leave Brier Hill?[25]

To restate the matter with the clarity of hindsight, the problem was that both Sheet & Tube's mill at Brier Hill and J & L's mill in Aliquippa made components ("rounds") for seamless pipe. Even if the merged company elected to continue to operate the seamless pipe mill at the Campbell Works, that mill would probably obtain its "rounds" from Aliquippa where they were made by a BOF process less costly than Brier Hill's open hearths.

Advance Notice of a Shutdown But No Power

What does a local union do if it has good reason to believe, a year in advance of the event, that the merger of two conglomerates will cause its members to be put out of work?

What good is notice of a shutdown from your employer if you lack the power to make use of the advance warning?

The Brier Hill local began by asking the Justice Department not to approve the merger without conditions which would ensure the survival of Brier Hill. Mann and Dickey wrote to the Department on December 29, 1977:

> The central question we would have answered is, "Will the new corporation (Lykes-LTV) make a commitment to continue to operate the Brier Hill plant for a period of at least ten (10) years, while modernizing and updating the facilities?"
>
> Other questions we would like to have answered are: ["]If the new corporation is unwilling to make any commitments to keeping the Brier Hill plant open, can we demand that as a condition for approval of the merger, . . . Lykes divest itself of the entire Youngstown District, enabling an employee/community takeover to form a new corporation and operate these facilities including the shutdown portion?["][26]

The Justice Department responded by telephoning on January 9, 1978, and arranging for a meeting between its personnel and Local 1462 on January 23. Other steelworker locals in the area were then moved to act and arranged that they would attend the meeting also. District Director Leseganich and the District's attorney Daniel Thomas were also present.

Dickey kept notes on the January 23 meeting at the Justice Department. The union representatives were permitted to view but not to copy a memorandum submitted to the Department of Justice by Lykes and LTV in which the companies touched on the future of Brier Hill. The memorandum stated:

> In the opinion of J&L management, the merged company will have the option of (a) replacing the Mahoning Valley facilities because of improved cash flow and newly available financing or (b) following a modest capital expenditure, supplying steel rounds to the YS&T tube mills from J&L's Aliquippa plant at substantial estimated cost savings. The choice between those

alternatives will be made at a future date based on circumstances at that time.[27]

All representatives of Youngstown steelworkers at the January 23 meeting, including Director Leseganich and his attorney, flatly opposed the merger. The following statements are illustrative.

> Leseganich: . . . If this merger becomes a reality, it will wipe out the Youngstown District. We are working on an alternative. Can we develop a model demonstration in Youngstown? . . . Poor management by the corporation was the reason for failure in the Youngstown District. With good management, it can become a profitable place. . . .

> Atty. Thomas: At this point I would like to summarize the Union's position. We are opposed to the merger per se. . . .

> Leseganich: . . . We have alternatives, options to this merger. We are considering buy-outs, the unit train, common blast furnace. We want you to study the feasibility study when it comes out. This merger does not bring life to the Youngstown District. . . .[28]

The International Union Takes a Hand

Then the international officials of the United Steelworkers of America took a hand. On February 2, 1978, USWA president Lloyd McBride—who had yet to make the 75-mile trip from Pittsburgh to Youngstown since the closing of the Campbell Works—stated at Kent, Ohio that he would not oppose the merger if it were a matter of Lykes' survival.[29] On March 10, Jim Smith, an aide to McBride, called Rene Torrado of the Anti-Trust Division who recorded the conversation as follows:

> On Friday, March 10, 1978, I received a telephone call from Jim Smith, Assistant to Lloyd McBridge [sic], President of the United Steel Workers. Smith stated that the United Steel Workers might want to take a position concerning the Lykes-LTV merger. If the union took a position, it would be out of concern for the pension rights of the Youngstown Sheet and Tube employees. Smith stated that, with the demise of the Allen Wood Steel Company, the pension rights of the steel workers at Allen Wood were left unprotected. The United Steel Workers did not want to see

the same situation at Youngstown Sheet and Tube: their interest is in seeing that Youngstown Sheet and Tube does not go into bankruptcy. If the merger of Lykes and LTV is the only way to avert the bankruptcy of Youngstown Sheet and Tube, the union would feel compelled to support the merger.[30]

While the international union did not openly support the merger, the union made it clear that its principal concern was that Lykes might go bankrupt. If a merger was the only way to prevent bankruptcy then the international was for the merger.

Local Steelworker unions either opposed the merger or wanted conditions imposed before the merger was allowed. The concerns expressed by local unions ranged from outright opposition to the merger (Local 1211, J & L, Aliquippa) to a request that a decision be delayed until Sheet & Tube workers received assurances about both pensions and continued employment (Local 1418, Sheet & Tube, Youngstown) to a proposal that the companies commit themselves to complete the Indiana Harbor coke plant if the merger were approved (Local 1011, Sheet & Tube, East Chicago, Indiana).[31] Local 1462 at Sheet & Tube's Brier Hill Works urged no decision on the merger before consideration of the impact on the Mahoning Valley community, the possibility of a third-party buyout of the Campbell Works, and the forthcoming Coalition feasibility study.[32]

The Justice Department's Decision

With Lykes, LTV, and their associates pressing hard for a merger, only a handful of local unions opposed to the merger, and the international union somewhere in between, the outcome was predictable.

On June 21, 1978, the Department of Justice approved the merger. Attorney General Bell stated he had "decided to approve the merger as the only viable means for maintaining the Lykes' steel producing facilities and for saving the jobs of those concerned."[33]

No conditions were imposed.

Chapter Two. Fighting Both the Company and the International

After Attorney General Bell approved the proposed merger in June 1978, Local 1462 sought with increasing desperation to meet with the management of the company that (the local feared) was planning to close the Brier Hill Works.

The Company's Refusal to Bargain with the Local

Local 1462's first formal request for a meeting was made in a letter dated June 30, 1978. J & L management replied that since the merger had not yet occurred, it would be improper for them to meet with a local union representing employees of Youngstown Sheet & Tube.

Meantime, it appears, the *managements* of the two companies were meeting frequently to plan their future operations. According to *Business Week*, Thomas Graham, president of J & L,

> [l]ate last year . . . initiated regular meetings with Youngstown officials to explore how best to meld the companies' operations. They moved on to deal with staffing and organization. "By the time the merger was approved, Tom knew pretty well what he wanted," says Youngstown President Jennings R. Lambeth.[34]

The Youngstown press described at least one meeting prior to the merger of Jones & Laughlin and former Sheet & Tube executives with Karl Fetters, a retired Sheet & Tube vice president for planning and engineering. Thomas Graham was quoted to the effect that Fetters was invited to meet with J & L's engineering staff. And Fetters was said to have confirmed that he was brought in by the back door to a session with management representatives of the two companies so as to avoid meeting anyone he might know.[35]

Denied the opportunity for a face-to-face meeting with the decision-makers, Brier Hill steelworkers learned of their probable fate from a prospectus concerning the proposed merger mailed by Lykes and LTV to their respective stockholders in October 1978. Among the "anticipated . . . benefits" of the merger listed in the prospectus was the following:

> The combination of Youngstown's Mahoning Valley plants with J&L Steel's Pittsburgh and Aliquippa plants offers an opportunity to substantially reduce the cost of producing rounds for Youngstown's seamless tube operations. . . . In the opinion of J&L Steel management, after the Merger and following a limited modification of certain facilities at J&L Steel's Aliquippa Works, Youngstown's seamless tube mills will be able to obtain steel rounds from J&L Steel's plant at Aliquippa at substantial cost savings, thus permitting a phasing-out of Youngstown's iron and steelmaking and round producing operations in the Mahoning Valley during the latter part of 1979.[36]

The *Vindicator* made sure people got the news. "Proxy Confirms Plan To Close Brier Hill Works," its October 30 headline said.

Local 1462 immediately wrote again to J & L management, this time to Gordon Allen, who was to supervise the operations of the merged steel companies in Cleveland and Youngstown. The letter stated:

> You will recall that on June 30, 1978, representatives of Local 1462, United Steelworkers of America, contacted you requesting an immediate meeting about the future of the Brier Hill mill.
>
> At that time we were informed that a meeting could not be arranged until after consummation of the proposed merger between the LTV and Lykes Corporations.
>
> The *Wall Street Journal* for Monday, October 30, 1978, and *Youngstown Vindicator*, same date, carried stories about the joint proxy statement issued by LTV and Lykes to their respective shareholders.
>
> According to these stories, the proxy statement indicates that production at Brier Hill will be phased out in late 1979.
>
> The announcement comes as a shock to the 1200 members of Local 1462. Notwithstanding statements in the past about the

possibility of shutting down Brier Hill, recent expenditures on the Brier Hill open hearth shop, including installing oxygen lances on six of the furnaces, installing four bag houses for pollution clean up, and a waste heat recovery system, encouraged the hope that the mill might be kept open.

Therefore we urgently renew our request for a meeting about the future of Brier Hill. . . .[37]

Mr. Allen responded:

Dear Mr. Mann:

I have received your letter of November 20, 1978, requesting that we meet in early December. Responsibility for Union negotiations falls under the direction of John H. Kirkwood, Vice President of Industrial Relations, and I have forwarded your letter to Mr. Kirkwood.

Mr. Kirkwood advises me that he and Director Leseganich have been attempting to find an opportunity for the parties, including yourself, to meet. I understand that Director Leseganich's recent illness has prevented such a meeting. I know that John Kirkwood will continue his efforts to establish a meeting date through the District Director.[38]

The effect of this letter was not only to delay a meeting, but to ensure that when it happened union participation would be controlled by the international. Mann immediately wrote Leseganich: "The J & L management is passing the buck to you as being the hold up for a meeting. We would appreciate you setting up a meeting immediately."[39]

A meeting of sorts finally happened on December 14, nine days after consummation of the merger, and was composed of so many different locals that it was impossible to focus on the fate of Brier Hill. The meeting was called not by Leseganich but by Frank Valenta, Steelworkers director in the Cleveland area, a younger man than Leseganich whom the international may have considered better able to ride herd on Youngstown dissidents. At the meeting Gordon Allen stated, "There is no hope for Brier Hill beyond the end of 1979."[40]

Picketing for Jobs

On the evening of December 15, local officers reported to a tumultuous special meeting at the Union hall.

The call to the meeting, a leaflet passed out at the gates, stated:

FRIDAY NITE

We are having a Christmas Party, but there is not much to celebrate.

If things go according to plan (LTV/Lykes Plan), most of us will be unemployed at this time next year.

Friday night we'll have a party, but before we party, we are going to talk.

CAN BRIER HILL BE SAVED?

SHOULD IT BE SAVED?

WHAT ARE OUR ALTERNATIVES?

Come to the meeting and bring your ideas and opinions.

The time for talking is coming to an end. The time for action is near. . . .

The meeting focused on J & L's announced intention to move certain machines known as "peelers" from Brier Hill to Aliquippa at an unknown date. Peelers remove irregularities from the surface of the rounds assembled into seamless pipe. The reason for moving the peelers was that J & L planned to manufacture at Aliquippa the "rounds" presently made at Brier Hill. So, for those who worked at Brier Hill, moving the peelers was the concrete embodiment of the conglomerate's decision to take the tools of the trade out of the hands of members of Local 1462.

At the meeting, some of the younger men proposed to chain themselves to their machines rather than let the company move them to Aliquippa.

Father Ed Stanton, executive secretary of the Ecumenical Coalition, called on members of the local to do more "kicking ass."

A proposal was made but not acted on to picket the district and national offices of the Steelworkers union. In hindsight, Ken Doran is convinced that workers who are fighting a shutdown must be prepared to bring public pressure on their own union.

The meeting directed local union officers to use all methods possible to keep Brier Hill open. Following the meeting, the officers of Local 1462 moved in three directions.

First, they demanded the meeting between J & L and the Brier Hill local which had been sought since the previous June. A telegram went off, proposing that the agenda of the meeting should be: 1) What are the considerations that led the Company to decide to shut down the Brier Hill Works?, 2) Is the Company prepared to bargain in good faith about alternatives to a shutdown?[41] The indefatigable

Gerald Dickey put meat on the bones of this proposal by suggesting in the *Brier Hill Unionist* that a worker/community takeover of Brier Hill might consider installing a finishing mill to make rails. He even had a name in mind: "The Brier Hill Steel Company," the company's name before its absorption by Youngstown Sheet & Tube in 1923. It would, Dickey concluded, "be the best damn little steel company in the country."[42]

Second, the local organized the first direct action taken by steelworkers in response to the Youngstown shutdowns: a picket line. This action may seem very bland after so much strong language. But as Ed Mann commented throughout the next months, steelworkers were out of the habit of even the mildest direct action. There had been no national steel strike since 1959. Wildcat strikes, which Mann and John Barbero had both helped to lead,[43] were more and more rare in the steel industry even at Brier Hill. One had to walk before running, and the first step was a picket line.

An estimated 200 steelworkers picketed on Friday, December 29, in an open area near the Brier Hill clockhouse. Their signs said, "Keep Brier Hill Open," "People First, Profits Second," "Impeach Griffin Bell" (a reference to Attorney General Bell's approval of the merger without conditions), "Youngstown: Victim of Corporate Rape," "Where's Joe—In Houston?," "Justice for Youngstown," "Keep the Peelers in Youngstown," and "Save Our Valley." The press commented aptly that these pickets did not signal a work stoppage, but were picketing for the chance to work.[44]

The Local's NLRB Charge Called Unauthorized by the International

Third, the local reactivated an unfair labor practice charge originally filed in October 1977 with the National Labor Relations Board. The charge as originally filed by the six local union presidents alleged that Youngstown Sheet & Tube by its abrupt announcement of the closing of the Campbell Works had violated a duty to bargain over investment decisions. Sections 8(a)(5) and 8(d) of the National Labor Relations Act require an employer to bargain in good faith.

In 1977, when we filed the charge, a growing body of legal precedent held that where an employer engages in a partial shutdown there is a duty under the Act to bargain, not only about the effects of the shutdown, but about the shutdown decision itself. The charge stated:

> On September 19, 1977, the company unilaterally announced the termination of 5000 employees in the Youngstown area. There was no prior notice to the union. There was no effort on the part of the company to bargain in good faith with the union. No attempt was made to lay the company's difficulties before the union, and to seek the union's counsel about possible alternatives to the shutdown. . . .

The charge filed by the six local union presidents in Youngstown had asked for immediate action by the Board to halt the shutdown process. The charge concluded:

> We specifically ask the Regional Director to seek an injunction which would direct the company to stop the shutdowns, to reinstate and make whole persons already laid off, and to begin to bargain in good faith.

Instead of immediate action, what we got was indefinite delay. Normally the Board makes an immediate investigation and decides either to issue a complaint, or to refuse to issue a complaint, within 30 days of the filing of a charge. In this situation, because both a grievance and an NLRB charge had been filed, the Board made its investigation but decided to delay its decision about issuing a complaint until after arbitration of the grievance. The Board acted under a policy of "deferring" processing of an NLRB charge by the Board until after arbitration of a grievance dealing with the same problem. The underlying assumption is that it is preferable for labor disputes to be resolved by the machinery for dispute resolution set up by the parties to collective bargaining agreements, that is, by grievance-arbitration procedures, than before outside agencies such as the Board or the courts. Therefore, when a grievance and an NLRB charge concern the same subject matter, the Board will wait to see what happens to the grievance before making its own decision.

Arbitrator Crane's award was made on December 4, 1978, and on December 20, acting on behalf of Local 1462, I asked the Board to resume its consideration of whether a complaint should issue. I also amended the charge by claiming that Jones & Laughlin as successor to Youngstown Sheet & Tube had refused to bargain with Local 1462 before announcing the closing of the Brier Hill Works.

Local 1462's request that the Board review the arbitration award came to the attention of the international union. According to William Shuzman, the Board investigator who handled the complaint throughout, an international union attorney named James English stated in a conversation with Shuzman on January 15, 1979,

> that since the International Union was the exclusive certified and recognized collective bargaining representative for the employees at the Campbell Works, neither Local 1462 nor any other affected local had the authority to file the abovementioned charge. Furthermore, English stated that Local 1462 did not have the authority to request review of the arbitration award and in fact, the International Union did not desire such review.[45]

This was the end of the effort to do something about shutdowns in Youngstown by the conventional means of filing a grievance or an NLRB charge.

The International Denies the Local's Right to Self-Representation

A meeting between J & L and Local 1462 was tentatively set for January 19, 1979. At once a struggle began over the agenda.

In their telegram of December 19, the local officers insisted that the agenda should be the shutdown *decision*, and whether it could be reversed. They wanted at all costs to avoid a meeting focused on shutdown *benefits*, discussion of which would tacitly concede the inevitability of the shutdown itself.

District leadership of the Union had other ideas. On December 20, Director Frank Leseganich wrote to Director Frank Valenta: "It is my understanding that LU 1462 has requested that you arrange a meeting for that group separately. Therefore, when an agenda is necessary I will do all possible to prepare same."[46]

A second point of difference concerned who should attend the meeting. Local 1462 wanted to bring the community into the discussion. By letters of January 2, they invited to the meeting the Ecumenical Coalition, Congressman Lyle Williams, Senator Edward Kennedy (chairman of the Anti-Trust Subcommittee of the Senate Judiciary Committee), Senator Howard Metzenbaum, and Mayor Phillip Richley. The local had retained me as its attorney, and informed the company that I would be present at the meeting of the 19th.

As it turned out, none of the above were permitted to attend the January 19 meeting. The company dealt with the invitation to me by referring the problem to the international. This elicited a letter from none other than President Lloyd McBride, dated January 10, 1979, addressed to J. H. Kirkwood, Vice President—Industrial Relations, J & L, and copied to the officers of Local 1462, the NLRB investigator of the local's unfair labor practice charge, Senators Metzenbaum and Kennedy, Congressman Williams, Directors Leseganich and Valenta, staff representative Hinchcliffe, and myself. The letter stated:

> Dear Mr. Kirkwood:
>
> This is in response to your inquiry, received today, concerning our collective bargaining status at the Brier Hill plant. Your inquiry, I understand, was initiated because of the receipt of a letter from an attorney named Staughton Lynd who was purporting to speak on collective bargaining matters on behalf of our Local Union 1462 and the Ecumenical Coalition of the Mahoning Valley.
>
> In accordance with federal law and Article XVII, Sections 1 and 5 of our International Constitution, the International Union is the sole and exclusive collective bargaining agent for the employees in question. Our designated representatives for effectuating such collective bargaining relationship are District Director Frank Valenta, Chairman of our J & L bargaining committee, and District Director Frank Leseganich, who administers the affairs of the International Union in District 26.
>
> Attorney Lynd has not been designated to represent any members of the International Union. Nor will he be present at the scheduled January 19, 1979 meeting.
>
> Chairman Valenta and Director Leseganich will have the responsibility on behalf of the International Union for determining all matters concerning who shall attend and what shall be discussed at the January 19, 1979 meeting, and any dealings between the Company and any other individuals or organizations with respect to such matters would be in violation of legal and contractual requirements.
>
> Sincerely yours,
> Lloyd McBride[47]

Just as, in the fall of 1977, the District leadership's principal response to the shutdown at Campbell was to destroy the ad hoc committee of Sheet & Tube local officers and grievance committeemen organized by Gerald Dickey, so once again, in Brier Hill's moment of crisis, the most decisive action of the international union was to obstruct the local union's effort to reach out for help in the surrounding community.

Meantime an interesting insight into the company's attitude to the Brier Hill shutdown had fallen into the hands of Local 1462. During the Christmas holidays of 1978, a joint meeting of management and sales personnel of the combined J & L and Sheet & Tube steel companies took place in Pittsburgh. Thomas Graham, president and chief executive officer of J & L, addressed the meeting. His remarks were taped. A copy was obtained, played before the Local 1462 executive board, and later, played at a local union meeting. Graham said as follows about Brier Hill:

> The most noteworthy or newsworthy event in 1979 in the Central Division will come with the shutdown of steelmaking and hot rolling at Brier Hill. This is a very controversial matter. It's had undue attention from an irresponsible press, in many respects. And when we recognize that we intend to be a corporate citizen in Youngstown for many years to come, the management of this shutdown is a very formidable assignment.
>
> As most of you know, it's targeted for the first of October, 1979. And the real challenge in this Brier Hill shutdown will run to how well we do that job. Can it be handled, in recognition of the human factors, the politics, the socio-economic impact, in such a fashion that it will enhance our role with the surviving operation? That may seem like a conflict in objectives to you. But that's what our job is in Youngstown, and it's a very difficult job. Can this be managed in such a way that the quality of the surviving operations will be enhanced?

The Local Puts Forth its own Program and Scores a Public Relations Victory

Amid these conflicting pressures the Brier Hill local union prepared for the January 19 meeting. It did not help the general mood when J & L officials suggested that the Brier Hill Works might be used as a historical museum of the steel industry.[48]

My notes on a January 2 meeting indicate that the discussion ranged over the local's NLRB charge that the company had failed to bargain in good faith, the issue of whether to invite community representatives to the January 19 meeting, and above all, possibilities for modernizing and saving the Works. It was at this meeting that someone expressed the concept that the roughly $100 million required to modernize Brier Hill was "reparations." Gerald Dickey put this idea into a position paper which Ed Mann read when the January 19 meeting began:

> LTV owes a debt to the people of the Mahoning Valley as a price for the merger. The exact amount is certainly astronomical, but we expect that debt should easily total $100 million—the price of modernizing a steel producing facility. We want to see Brier Hill modernized with the installation of electric furnaces.

This careful preparation paid off when the meeting finally transpired. Valenta, Leseganich, the local union officers and committeemen, and staff representative Hinchcliffe, met before the J & L representatives arrived. The 1462 people read their position paper and insisted that the meeting begin with a discussion of alternatives to a shutdown. After the J & L men joined the meeting, the local put the following specific proposals on the table:

> The company should make capital expenditures to improve productivity, such as the installation of additional soaking pits and new table rolls leading to the intermediate mill in the blooming mill department.
>
> The company should extend the timetable for a shutdown at least two years, so that the Union can develop a viable alternative and keep the plant operating.
>
> The company should consider transferring the property to a worker/community group and assist the new company to install finishing facilities, such [as] a rail mill or merchant mill.
>
> The company should be prepared to produce slabs for the Campbell Works, if the Ecumenical Coalition is successful in reopening the hot and cold strip mills.[49]

J & L, in an effort to restrict the agenda of the meeting to benefits, sent only industrial relations representatives to the January 19 meeting. They could only promise to get back to the local union about the more fundamental questions that the local raised.

Publicly, the big news about the January 19 meeting was that Mayor Richley, Kennedy aide Jonathan Orloff, and Congressman Williams' aides Marlin Ford (president of the UAW Lordstown local) and Anthony Centofanti (former mayor of Struthers), all showed up and were all excluded from the meeting. Minutes before the meeting was to begin, each was handed a hastily-composed statement reading:

> Today's meeting was scheduled as a routine Company-Union meeting to discuss local matters relating to the Brier Hill Works. A similar meeting was held with the local Unions representing Campbell Works employees last Monday.
>
> Reports that the meeting today was for the purpose of resolving the future of the Brier Hill Works are unfounded.
>
> The Company believes the problems between the Company and the Union should be discussed within the normal procedures rather than in a public meeting.

The representatives, invited by Local 1462 with the knowledge of J & L, were unpersuaded. "I'm frankly disappointed," Senator Kennedy's assistant was quoted as saying. "Senator Kennedy is profoundly interested in what is transpiring here." The same front-page news story reported Mayor Richley to have asserted: "If Senator Kennedy's representative is disappointed, well I'm damn mad."[50]

Local 1462 had scored a considerable public relations victory, which the international at once moved to defuse. Frank Valenta told the media the next day: "I didn't care for Ed Mann's handling of the matter. The company was right to keep the outsiders from the meeting."[51]

Company Officials are Picketed at the Country Club

Three days later, on January 22, those present at the January 19 meeting reported to the union membership at the Local 1462 hall. By coincidence it also happened that on the same evening Sheet & Tube superintendent Gordon Allen addressed the Youngstown district section of the Association of Iron and Steel Engineers at the Mahoning Country Club, not far away.

It had grated on members of the local that Mr. Allen, after helping to arrange the January 19 meeting and indicating to Ed Mann that he would attend it, did not come.

The executive committee of Local 1462 met before the larger meeting began, and voted not to recommend confronting Allen at the

Country Club. The officers felt themselves bound by a tacit agreement with the company to wait for J & L's response to the questions raised by the union on January 19.

However, after reporting to the members what happened on January 19, Ed Mann mentioned the fact that Allen was speaking nearby. There was no clear response. The discussion turned to the role being played by Director Frank Valenta, as to which there was a sharp exchange. Then one of a group of Puerto Ricans took the floor and urged immediate action. Mann again mentioned that Allen was speaking only a short distance away. He added that he still had the signs from the December 29 picket line in the back of his pickup truck. As if by common consent people began moving toward the door. Gerald Dickey, watching the action from his officer's chair at the front of the hall, was even then unsure whether the crowd would really go to the Country Club or just go home. (Some officers and members declined to go to the Club.)

A picket line formed spontaneously outside the main door to the Country Club, and people began to chant. Ken Doran moved up and down the line, saying "let's go inside." Finally, Doran opened the door, and John Barbero led the group through. Some members did not go inside, feeling that to do so was trespassing on private property. The intruders came to a halt in the lobby, completely blocking access or egress. Allen's voice could be heard in the ballroom, concluding his remarks. Those waiting in the lobby set up the chant, "Where's Gordon Allen?" It was a way of saying, will we ever get to talk to someone who can make a decision about saving our plant?

The management of the Country Club called the Girard police. The police arranged themselves inconspicuously and made no attempt to interfere.

Roger Slater, J & L's Youngstown District Manager, and Gary Wuslich, Superintendent of Industrial Relations, pleaded with Ed Mann to keep the demonstrators outside. Then:

> After a heated discussion, Mann agreed to hold the steelworkers in the lobby until Allen came out.
>
> The demonstrators waited 10 or 15 minutes. When Allen approached the group, he paused and said to Mann, "Now, Ed, you know we are handling this through the Union."
>
> "But we are the Union," Mann [and several others] emphatically replied.
>
> "I'm tired, I'm going home," Allen said, hastily pushing through the steelworkers.[52]

Later, union members learned that some of their immediate super-visors had welcomed the action. One supervisor suggested that the demonstration could have been even more effective if the union had bought a few tickets to the speech, and so been in a position to ask questions of Mr. Allen inside the ballroom, while at the same time doing its thing in the lobby.

Chapter Three. The End at Brier Hill

When we returned to the union hall from the Country Club, to resume the "adjourned" meeting, Ed Mann reflected on the fact that the December 29 picket line had been followed within a month by the Country Club confrontation.

"We're beginning to get in practice," he told the group. "We're beginning to get used to the idea of demonstrating. Now we can go on building."

But it didn't work out that way.

At the January 19 meeting, J & L had promised to respond to Local 1462's demands but left somewhat uncertain when that would happen. The planning group at the local—the officers, grievance committeemen, and myself—found ourselves somewhat in limbo. There was not the same sense that there had been before the January 19 meeting of urgently preparing for a definite future event. One result was that decisions tended to be made in a more routine manner, by a smaller number of persons.

In this way, it was decided to hold a downtown rally on Saturday, March 17, St. Patrick's Day.

It may be that the March 17 rally was the turning point in the entire Youngstown effort. At the time of the rally, the Federal government had not yet announced its decision on the Ecumenical Coalition's request for funds and guarantees to make possible the reopening of the Campbell Works. Moreover, as a pamphlet prepared by Dickey pointed out, U.S. Steel was also watching the reaction of people in the Valley.

> US Steel has already indicated through the media and by their failure to modernize, that they intend to close their Mahoning

Valley plants—the Ohio Works and the McDonald Mills. If LTV makes an easy escape, it will be a clear message to US Steel that they can simply shut down and walk away, leaving another 4,000 people jobless.[53]

From this point of view, our inability to produce a really massive outpouring on March 17, 1979 may have doomed all three resistance efforts: the attempt to reopen the Campbell Works and the effort to prevent shutdowns at U.S. Steel's Youngstown Works, as well as the struggle for an alternative at Brier Hill.

Certainly Local 1462 systematically sought to call in its IOUs, as Ed Mann put it, from community and union groups it had assisted over the years. As I write I am looking at the literature which sought to spread the word: a one-page leaflet, "Join the Rally"; a letter from Ed Mann to "Brothers and Sisters" in Local 1462, "asking each one of you, your family and your friends to attend the rally"; Gerald Dickey's thoughtful pamphlet, already quoted; a professional press release, suggesting that photographers wishing to view the (presumably vast) crowd from above could use the offices of Northeast Ohio Legal Services. The Ecumenical Coalition added a letter to its own mailing list, correctly stating:

> This is the crucial moment. Campbell Works men and women are joining hands now with the Ecumenical Coalition and with their brothers and sisters at Brier Hill. Let's show them that we believe in them, and by doing so, show the nation that we intend to help save the Mahoning Valley. Remember, the people who paint a rosy future for this Valley expect you to do nothing. Don't believe them! We have to help ourselves.

Nor was this barrage of literature confined to the mails. I recall particularly that leaflets were handed out at the gates of the U.S. Steel mills.

Yet less than 500 persons turned out March 17. The *Vindicator* estimated the crowd at 250, and topped its story with a headline as demoralizing as it was awkward: "Poor Jobs Rally Turnout Laid to 'Hunger' Lack."

Management's So-Called Compromise

March 17 was still in the minds of Local 1462's officers when, on March 30, the follow-up meeting with J & L occurred in Pittsburgh.

One of the participants, Jim Davis, later said explicitly that March 17 showed it would not be possible to make a fight and so the local was obliged to cut the best deal that it could.

On March 30, the day of the meeting, J & L mailed a letter to the Local 1462 membership. Frank Valenta and others later claimed that concessions in the letter were obtained in exchange for the local's promise to work with the company in making possible an "orderly shutdown." This is demonstrably false. The union did not know it, but J & L's letter containing the concessions was already in the mail to the membership *before* the March 30 meeting at which the union leadership agreed to an orderly shutdown.

The J & L letter made the following main points:[54]

> At present, we plan to continue to operate the Brier Hill steel-making facilities and Blooming mill at least through the end of 1979, and beyond depending on market conditions. . . .
>
> In addition, we have considered carefully the request of the Union that additional time be provided so that the Union and/or civic groups, such as the Ecumenical Coalition, have additional time within which to arrange for an alternative use of the Brier Hill Works. To accomodate that request, we have advised the Union that we will incur the additional expense of maintaining the Brier Hill Works as an idled but not permanently shutdown facility for a six month period after the termination of steel-making and bloom production. . . .
>
> Our Seamless operation at Campbell supplied with Open Hearth steel from Brier Hill, contrary to popular misinformation, is not a profitable operation. . . . With the modern steel-making capacity that J&L has at Aliquippa, Cleveland, and Pittsburgh (where new Electric Furnaces are about to go into operation), our Company cannot justify another large investment which would be necessary to modernize steelmaking at Brier Hill. . . .
>
> Because of the past efforts on the part of your Union and Management, many of you at Brier Hill will be eligible for 70/80 pensions provided the Mill is eventually shutdown and that such shutdown occurs in an orderly fashion. In fact, about 500 of the 1200 employees that would likely be affected by an eventual shutdown of Open Hearth and Blooming facilities will be eligible.. . . .

Orderly Shutdown Agreed to by Local Leadership

A majority of the local union's representatives at the March 30 meeting felt that the contents of J & L's letter was all that realistically could be achieved. John Barbero felt differently, and argued that to be consistent with the local's longstanding support of rank-and-file ratification of contracts the question should be brought back to the members before it was finally decided.

Accordingly, a meeting took place at the local union hall on Sunday, April 1. Ken Doran argued forcefully that having won this much, it was possible to win more. Jim Davis, perhaps sensing that Doran's position would win majority support at that meeting, proposed that to be truly democratic there should be a referendum vote.

The referendum vote occurred on April 10. The local union officers distributed the following ballot:

> . . . You have received a letter from J&L management dated March 30, 1979, stating that the company plans to keep Brier Hill open through 1979, and possibly into 1980, depending on market conditions. The company has also indicated that they will not declare the plant shut down until six (6) months after they cease steelmaking operations. The company wants an orderly shutdown and removal of equipment (peelers and saws) sometime after July 1, 1979.
> Indicate below if you are . . .
> _____ FOR the Proposal
> _____ AGAINST the Proposal

John Barbero and Ken Doran handed out a leaflet urging people to vote, "Against." The leaflet stated:

LET'S KEEP THEM TALKING

Our Union Officers have been negotiating with J & L since January 19. Other activities have taken place since Christmas. As a result we received a letter from J & L which grants a six month extension of the formal announcement of the BRIER HILL PLANT SHUTDOWN.

IS THIS A GOOD DEAL?

The answer is Yes. BUT IS IT GOOD ENOUGH? The answer is "N O." In reality, this partial gain is only a reprieve—a temporary stay of execution. Brier Hill's most valuable tools, four of the five saws and four of the five peelers will be removed after

July 1. Soon afterwards many workers will be let go in the Open Hearth, Blooming Mill, Peelers, Conditioning Yard and Shops.

NO WINNERS WHEN BRIER HILL SHUTS DOWN

When the shutdown comes, many will be forced to retire early, during their best earning years while not ready to quit working or financially unprepared for old age. Rule 65 people will be kept hanging for two years. Those with under 20 years will get unemployment compensation and SUB, IF THERE IS ANY. Many of us will be forced to uproot our families, sell our homes and relocate. We deserve some thing better (in exchange for the best years of our lives.)

THE NEXT MOVE

The decision to continue the fight for Brier Hill is now up to us, the membership. This is as it should be.

Company's Proposal Accepted by the Membership

In light voting, the membership voted 2–1 to accept the company's proposal. Although the open hearths did not go out until the end of December 1979, and the shutdown was not formally announced (as the March 30 letter promised) until eight months later, the fight at Brier Hill was over.

Chapter Four. Lessons

Why was the turnout so poor at the rally on March 17? Why did the Brier Hill membership not vote to continue the fight?

The Downtown Rally

The problem was not the *place* of the demonstration. There is nothing inherently wrong with a downtown rally. The great protest of December 1978–August 1979 of steelworkers in Longwy, France, directed against the announced layoff of 20,000 steelworkers and culminating in the most extraordinary mass actions, began with a demonstration of 25,000 people on the main square of Lower Longwy "in a burst of mobilization never before equaled in the basin."[55]

A more likely explanation is the *timing* of the demonstration. In Longwy, the layoffs were announced on December 11 and 12, 1978, and the downtown rally took place one week later, on December 19.[56] In Youngstown, by contrast, J & L definitively announced the closing of the Brier Hill Works on December 14, 1978, and the rally did not take place until three months later.

A plant closing struggle is totally unlike, say, the struggle for the right to vote in the South, or resistance to the Vietnam War. There, no matter how small a movement's beginnings (one person in one town refusing to go to the back of a bus, four young men sitting in at a lunch counter, a handful of individuals burning their draft cards), one could proceed with some confidence that the same causes which led that first person to resist would also prompt more and more resistance with the passage of time. I recall, for example, picketing with one other person at the Pentagon in June 1965. We were instantly surrounded by numbers of military policemen, who asked, with incredulity, what we thought we were doing. Summoning all my dignity I replied: "You don't understand. We're just the first of thousands." And we were.

In a plant closing struggle the movement may grow weaker rather than stronger as time goes on. When the closings in Youngstown were first announced there were, in each instance, angry mass meetings at which young persons especially talked about chaining themselves to machines, or blowing things up. And in each instance there were fairly militant actions in the first days or weeks after the announcement. At the Campbell Works, more than 100,000 signatures were collected between Tuesday and Thursday and dozens of angry men took them to Washington. At Brier Hill, local union members first picketed outside the plant, and then barged into the local country club to confront the company's area superintendent. And at U.S. Steel's Youngstown Works, the company's Pittsburgh headquarters was occupied three days after the closing was announced, and the company's Youngstown headquarters two months after the announcement (as will be told in Part III).

The evidence suggests that, in the case of Brier Hill, the leadership waited too long. An impending shutdown prompts each affected person to think about his or her personal survival. Try as one may to postpone discussion of "benefits," and to concentrate on collective struggle against the shutdown itself, this requires an effort of will, endlessly repeated, against the fear which leads a person to ask, What will happen to me? As time goes on, collective outrage dims and personal survival takes over. The failure to produce a quick change in the company's decision leads to a mood of resignation and a focus on looking after oneself. The rhetoric of struggle is replaced by a rhetoric of benefits. Since each union member is slightly differently situated with respect to the benefits available, the pain of the plant closing becomes privatized.

I think this is what happened at Brier Hill, and is likely to happen anywhere. As soon as it was known that J & L definitely intended to close Brier Hill, the local union dutifully advised its membership to begin to prepare. "Get In Shape," warned the *Brier Hill Unionist*.

Don't make any big bills. Save your money. If the threatened Brier Hill shutdown comes next year, be prepared for it. Fill your needs, but be cautious of your desires. Do you really need that new car? It's a bad time to be borrowing money—a bad time to go into debt.

What kind of shape are you and your family in? Physical shape, that is. It's a good time to see your doctor and get a complete physical exam. If you have any problems, get them taken care of while you still have hospitalization benefits. Get your teeth examined, get the cavities filled. And if you need dentures and have been postponing it, don't delay any longer.

Start behaving as if a shutdown is coming, and if it does, you should be prepared for it. . . .[57]

The lesson appears to be this: *It is humanly very difficult to "start behaving as if a shutdown is coming," and at the same time take daring action, with unpredictable consequences, to try to stop the shutdown.* People calculating their benefits are unlikely to chain themselves to their machines.

The Role of the International

If the March 17 demonstration failed (at least in part) because of poor timing, however, the overall failure of the Brier Hill struggle to accomplish more than it did must be laid at the door of the international union. This was memorably expressed by Ken Doran in the following letter to the editor:

This is in regard to the closing of old, but profitable steel mills in Youngstown and other areas.

As the average steelworker in Youngstown prepares him or herself for a new life as a non-poor welfare recipient, they surely must wonder why. I wonder why not?

The United Steel Workers of America, a major labor union possessing a power base from which they could influence corporate decisions on plant shutdowns and the modernization of the steel industry, has remained virtually silent.

I think over the years many factors have led to this position by the U.S.W.A. Its development as a narrow-interest trade union association instead of a class-conscious labor organization was one factor. Union acceptance of corporate capitalism at home and allegiance to corporate economic expansion overseas are other factors.

The union's independence and integrity have been sacrificed to corporate policies that have provoked wars and the associated negative aspects of such wars. In the process the steelworkers union has assisted in the creation of multinational corporations which now threaten the economic and psychological security of the very workers the Union should protect.

What can be done? The answer is not easy. Changing union leaders will make little difference unless the values held by the new young leaders are also changed. A reordering of priorities must take place. The modernization of existing plants, called "brownfield" as opposed to the opening of new plants, called "greenfield" should be a top union priority. Why not start in Youngstown? A conversion from narrow-interest policies to one dedicated to the interest of the whole community is in order.

Again the U.S.W.A., a major labor union, possesses the means to turn things around. Will they become the sleeping giant that suddenly awakens in Youngstown? I wonder, why not?

Ken Doran[58]

A year later, after Brier Hill poured its last heat of steel and the mill was closed, John Barbero penned a similar testament.

I worked my last day Thursday. I went in with three production workers and 20 maintenance people supposedly to mothball and to ship out tools and unusable equipment to other plants. The first day back after the last steel was tapped was a shock. Our normally clean locker wash room resembled a garbage landfill. Looters had come in over the weekend and had taken everything that was useful. Everything else—unwanted workshoes, left behind clothes, tools and toilet articles—was strewn about in one hellish mess.

The next two weeks our crew acted as scavengers and vultures stripping the Open Hearth Department clean of anything that still could be used anywhere else but Brier Hill. We first and everyday burnt benches to keep warm, the Open Hearth is cold when the furnaces are dead. We then tore open the maintenance people's lockers throwing tool belts, pipe wrenches, slings, and thousands of tools into piles. Later we moved and sent out nearly all electric motors and welders and then all the moving equipment. Trucks appeared regularly hauling this plus moulds and stools to Aliquippa.

The last day I burned all the production records—"100,000,000 tons by 1970"—and the attendance and work records of the thousands of people who worked here for over 70 years. We have become non-persons. By the time we left, the once awesome open hearths stood as skeletal ruins picked clean and probably abandoned forever. It reminded me of Hiroshima where I worked for a few months immediately after the bomb was dropped.

The International's absence in Youngstown from the day Campbell was shutdown, through Brier Hill's shutdown and now to the eve of the Ohio and McDonald shutdown is not only callous, it is disgraceful. 10 to 12 thousand steelworkers will have lost their jobs here and the International has remained silent.

This should be a signal to all other steelworkers wherever they are in the U.S. They, too, will be allowed to hang separately, each in their turn, without the Internatio..al lifting a finger to help. Don't think that this message didn't penetrate clearly to every steelworker losing their jobs here. This message has laid a smothering blanket over the coalition's effort to reopen Campbell and over Brier Hill's fight to stay alive. It is now the cloud over the Ohio Works' and McDonald struggle.[59]

Later still, in the fall of 1980, a local fabricator named Syro Steel bought the former tube and electric weld plant at Brier Hill. Syro also owns a plant in Salt Lake City, Utah. Joseph Krulich, secretary-treasurer of Syro, explained why the company had decided to expand its operation in the Mahoning Valley.

> There's a more cooperative and dedicated labor feeling among the labor force. There's not as much militancy among the unions any more. We decided that we'd like to stay here.[60]

Another portion of the Brier Hill Works is being reopened by a second local company, Hunt Valve. Hunt plans to install electric furnaces exactly as Local 1462 proposed. Hunt is being greeted as another Messiah in the community. Yet Hunt, like similar entrepreneurs at the Campbell and Youngstown Works, is simply starting over again the process which led to the closing of Mahoning Valley mills. There is nothing in Hunt's relationship to the community or to its workers to prevent Hunt from closing Brier Hill again, twenty-five or thirty years from now.

Part III. The Battle for U.S. Steel's Youngstown Works

Chapter One. The Shutdown

The pickets at Brier Hill on December 29, 1978 had carried signs saying: "Campbell Yesterday! Brier Hill Today! Ohio Works Tomorrow!" After the Campbell and Brier Hill Works struggles were lost, everybody knew that the next battle would be at U.S. Steel's Youngstown Works, comprising the Ohio Works in Youngstown and the McDonald Works in nearby McDonald. Those who had been active in both previous struggles turned their attention to U.S. Steel. I recall feeling that just as George Washington's army retreated southward across New Jersey in the summer and fall of 1775, losing one battle after the other, so our little band of resisters was withdrawing north up the Mahoning Valley.

As at Campbell Works and Brier Hill, so also at U.S. Steel's Youngstown Works the issue was whether the company would invest in modernization of the facilities. At least one steam engine still in operation at the Ohio Works had first been installed in the nineteenth century. The Ohio Works made steel in open hearths, just as had both the other mills which were shut down. Mike Kaufman, grievance committeeman at Local 1330, wrote in the union newspaper:

> The sad fact is that a team of supermen led by a battery of geniuses cannot keep this district going indefinitely. What is needed is an infusion of new capital to modernize the facilities. Pittsburgh, however, is adamant in its refusal to invest here. [1]

The concern of U.S. Steel's Youngstown employees about the company's failure to modernize its Youngstown facilities was heightened by U.S. Steel's apparent intention to make its new investment in a huge new mill at Conneaut, Ohio, on the shore of Lake Erie. The principal product to be made at the proposed Conneaut mill was hot-rolled steel sheet, also produced at the McDonald Works. The company's Youngstown employees felt threatened. In June 1979, the United States Army Corps of Engineers approved a permit which would allow U.S. Steel to begin construction at Conneaut as soon as a PSD (Prevention of Significant Deterioration) permit was obtained from the United States Environmental Protection Agency. In July 1979, Local 1330 (Ohio Works) joined with Local 1397 (the Homestead Works in Pittsburgh), and several environmental groups, to bring suit seeking to set aside the Corps of Engineers permit.[2] Our theory was that the Corps had failed to explore rigorously and to evaluate objectively the alternative of putting the new steelmaking capacity in Youngstown and/or Pittsburgh.

Promises to Stay Open

Yet workers at U.S. Steel's Youngstown Works were not expecting a shutdown in the fall of 1979. They felt that the company had promised to keep the mills open if the workers could make them profitable. "It's a betrayal," George Denney, a machinist at the Ohio Works for seven years, told the *New York Times* after the shutdown announcement.

> They made a promise to the employees that as long as it's profitable they would stay open.[3]

Moreover, U.S. Steel workers in Youngstown understood that their mills *were* profitable in the spring and summer of 1979. The wife of one U.S. Steel employee wrote to the *Vindicator* after the shutdown announcement:

> These shutdowns are a disgrace and a bewilderment. One day the mills are making profits and the next day they are closed down.

Another woman, herself a McDonald Works employee, asserted:

> Although U.S. Steel has the right to phase out antiquated facilities . . . we have proven ours can be run profitably.[4]

On what evidence did Youngstown steelworkers base their conviction that U.S. Steel had promised to keep its Youngstown mills open so long as they made a profit, and had additionally told them that the mills were, in fact, profitable? The following were among the company's statements:

September 14, 1977. According to the *Warren Tribune*, Randy Walthius of U.S. Steel's Cleveland office said there would be a consolidation of operations at the Ohio and McDonald Works. Walthius stated:

> "Studies are being made. . . . The studies are aimed at making the Youngstown facilities profitable, *and it is on the basis of the plants' profitability that they will continue to operate.*" (Emphasis added)

January 4, 1978. Again according to the *Warren Tribune*, U.S. Steel repeated the company's September 1977 statement in the following words:

> "At that time . . . U.S. Steel did say that *continued operation in Youngstown would depend on the plant's ability to become profitable.* Since that time progress has been made in reducing losses.
> This effort will continue. *When and if there is a phaseout will depend on the plants' profitability.* . . ." (Emphasis added)

April 17, 1978. According to the *Warren Tribune* once more, U.S. Steel officials announced that in March 1978 the Ohio and McDonald Works had made a profit. This was said to be the first monthly profit at the plants in over a year. U.S. Steel Youngstown District Superintendent Kirwan said: "We'll be doing business here for some time to come." Spokesman Randy Walthius concurred, stating:

> "*Company management has repeatedly said that the works will stay open if they become profitable. Well, now they are profitable.*" (Emphasis added)

June 5, 1979. According to the *Wall Street Journal*, U.S. Steel's Youngstown Works "is profitable and can turn out about one million tons of steel a year." The article continued:

> "The *Youngstown Works finished 1978 in the black* and, Mr. Kirwan says, *even managed to win a profitability contest against U.S. Steel's much-newer plant in Baytown, Texas, which produces many of the same kinds of products.*" (Emphasis added)

June 18, 1979. David Roderick, chairman of the board of U.S. Steel, stated on ABC television that U.S. Steel's position on its Youngstown mills had been consistent.

"We have no plans for shutting down our Youngstown oper-
ation. . . . The Youngstown plant is profitable. We're operating
in the black there." (Emphasis added)

These statements to the media were echoed by company representatives at the Works. At a meeting and beer party for newly elected
local union officers in May 1979, Youngstown Works superintendent
Bill Kirwan stated that if the plant could be kept profitable it would
stay open; that the plant was presently profitable; and that there was
no intention to shut it down.[5] In June 1979, four union representatives
at the McDonald Works were told by a supervisor that the Youngstown Works had made $3 million during the first half of 1979.[6] In
September 1979, the company hosted a party at Sokol's Restaurant
on Midlothian Avenue for employees at the Ohio Works burning
yard. Superintendent Kirwan told the men that they had saved their
jobs through their hard work.[7]

The Promises Repeated

Only in October 1979 did rumors begin to circulate of impending
crisis at the Youngstown Works. On October 23, Mr. Kirwan told
union president Bob Vasquez that the Works were not on the 18-
month or 5-year investment plans of U.S. Steel, and that orders for
the next three months were running at levels below the Works' break-
even volume of 55,000 tons a month.[8] Alerted by Mr. Vasquez, the
Tri-State Conference on the Impact of Steel (a successor to the Ecumenical Coalition, made up of steelworkers and clergy in Youngstown and Pittsburgh) issued a press release calling on "steelworkers,
clergy, and people of good will in the steel-making communities" to
join in an emergency effort to save the Ohio Works.[9] Bishop Robert
Appleyard, Episcopal Bishop of Pittsburgh and chairperson of the
Tri-State Conference, wrote to David Roderick of U.S. Steel requesting a personal meeting. Specifically, the Bishop wrote,

> we want to discuss with you . . . your plans for capital invest-
> ment and modernization of the existing facilities of your corpo-
> ration. . . . I am sure you will agree that if major changes in the
> mobility of any plant facility are on the horizon, it is in the in-
> terest of everyone to know clearly what the future holds and to
> plan accordingly.[10]

Roderick did not answer the letter and, through a spokesman, declined to meet with Appleyard.

In an effort to obtain confirmation or denial of rumors about the Youngstown Works, officers of Locals 1330 (Ohio Works) and 1307 (McDonald Works) and steelworkers from other locals attended a public forum in Cleveland on the evening of November 1, 1979, where Frederick Foote, a public relations representative of U.S. Steel, was scheduled to speak.

Mr. Foote denied that the Ohio Works was in trouble. He stated at the November 1 public forum, and repeated to a reporter for the *Warren Tribune* the next day, that:

> We've said all along the Ohio Works has been profitable and there are no plans for a shutdown.[11]

U.S. Steel's Decision

So matters stood for the next three and a half weeks. It seemed that the public alarm sounded by the religious community had at least produced a reprieve for U.S. Steel's Youngstown mills. On Sunday, November 25, the *Vindicator* carried a sentimental letter by Jim Colella, recording secretary of Local 1330 (Ohio Works). Colella recognized that "we are in some very critical times at the Ohio Works plant." The bulk of his letter gave thanks for the jobs which the Works had provided over the years. "Why am I thankful?," Colella asked. He said that his wife, his son, and a brother had worked at the plant. Still working there, he continued, were his father-in-law, four brothers-in-law, and some of their sons. Colella calculated that his immediate family had provided more than 275 years of service, and added that there were many families who could match or surpass that figure. Colella concluded that he saw steelmaking "being around forever." We have made many millions of tons here at the Ohio Works, he went on. He was thankful that "the Ohio Works of U.S. Steel, and Local 1330—representing the production and maintenance workers—will never die."[12]

Two days later, on Tuesday, November 27, the Board of Directors of U.S. Steel meeting in New York City announced the permanent shutdown of the Youngstown Works together with more than a dozen other smaller facilities. 13,000 employees, the statement said, "will be affected."[13] Subsequent statements projected the physical closing of the Youngstown Works for June 1980.

There is some question as to when the decision to close the Youngstown Works was actually made. U.S. Steel's top executives testified in court that there was no decision until November 1979. Yet nine months earlier, on February 12, 1979, the following "Confidential Memo to the File" was dictated by a staff member of the Ecumenical Coalition:

> Last week there was a meeting at Bill Cafaro's office, attended by three bank presidents (Brauninger, McGowan and Young), Forrest Beckett [the president of the Mahoning Valley Economic Development Committee], and Bill Brown [editor of the *Youngstown Vindicator*]. The five were there to persuade Cafaro into running Phil Richley for a second term as mayor.
>
> Apparently, U.S. Steel is going to close down the Ohio Works and McDonald Works this year, laying off 5,000 steel workers. A major economic decline is predicted for the Youngstown area. The above city leaders believe Phil Richley is the only one who can lead Youngstown through the decline. One bank president fears a total economic collapse. A city planner predicts a fifteen year decline.
>
> Cafaro does not want Richley to run again. He doesn't want Richley "holding the bag." One area banker, a former mayor, advised a close friend of his, rumored to be interested in the mayoral election, not to run because no one will be able to avert the tragedy, and *any* mayor is going to take a lot of blame.[14]

Even this may not be the whole story. In the course of pretrial proceedings in the Conneaut case, plaintiff steelworkers discovered a U.S. Steel planning document dated *February 13, 1975* which in forecasting the company's need for hot strip mill production stated that the McDonald Works would be "relieved of all Hot Rolled Sheets by 1980" and "relieved of all Hot Rolled Strip shortly after 1980."[15]

In all probability the turning point for Youngstown came in the spring of 1979 when U.S. Steel appointed a new top management team. David M. Roderick, previously president and chief executive officer, became chairman of the board. William S. Roesch, a much-travelled troubleshooter from outside the company, became president. Roderick and Roesch took over from men who had spent their working lives making steel at U.S. Steel facilities and who were sentimentally attached to the mills. Indeed Edgar B. Speer, Roderick's predecessor as chairman, had gotten his start at the Youngstown Works. In contrast, Roderick's background was in finance: he came to stand for a philosophy of putting investment dollars where they make the most return, whether in or out of the steel business. Roesch was a specialist in making hard-headed decisions about obsolete mills. Despite Roderick's statement in June 1979 that his policy toward Youngstown was "consistent" with that of his predecessors, there is every reason to believe that he initiated a new point of view. According to the *Wall Street Journal*, one of Roderick's first actions as chairman of the board was to ask Roesch

> to evaluate every steel mill with an eye toward paring the hopeless cases. The result . . . was the permanent closing of all or parts of 15 facilities and the elimination of some 13,000 jobs.[16]

Workers were the Last to Know

One thing is certain. Before the announcement on November 27, 1979, the company told the international union that it was considering closing the Youngstown Works. David Roderick, chairman of the board, testified in March 1980 that in late October or early November 1979, and in any event before November 12, Bruce Johnston, Vice President and General Manager of Industrial Relations, notified Lloyd McBride of the impending shutdown.[17] But nobody told the workers directly "affected" or their local union officers.

The news reached each family differently. Frank Georges was a 37-year-old machinist at the Ohio Works. He had spent most of November 27 at the bank in Beaver Falls, Pennsylvania, completing the "closing" on a new house. He and his wife had decided to buy a larger home so as to be able to invite his wife's parents, who were ill, to live with them. Georges started looking for a new home, he later testified, after he saw David Roderick make a statement on TV that the company had no plans for closing the Ohio Works, and after he heard William Kirwan, the plant superintendent, state on the mill "hot line" that the Works were profitable. As he drove home from the bank November 27 Georges heard on the car radio that the mill was to close. "I felt like someone pulled a rug out from under me," he said. "Then I got angry. . . ."[18]

Mrs. Kathy Green wrote a letter to the editor on the day of the shutdown announcement. She said her husband was an employee at the McDonald Works. This is the year of the child, she went on, and asked who would help to feed their three children. Mrs. Green told a story common to Youngstown: the last time her husband had been laid off, he had been told by the welfare office that he collected too much unemployment compensation to be eligible for food stamps or Aid to Dependent Children. There was very little money left in the SUB fund (Supplemental Unemployment Benefits provided by the company) at the McDonald Works, Mrs. Green continued. Both her husband and she had only high school educations, she said. They were unable to find jobs to support their family and pay their bills. They did not have money for further education. Mrs. Green concluded: "I feel very angry."[19]

How the Local Unions Took the Lead

A meeting of persons from the old Ecumenical Coalition network who were still interested in plant closing issues had previously been planned for the afternoon of Wednesday, November 28, at the Local 1462 hall. By tacit agreement it became a meeting on the new crisis at U.S. Steel.

The meeting had been in progress about half an hour when the executive committees of the U.S. Steel production and maintenance locals, Local 1330 (Ohio Works) and Local 1307 (McDonald Works), walked in. Bob Vasquez, president of Local 1330, spoke for the group. Even more clearly than in the case of Brier Hill, it was made plain that the U.S. Steel struggle would be led by the affected local unions.

The recommended first step was a mass meeting at the union hall on Thursday evening, November 29, and a picket line outside U.S. Steel's Pittsburgh headquarters the next day.

The Thursday meeting was by far the largest which had thus far taken place, in any of the shutdowns. The meeting room at the Local 1330 hall held about 1,000. Hundreds more milled in the corridors and doorway, unable to get in. Picket signs, hand made at the hall that afternoon in anticipation of next day's picketing, decorated the stage. Some of them read: "Merry Christmas from U.S. Steel,"

"U.S. Steel gets the gold mine, we get the shaft," "From steel city to cobweb city," "I gave my life to U.S. Steel, they gave it to Japan," "Khomeini Roderick holds 13,000 hostages."

The leaders of the continuing struggle in Youngstown addressed the crowd: Reverend Rawlings, principal organizer of the Campbell effort; Ed Mann, president of the Brier Hill local; Bob Vasquez, president of the local at the Ohio Works. The speeches applied the analysis previously reserved for steel companies acquired by conglomerates to U.S. Steel as well. Marvin Weinstock, a former president of the local union at the Ohio Works, said:

> They've taken money out and milked us dry. Money that came out of your sweat, backs and muscles.[20]
>
> Out of your sweat, out of your muscle, they took millions and millions, hundreds of millions and put it in hotels, Disneyland, everywhere except in Youngstown.[21]
>
> We put our lives into the valley. We built the homes and the churches and the hospitals. Now they're cutting us off.[22]
>
> You invested here. You built houses and paid taxes that built the schools and highways. And we want U.S. Steel to invest here, right here. That's the issue.[23]

Reverend Rawlings said what U.S. Steel had done to Youngstown was "economic genocide."[24]

District 26 Director Frank Leseganich spoke, too. He was asked from the floor whether he would join the picket line in Pittsburgh the next day. He said No, and urged his audience not to "overreact."[25]

An Unplanned Occupation of U.S. Steel's National Headquarters

Early the next morning seven chartered buses left the Local 1330 parking lot for Pittsburgh. The ride was something of a traveling seminar. Chuck Rawlings recalls John Barbero commenting, "It takes you years to learn something and then you try to get it across in a couple of hours."

The buses unloaded in front of the rust-colored skyscraper at 600 Grant Street in Pittsburgh which houses U.S. Steel's national headquarters. It was snowing lightly, and cold. As the line formed and began to circle the sidewalk dozens of Pittsburgh steelworkers, most of them from the Homestead Works local, joined in.

Whether because it was cold, or because some people had planned it that way, or because, in the moment, the occasion seemed to call for something more, the line suddenly broke up and the participants streamed into the lobby of the building. Within moments the lobby was all but filled with sign-carrying steelworkers. An escalator ran from the lobby to a mezzanine, from which elevators led to the rest of the building.

Company security personnel, with walkie-talkies, barred the way up the escalator. They were brushed aside. Led by Kathy Centofanti, wife of a Youngstown steelworker, among others, the demonstrators surged up to the mezzanine and began to walk around and around it, unsure of what to do next. They had more power than they knew. It later appeared that the company turned off the elevators leading from the mezzanine to the offices on higher floors. While this effectively prevented the demonstrators from going up, it also prevented the U.S. Steel executives from coming down. Had the demonstrators held their ground the only means of exit for the executives might have been by helicopter from the roof.

Action, however, had run far ahead of what any one was intellectually or emotionally ready for. The most that the collective wisdom of the crowd produced was a stubborn determination not to leave the building. A number of individuals, some of them union leaders, repeatedly urged every one to go back out on the street. They were ignored. At one such moment, there swept through the lobby of the U.S. Steel building the chant of draft resisters in the 1960s: "Hell No, We Won't Go."

But eventually we did go. About four in the afternoon, with a feeling that all had been done which could be done on that occasion, people got back into the buses and rode home to Youngstown.

Chapter Two. The Fight Continued by Legal Means

From the occupied escalator in the U.S. Steel Pittsburgh head-quarters I had sketched out a possible law suit against U.S. Steel. I said that the steel company might have broken a verbal contract with steelworkers to keep the mills open so long as they were profitable, and that legal action might be taken to open up the company's books.[26]

It was actually not I but my Legal Services coworker Jim Callen who first suggested the theory of the suit. Workers at U.S. Steel's Youngstown Works felt the company had broken a promise to keep the Works open so long as they were profitable. Jim suggested that if the workers had "detrimentally relied" on this promise, that is, had made sacrifices and concessions because of the promise, the promise might be a legally enforcible contract. And Section 301 of the National Labor Relations Act permits local unions or individual employees to sue a company for violating a contract.

Bob Vasquez had asked our office to suggest any legal possibilities that occurred to us. We immediately shared Jim's idea with him. He, in turn, ran it past the international union's lawyers. Their reaction was skeptical, according to Vasquez.

Going to Court with the Help of a Congressman

Then help came from an unexpected source. In November 1978, incumbent Democratic Congressman Charles Carney had been defeated by a Republican challenger, Lyle Williams. Williams was the first Republican to represent the Youngstown area in Congress since the 1930s. The vote for him was a protest vote against Carney, and a measure of the Valley's disenchantment with the promises of the Carter administration. Williams himself was an unknown quantity. Williams came from West Virginia, and it was vaguely supposed that he had first-hand knowledge of hard times. Before going into politics he had worked in Warren as a barber. It was a pleasant surprise when he invited the U.S. Steel local union presidents and attorneys to meet with him about a possible law suit.

We met with Williams three consecutive Sundays (December 2, 9, 16) at a local Holiday Inn. What he sought from the law suit was a delay in implementation of the shutdown long enough for Congress to provide capital needed to modernize the Youngstown Works. Williams said he had an attorney. The gentleman was listed on the papers we filed in court, but he never made it from Aliquippa, Pennsylvania to Youngstown and the management of the litigation fell wholly on Youngstown lawyers: Jim Denney, brother of George Denney who worked at the Ohio Works, representing most of the plaintiff local unions; and Bob Clyde, Jim Callen, and myself, representing the Tri-State Conference, and the Brier Hill Works local union, Local 1462.

Williams announced that he planned to file suit at a press conference in the William Penn Hotel in Pittsburgh on December 11. "The action we are announcing here today is in many respects a radical one," his press release stated. "But it is in response to an action that I consider to be equally radical."[27] At the press conference, Williams played a tape recording of David Roderick's television appearance in June, when Roderick said, "We have no plans for shutting down . . . Youngstown." He gave a rough description of the law suit's theory. Referring to Roderick's oral promise,

> Williams called his coalition "pretty sure we can document this promise. The union made some concessions because of it. We think that's unfair."[28]

Labor and community leaders reacted critically. William Edwards from the international union's Public Relations Department told the press: "I don't think we can force the company to keep the plants open."[29] Forrest Beckett, chief executive of an airline catering to business executives and chairman of the Mahoning Valley Economic Development Committee, stated that Congressman Williams "did a great disservice to this valley" in supporting the law suit.[30]

Congressman Williams did not back off. The evening of Thursday, December 20, there was another mass meeting at the Local 1330 hall. Williams told the crowd: "I plan to lead the fight to make U.S. Steel live up to its verbal . . . commitment . . . it made for the last two years since September 1977."[31] A form was passed out which stated:

> I believe that United States Steel promised to keep the Ohio and McDonald Works open so long as they were profitable. I also believe that the Ohio and McDonald Works were profitable when United States Steel announced that it was shutting them down. Therefore, I believe that United States Steel has broken its promise, and I wish to join Congressman Lyle Williams, Local 1307, and Local 1330, as a plaintiff in a law suit to be filed in United States District Court which will seek an injunction to keep the mills open.

The suit was filed at the Clerk's office in Youngstown at noon the next day, Friday, December 21.

The Theory of the Law Suit

The plaintiffs were: Congressman Williams; the four local unions representing production, maintenance, office and technical workers at the Youngstown Works (Locals 1330, 1307, 3073 and 3072); Local 1462, USWA, representing production and maintenance workers at Brier Hill, on the theory that the Brier Hill Works was just across the river from the Ohio Works and could be purchased and modernized with it; Local 1112, UAW, representing production and maintenance workers at the General Motors plant in Lordstown, who argued that their plant could get steel more cheaply if it were made locally; the Tri-State Conference on the Impact of Steel, composed of clergy and steelworkers with a special interest in "brownfield" modernization; and sixty-five individual steelworkers at the Youngstown Works.

We knew that the Court might eventually hold that some of these plaintiffs did not have enough connection with the shutdown of the Youngstown Works, and thus lacked "standing" and should be dismissed. But we felt that it was important for the judge to understand the breadth and variety of the coalition concerned to keep the mills open. As it turned out, the only plaintiff to be dismissed in the first phase of the case was Williams himself.

After listing the plaintiffs and describing how each was interested

in the impending shutdown, the Complaint set forth the three elements of the contract claim on which the suit was based. First, there
was the promise:

> During a period beginning no later than September 14, 1977
> and ending no earlier than November 2, 1979, Defendant by its
> agents Randy Walthius, Edgar Speer, William Kirwan, David
> Roderick, and Frederick Foote, as well as by various super-
> visors at the Ohio and McDonald Works, repeatedly and con-
> sistently promised Locals 1330, 1307, 3073, and 3072, and their
> members, that the Ohio and McDonald Works would be kept
> open so long as they were profitable.

The second element of the claim was that steelworkers at the two
mills had "detrimentally relied" on the promise, that is,

> acquiesced in proposals by Defendant concerning work practices
> at the Ohio and McDonald Works which were injurious to the
> interests of one or more members of the locals and to the interests
> of the locals themselves, and which the locals would have opposed
> had it not been for the promise by Defendant to keep the Ohio
> and McDonald Works open so long as they were profitable.

Also, the Complaint went on, individual steelworkers (like Frank
Georges)

> gave up opportunities to take other employment and committed
> themselves to major, long-term expenditures such as the pur-
> chase of homes.

It was this detrimental reliance which, according to the theory of the
suit, turned U.S. Steel's promise into a contract. (The legal doctrine
on which the plaintiffs relied is set forth in the Second Restatement
of Contracts, section 90: "A promise which the promisor should
reasonably expect to induce action or forbearance . . . and which
does induce such action or forbearance is binding if injustice can be
avoided only by enforcement of the promise.")

Finally, the Complaint asserted that U.S. Steel had broken the
contract by closing the mills when they were profitable. At the time
the suit was filed we had no detailed, authoritative evidence for this
element of the suit, and indeed, filed together with the Complaint a
"Request for Production of Documents" intended to obtain the
Works' profit data. So, in this first version of the Complaint, we said
only what the company had itself admitted in its statements in the
press:

In March 1978, for the first month in a year, the Ohio and McDonald Works made a profit. They have continued to be profitable and in 1978 won a profitability contest sponsored by Defendant against Defendant's newer mill in Baytown, Texas.

The Complaint then made the necessary assertions to justify an injunction: that plaintiffs would be more damaged if the mills were closed than U.S. Steel would be damaged by an order preventing them from closing.

> Since the Ohio and McDonald Works are profitable, Defendant will be less harmed by keeping the Ohio and McDonald Works open while governmental representatives and agencies seek capital for their modernization, than Plaintiffs, and especially the approximately 5,000 members of Locals 1330, 1307, 3073, and 3072 who work at the Ohio and McDonald Works, would be harmed by an abrupt and perhaps unnecessary shutdown.

We especially emphasized the work that Williams and other Congressmen were doing to make funds available for modernizing the mills:

> Plaintiff Williams, and other United States Congressmen, together with members of the Ohio legislature and of city governments in the Mahoning Valley, are seeking the capital necessary to modernize the Ohio and McDonald Works. On December 5, 1979, the City Council of Youngstown adopted Resolution 79–153 which called for support of H.R. 4646 before the Congress of the United States to provide additional capital for industry by permitting accelerated depreciation and other tax incentives, on condition that "every penny provided to the steel industry is reinvested in communities like Youngstown where steelworkers already live and work." Resolution 79–153 also called for an amendment to legislation before the Congress of the United States to authorize new funds for loan guarantees to distressed steelmaking communities, which amendment would permit up to $225 million in loan guarantees "to a single community such as Youngstown which is experiencing economic genocide from plant shutdowns." The Commerce, Consumer and Monetary Affairs Subcommittee of the Government Operations Committee of the United States House of Representatives, of which Plaintiff Williams is ranking minority member, held a hearing on the steel crisis on December 20, 1979, and as this Complaint is being filed, the Steel Task Force of the Ohio legislature and the Sub-

committee on Trade of the Ways and Means Committee of the United States House of Representatives are expected to hold hearings in Youngstown within the next week.

Political Support for the Suit

As this language suggests, the law suit was a part of a larger political effort by steelworkers and their supporters to focus attention on Youngstown and to find a way to keep the Youngstown Works alive. On December 5, 1979, steelworkers drafted and pushed through the Youngstown city council the resolution quoted in the Complaint. On December 22—the day after the suit was filed—an emergency Steel Task Force of the Ohio legislature appeared at the Local 1330 hall and took testimony. Once again the tale of the promise was told. Mike Farah, a grievance committeeman at Local 1307,

> said steelworkers made concessions in the interests of keeping the plants profitable, based on U.S. Steel's pledge to keep the plants operating.
> "Frankly, I feel we've been lied to," he said. "We've been given a lot of empty hopes."[32]

Caught up in the spirit of the occasion the Task Force publicly announced its support of the law suit filed the day before.[33]

On December 28, a Subcommittee on Trade of the Committee on Ways and Means of the United States House of Representatives, chaired by Congressman Charles Vanik, held a hearing on steel in the chambers of the Youngstown City Council. That hearing was helpful in several ways. Reverend Rawlings presented carefully documented testimony on the way in which the Economic Development Administration (EDA) had deceived the Ecumenical Coalition. The Congressmen were openly sympathetic. Quite frankly, said Rep. Thomas Downey (D.-N.Y.), "I think they [the Coalition] got screwed. . . . I would hope the committee doesn't let this issue die."[34] When an EDA representative rebutted by saying that Youngstown had been the agency's No. 1 priority for the past three to four years, Congressman William Fenzel (R.-Minn.) commented: "I'd hate to see what the EDA did for communities that weren't a No. 1 priority."[35] Chairman Vanik concurred in language that seemed to revive the Alperovitz-HUD proposal of a Youngstown demonstration project. There were signs of a determination and resilience in Youngstown that would make the risk less, and such determination deserved a chance to demonstrate its potential. America, Congressman Vanik was reported to have said, could "look upon this community as a laboratory." Surely there were going to be problems similar to Youngstown's in other industries.[36]

Also at the December 28 hearing, Bob Vasquez presented to the Congressmen a six-point plan for saving the U.S. Steel plants in Youngstown. Some key items included a call for U.S. Steel to bargain with local unions in an attempt to prevent the shutdowns and a plea for them to explore the possibility of purchasing the nearby J & L Brier Hill Works and renovating both it and the Ohio Works.

For any of these possibilities to have a chance to materialize we needed time. If U.S. Steel were permitted to proceed to close its Youngstown mills, disperse the machinery, and sell off the property piece by piece, all projected alternatives would become moot. This is why the law suit focused on an injunction. In the language of the Complaint as initially filed, the injunction would

> direct Defendant to keep the Ohio and McDonald Works open until this Court, after an adversary hearing, has determined that the Ohio and McDonald Works have ceased to be profitable.

The Judge

When a suit is filed in Federal court, the Clerk assigns a judge to the case. This is supposed to be done on a wholly random basis. Youngstown cases, although they could be filed in Youngstown, were ordinarily heard in Cleveland. Accordingly, when a case was filed at the Clerk's office in Youngstown a telephone call was placed to the Clerk's office in Cleveland, where the assignment of a judge was made. Usually this took a matter of seconds. But when Williams v. U.S. Steel was filed there was a wait of close to fifteen minutes. Then the Clerk told me: Judge Lambros.

I was overjoyed. I had previously been before Judge Lambros in 1977 when Kent State University sought to build a new gymnasium on the site where four students had been shot and killed by National Guardsmen in May 1970. I represented the teachers' union at Kent State, which supported several student groups in opposing construction of a gym in that place. There was a vivid memory in my mind of

Judge Lambros, in his shirtsleeves at one or two o'clock in the morning, trying to arrange a negotiated settlement. We had drawn a judge with more than the ordinary share of human feeling.

Had I thought longer I might have remembered something else about the Kent State case. In that litigation, Judge Lambros granted a preliminary injunction to stop construction of the gym until he could hear the merits of the dispute. But when he reached the merits he permitted the gym to be built.

Chapter Three. The Sit-In: Youngstown's Last Stand

The events of January 28, 1980 represented a last effort on the part of the Mahoning Valley's steelworkers and community to fight back. At the height of the January 28 events, steelworker Pat Madden looked out of the occupied U.S. Steel administration building and was asked what he thought about the protest. "This is the last stand," he said. "The whole city should be down here."[37]

A Futile Attempt to Bargain

The prelude to what happened on January 28 was an attempt to get U.S. Steel to reconsider the decision to close its Youngstown mills.

Almost from the moment U.S. Steel announced the closing of the Youngstown Works the workers there had asked the company for an opportunity to propose alternatives. A meeting was finally arranged for December 20 at U.S. Steel headquarters in Pittsburgh. The participants were: for the company, Bruce Johnston, General Manager of Industrial Relations, and another labor relations executive; for the unions, Bob Vasquez and Reno DePietro, presidents of the principal affected locals; for the public, State Senators Harry Meshel and Thomas Carney.

Bob Vasquez described what happened in his testimony at trial the next March:

> Me and Reno and the two State Senators went in and Mr. Johnston talked to us, made a presentation to us about an hour

or so as to why the facilities were shut down and the extensive amount of capital that the corporation needed to [equip] their fleet on Lake Erie . . . with holding tanks, wasn't allowed to dump into the Lake any more, and what they needed at Provo, Utah, and the emissions standards on the coke battery, and if you filled a thimble full of dust and threw it into the Houston Astrodome, that's the standards they had to meet.

Then he excused himself and said he had to go to a luncheon meeting at one of the colleges there. . . .

The steelworkers were left to make their presentation to Mr. Johnston's lesser-ranking associate, a Mr. Miller.[38]

Vasquez also described the package which he and DePietro suggested in an effort to save the mill.

We have an existing package of approximately $500,000 a month in incentives, and what we were offering was to give up these incentives on a deferred basis and take them in the form of stock at a later date if they would use that money we were giving up to plow back into our facilities and bring them up to date and modernize them and let us have an opportunity to continue to live and work in the area where we wanted to, where we were born and raised.[39]

The workers' offer amounted to $6 million a year (12 times $500,000). As would become apparent at the March trial, this was far in excess of the Youngstown Works' loss in 1979 by any suggested method of accounting.

There was good reason to believe that these proposals might be accepted. Among the plants which U.S. Steel on November 27, 1979 announced that it would close were American Bridge plants at Ambridge and Shiffler, Pennsylvania. The American Bridge plant at Gary, Indiana was not mentioned in the announcement, and was presumably to be spared. A month later, however, U.S. Steel reversed its decision: the Ambridge (about 1,200 workers) and Shiffler (about 285 workers) plants would stay open, while the Gary plant (about 750 workers) would be closed. The company changed its mind when the Ambridge and Shiffler unions voted to accept a three-year wage freeze and a 25 per cent "cap" on cost of living adjustments, taking them out from under the Basic Steel Contract. An hour after the Ambridge vote, David M. Roderick of U.S. Steel announced the company's new decision. Ambridge could continue to be a source of "first-rate jobs" and employment opportunities, he said, if the agreement was carried out "in a spirit of cooperation and sustained productivity." As for Gary, he stated that the refusal of its employees

> to make any compromise in the same direction means that the Gary plant will be phased out as existing work can be completed or relocated.[40]

The company's employees in Youngstown who had for twenty-six months responded to such rhetoric with one sacrifice and concession after the other now offered still greater concessions in hope of reversing the company's decision about Youngstown.

But U.S. Steel said No. Vasquez and DePietro received phone calls between Christmas and New Year's in which they were told that the company saw no useful purpose in continuing to meet.

Planning the Sit-In

Vasquez now turned to the idea that if U.S. Steel would not run the Works itself, it should give the workers a chance to buy them. But the company refused to meet with him to talk about this alternative. Accordingly, serious planning began for a rally and building occupation on an arbitrarily chosen date: Monday, January 28.

A first question was, Where? It was attractive to think of going back to Pittsburgh and completing what had been only begun November 30. This option was rejected because the Youngstown police were thought more likely to be friendly. (This judgment proved to be correct.) Occupation of the company's Youngstown administration building was preferred, perhaps mistakenly, to an occupation of the mill. The real stroke of genius in planning for the 28th was the decision to begin the day with a rally to which all the prominent politicians would be invited. Thus one got the best of both worlds. On the one hand, the grapevine carried the message that this was not to be one more rally, that something was going to happen, that this was D-Day. On the other hand, a dozen political leaders found themselves in the position of having told a mass audience that they were willing to do *anything* to help just before that same crowd trespassed on U.S. Steel property and occupied the company's Youngstown headquarters.

Since the headquarters was just down the hill from the Local 1330 union hall, it was determined that the morning rally would be at

Local 1330. So as to make clear that the McDonald Works was equally involved there was a preliminary rally on Sunday, January 27, at the McDonald Works local union hall. The energizing event on that occasion was a statement a few days earlier by Lloyd McBride, international union president, that those involved in resisting shutdowns in Youngstown were "phonies."[41] Whatever McBride intended the members and officers of Locals 1307 and 1330 understood their union president to be talking about them. Joe Saunders, one of the Local 1307 officers, read a heated response to the January 27 meeting.

Also on January 27, the *Vindicator* carried a front-page story to the effect that steelworkers at the Youngstown Works would be denied Trade Readjustment Assistance (TRA) benefits. Campbell and Brier Hill workers had received TRA benefits when their plants closed. The effect of the TRA benefits was to continue for a full year unemployment compensation which otherwise terminated after six months. It was even possible to extend TRA for yet a third six-month period by enrolling for an approved job training program. But to qualify for TRA the Department of Labor had to certify that a plant closing was caused by imports. The Department told the *Vindicator* that it would decline to do this in the case of the Youngstown Works. Members of Locals 1330 and 1307 were thus given a short-term reason for turning out on the 28th in addition to the long-term purposes which to many seemed unreal. The crowd on the 28th would include persons desperate to increase their benefits as well as men and women who still hoped to prevent the mill from closing.

A smaller, private meeting, to make final plans for the 28th, occurred the evening of the 27th at Local 1330. The next day was to show how much had not been foreseen. Yet an earnest effort was made that evening to anticipate all possible contingencies. How many steps ahead of the present could one confidently plan? It wasn't known whether enough people would show up at the union hall to do anything after the rally. It wasn't known whether the politicians would capture the crowd in such a way as to defuse any thought of action. If people tried to get into the building, it wasn't known whether they could actually do so or not. Actually occupying the building seemed so wild a dream that the group could not bring itself to plan with precision how the occupation would be conducted, who would make the decisions, how those within would communicate with those who stayed outside. No one imagined U.S. Steel would permit persons to wander in and out all afternoon. This was a critical failure, yet a very understandable one.

"I'm Going Down That Hill"

The rally on January 28 began with singing. My one contribution to the day was to recruit the singers: two actors from the Iron Clad Agreement, a Pittsburgh theater group, who agreed to double as folk singers for the occasion. It helped. The crowd took a long time gathering, yet it was obvious early that the crowd would be large.

Bob Vasquez chaired, as president of Local 1330 and as recognized leader of the Youngstown Works struggle. The politicians talked for a long time. Michelle DePietro, representing Senator Metzenbaum, was fiery in demanding Trade Readjustment Assistance for the Youngstown Works. State Senator Harry Meshel was long-winded and irritated the crowd, while Congressman Williams got a hand for his role in the law suit. Yet even as the television cameras ground away to record the political speeches, the feeling hung in the air that speechmaking was not the real business of the day. Nobody drifted away. Everybody waited, most of them for something which had only been described to them in the most general terms. Then Bob Vasquez introduced Ed Mann.

His own mill down, his own local union all but disbanded, Ed Mann could speak for himself in a way that had been difficult when he was representing the many interests within Local 1462. He began by saying: "You know we've heard a lot about benefits this morning but I thought we were here to save some jobs." Then he went on:[42]

> And I'm not interested in calling a lot of people together and just talking to them and going home. I think we've got a job to do today. [Responsive noises from the crowd.] And that job is to let U.S. Steel know that this is the end of the line. No more jobs are going to be shut down in Youngstown.
>
> You've got men here, you've got women here, you've got children here and we're here for one purpose. Not to be talked to about what's going to happen in Congress two years from now. What's going to happen in Youngstown today? There's a building two blocks from here. That's the U.S. Steel headquarters. [Laughter.] You know the whole country is looking at the voters, the citizens. What are you going to do? Are you going to make an action, or are you going to sit and talk and be talked to?
>
> The action is today. We're going down that hill, and we're going to let the politicians know, we're going to let U.S. Steel know, we're going to let the whole country know that steelworkers in Youngstown got guts and we want to fight for our jobs. We're not going to fight for welfare! [Cheers.]

In 1919 the fight was on for the 8-hour day and they lost that struggle and they burned down East Youngstown, which is Campbell. Now I'm not saying burn anything down but you got the 8-hour day.

In 1937 you wanted a union and people got shot in Youngstown because they wanted a union. And everything hasn't been that great since you got that union. Every day you put your life on the line when you went into that iron house. Every day you sucked up the dirt and took a chance on breaking your legs or breaking your back. And any one who's worked in there knows what I'm talking about.

Then came the most remarkable part of Mann's speech. Addressing an audience which included many blacks but was primarily made up of white middle Americans, Ed Mann said:

Now, I don't like to read to people but in 1857 Frederick Douglass said something that I think you ought to listen to:

"Those who profess to favor freedom and yet discourage agitation are men who want crops without plowing up the ground. They want rain without thunder and lightning. They want the ocean without the awful roar of its waters. This struggle may be a moral one (and you've heard a lot about that) or it may be a physical one (and you're going to hear about that) but it must be a struggle. Power concedes nothing without a demand. It never did and it never will. Find out what people will submit to and you will find out the exact measure of injustice and wrong which will be imposed upon them. And these will be continued until they are resisted with either words or blows or with both. The limits of tyrants are prescribed by the endurance of those they oppress."

This was said in 1857 and things haven't changed. U.S. Steel is going to see how much they can put on you. And when I say "you" I mean Youngstown, you know. We've got lists. We've got an obituary of plants that were shut down in the last twenty years. When are we going to make a stand?

Now, I'm going down that hill and I'm going into that building. And any one that doesn't want to come along doesn't have to but I'm sure there are those who'll want to. And one thing we're going to do when we get in there, we're going to stay there until they meet with Bob Vasquez.

When Ed Mann finished, Bob Vasquez said:

Like Ed told you, there's no free lunch. You've got to fight for what you want.

We've been trying to talk to U.S. Steel. They won't listen to us. We've been trying to talk to Jimmy Carter. He won't talk to us. We have to make these people listen!

If U.S. Steel doesn't want to make steel in Youngstown, the people of Youngstown will make steel in Youngstown! We're going down that hill!

With the exception of the politicians on the platform, only one of whom (State Representative Joe Vukovich) made it down the hill that day,[43] the crowd streamed out of the hall and down the few hundred yards to the large, squat, red brick administration building, with the neat steps leading up to the glass front door.

Someone broke down the door. There are different stories as to who did it, and perhaps it hardly matters, because the pictures of that moment of entry make it clear that the crowd would probably have pushed their leaders through the door had it not been broken.

People divided spontaneously into two groups. Those who were not "up" for trespass set up a picket line. Half forgotten skills were put into practice and a barrel was found, stoked, and lit. It provided some relief on a very cold day. Among those who picketed were many workers from other unions who showed up in support of the embattled steelworkers. I personally saw a local union officer of the Conrail workers union; several friends from Utility Workers Local 118; and a former client who had been fired from Schwebels Bakery. It seems that steelhaulers (truck drivers who haul steel) had planned to put in a dramatic appearance with their rigs, but were told not to participate by the steel companies on whom their livelihood depended.

Inside the building, an executive recreation room was found on the top floor and became, by common consent, occupation central. This discovery embarrassed U.S. Steel which subsequently issued a statement that the recreation room was available to everyone in the mill, a claim no one believed. I can recall seeing golf clubs on the picket line and wondering whence they came. It turned out they were from the executive rec room. (When Superintendent Kirwan met with union leaders the next day he began by complaining about the disappearance of his favorite putter.)

Some of the occupiers played pool in the rec room. A picture shows Ed Mann's daughter changing the diaper of her baby son there. Meantime many occupiers climbed to the roof and held up their picket signs, demanding "Work Not Welfare." A huge banner with the message "Keep Our Mills Open" slowly billowed out of several upper windows.

Down below in the street the Youngstown police arrived. Within minutes several were chatting with their former high-school classmates on the picket line.

Although Frank Leseganich was once again conspicuous by his absence, Russ Baxter, president of Local 2163 at the time of the Campbell Works shutdown and now president of the AFL-CIO council for Mahoning County, spent the entire afternoon in the building with the occupiers, and said: "We mean business. This occupation is good and it's for real. This had to be done."[44]

Another feature of the occupation was the large number of women who both entered the building and walked on the picket line. Most were steelworkers' wives, and their presence was due to the work of an organization called Save Our Jobs which they had started. One of these was Arlene Denney. Her grandfather had worked in the mills, and her father for an area steel fabricator. Her husband George had worked at the Ohio Works, and after the reopening efforts failed, would commute to the U.S. Steel mill in Lorain, Ohio. Ms. Denney recalls that, like many others, she and her husband had just bought a house when the shutdown was announced. At first she felt helpless and upset. Then she went to work as a bank teller to help pay the mortgage. Her wages were so low that, working full time, she was still eligible for food stamps. She began her effort to get wives involved

> because there were only a handful of women at the takeover of the U.S. Steel building in Pittsburgh. It looked like none of the steelworkers had families. That night I decided to get something started. Before working on the Save Jobs coalition, I was involved in the PTA. I got started organizing in the PTA. I just called my friends and the wives of George's friends and said, would you like to do something, to get something started? Some wanted to help and some did not.[45]

The presence of women in the occupied building may have been one reason that U.S. Steel apparently directed the police not to make arrests.

At least once that afternoon a U.S. Steel helicopter from Pittsburgh travelled back and forth over the building, no doubt trying to determine what was going on.

The Sit-In Abandoned

No one else was quite sure either. Bob Vasquez moved back and forth between the occupied building, the picket line, and the union hall, trying to hold things together. At one point he took Chuck Rawlings and myself aside and asked what we thought he should do. Ed Mann, John Barbero, and Ken Doran were all inside the building, but as members of another local they were hesitant to take the lead. There were a number of people in the building from out of town, whom few people knew. By the end of the afternoon some beer drinking was going on inside the building. There was some talk about setting the building on fire when it got dark.

It began to get dark about 5:30. Vasquez stood on the steps outside the front door, and gathered around him those who were still picketing. He said we were staying overnight. Reno DePietro, president of Local 1307, left the building to buy provisions. John Barbero left to get a newspaper.

As Vasquez made his way back into the building he was confronted by Superintendent Kirwan. (Most of the company personnel had long since gone home.) Kirwan told Vasquez that if Bob could get people out of the building, the company would meet with the local union presidents the next day. Vasquez consulted Ed Mann and June Lucas, Youngstown organizer for the Ohio Public Interest Campaign, among others. He decided to end the occupation.

The demonstrators went back to the Local 1330 union hall to debate their leader's decision. Unlike the eventual decision on November 30 to leave the U.S. Steel building in Pittsburgh, this decision was bitterly protested. One Local 1330 grievance committeeman protested again and again. Finally a fight broke out between this man and a supporter of Vasquez's decision.

I had gone home to eat supper and arrived at the union hall just as the meeting was breaking up. So did Reno DePietro who was beside himself with anger. With his arms full of the groceries which were to have sustained an overnight occupation, and wrongly imagining that I was part of the decision to leave the building, he asked me bitterly what I thought I was doing.

At 6:55 Walter Cronkite announced that a U.S. Steel building in Youngstown had been occupied briefly, but was now cleared.

Another Promise Broken

For three days after the memorable afternoon of January 28 it seemed that the decision to leave the building might have been a good tactic.

On Tuesday, January 29, Mr. Kirwan met as promised with the presidents of the Ohio and McDonald Works locals. He told them that U.S. Steel's realty subsidiary had begun the process of appraising the Works, and that a price for the entire facility would be named. He stated that the machinery would be kept intact at least until June. And he said that steelworkers would have the same chance to buy the mills as any one else.

The last point was the crucial one. Steelworkers had occupied the administration building on the 28th with the attitude: If U.S. Steel won't agree to keep the mills open, then we should have a chance to buy and run them ourselves. On the 29th Kirwan told them that they would have this chance.

There is no misunderstanding or controversy that Kirwan did say this. Reno DePietro took notes at the meeting which included the statement by Kirwan: "We [steelworkers] do have a shot at this." Randall Walthius, a company public relations man, told the press that U.S. Steel's realty representatives would meet with steelworkers and "any other potential buyers."[46] And later at trial, I asked Kirwan if he remembered Vasquez asking him on the 29th whether employees would have the same chance to buy the facilities as any other prospective buyer. Kirwan answered: "He asked me if I would give him the same chance and I said yes."[47]

On Wednesday, January 30, the general understanding was summed up in nearly identical language by the *Warren Tribune* (in an editorial entitled "Union gets answers") and by Chuck Rawlings, in a memo to members of the Tri-State Conference. In the words of the newspaper: "The four USW union locals have until June to draft a plan to buy any or all of the corporation's two steel mill works that will be closed."[48] The *Cleveland Plain Dealer* was more colorful. Its front-page headline on the 30th read: "Buy or bye-bye, steel union told."[49]

Momentum was building. I was invited to Columbus to testify before the legislature's Steel Task Force on Thursday the 31st. Rawlings, Greenman, and I were asked to go to Washington, Friday,

February 1 to testify before the Anti-Trust Subcommittee of the House Committee on Small Business. Youngstown steelworkers made plans to travel en masse to Washington on February 5 to testify before the Senate Committee on Small Business.

And then, as so often before, the door which had begun to open was slammed shut in our faces. On Thursday, January 31, the chief executives of American steel companies gathered in Washington for the release of a "white paper" by the American Iron and Steel Institute on the industry's needs. After the press conference, David Roderick, chairman of the board of U.S. Steel, was asked a question by Jan Hopkins, reporter for the Youngstown CBS affiliate. She asked him what he thought about the proposal for employees to buy and operate the Youngstown Works. The following ensued:

> Mr. Roderick: I don't believe those are really viable options. We obviously would not be interested in selling the plants to a group of people that can only be successful if they were massively. subsidized by the Federal government.
>
> We are not, in other words, interested in creating subsidized competition for ourselves at other locations.
>
> Ms. Hopkins: So you are refusing to sell?
>
> Mr. Roderick: I would certainly not be interested in selling to a coalition that would be subsidized by the Federal government in order to keep them into existence.[50]

Chapter Four. Back to Legal Action

Roderick's January 31 statement greatly lessened the chances of continuing to operate the Youngstown Works. At the Campbell Works, it will be recalled, Lykes/J & L had been pressured into offering the Works to the Ecumenical Coalition and giving the Coalition a six-month exclusive option to try to raise the money. Similarly at Brier Hill, J & L had agreed to "mothball" the mill from January to June 1980 in case the union and its coworkers could come up with the wherewithal to buy it. U.S. Steel was taking the position that it would not sell the mills to its workers even if they could raise the purchase price.

Yet there seemed one possible scenario. Roderick's refusal to deal with his employees had shocked public opinion. Senator Metzenbaum stated: "I don't think that will fly in the face of antitrust laws."[51] Congressman Williams asked the Federal Trade Commission to investigate.[52] Congressman Benjamin Bedell (D.-Iowa), chairman of the Anti-Trust Subcommittee of the House Committee on Small Business, was clearly disturbed and said that his subcommittee would consider whether new legislation was needed to cover a company's refusal to sell to a possible competitor.[53] Bill Mauldin published a cartoon showing a worker standing before the mill gate while a dog labelled U.S. Steel looked out through the smoke stacks; the title was "Dog in the Manger."

Our suit could be broadened to include this second broken promise. The Court might order U.S. Steel to give us a chance to buy, putting us in the same situation as we had been at Campbell and Brier Hill.

Accordingly plaintiffs filed a First Amended Complaint. The original Complaint was expanded in the following ways.

First, at the request of U.S. Steel, we were more specific about the company's promise to keep the plants open so long as profitable. We could do this because U.S. Steel had produced a number of the documents requested, including transcripts of its "hot line" messages to employees over the in-plant telephone. Thus Bill Ashton, superintendent before Bill Kirwan, told Works employees in September 1977:

> Hello, this is Bill Ashton.
>
> In response to many rumors, I want to tell you that there are no immediate plans to permanently shut down either the Ohio Works or McDonald Mills.
>
> However, steps will have to be taken to improve these plants' profitability. . . . The continued operation of these plants is absolutely dependent upon their being profit-makers.

After Bill Kirwan became superintendent in February 1978 the message was the same. For example, his Christmas message on the "hot line" at the end of 1978 stated in part:

> Hello, this is Bill Kirwan.
>
> You will recall that early in 1978 we initiated significant changes in our operations in order to make Youngstown Works profitable and once again a viable plant. Our efforts took many turns, but we have attained our 1978 goal which was "survival" and now we embark on the 1979 goal which is "revival."

Second, the new Complaint added a "Second Cause of Action" setting forth the facts concerning Kirwan's promise of January 29 and Roderick's repudiation of it two days later. This part of the Complaint began by pointing out that since December 21, when the suit was first filed, U.S. Steel had made a "seemingly irrevocable decision . . . to proceed with shutting down the Ohio and McDonald Works." For this reason, we went on,

> Plaintiff Locals have communicated to Defendant that an entity including Youngstown District employees desires to acquire the facilities and operate them itself.

Then the Complaint detailed what Kirwan had said and what Roderick had said.

Third and finally, the Complaint offered the Court two possible forms of relief:

Injustice to Plaintiffs, and particularly to Plaintiff Locals and
their members, can be avoided only by equitable relief enforcing
either Defendant's original promise to keep the Ohio and
McDonald Works open if they became profitable, *or* Defendant's
subsequent promise to offer the Ohio and McDonald Works for
sale to its Youngstown District employees. (Emphasis added.)

U.S. Steel paid no attention. The company announced that it
would close down the Ohio Works on March 11, six days before the
case was scheduled to go to trial.

The Injunction

Judge Lambros ordered a pretrial hearing for February 28. In
preparation, plaintiffs filed a motion asking for an immediate injunction to prevent the company from closing the mills; filed two
more motions asking that trial be held in Youngstown, and that plaintiffs be permitted to depose (ask questions in the presence of a court
reporter) David Roderick; and announced that Ramsey Clark was
joining the team of plaintiffs' attorneys.

Local 1330 chartered a bus to take steelworkers to Cleveland for
the hearing on February 28. It was only about a third full. The fact
underlined the essential weakness of our strategy after the building
occupation a month earlier. It was now three months since U.S. Steel
announced its intention to close. When earlier militant actions on
November 30 and January 28 failed to shake the company's resolve
to close the mills, the average steelworker had given up hope for his
or her job, and turned to the task of building a new life.

The law suit, originally one front of a much broader campaign,
was now all that we had going.

Judge Lambros, however, had no way of knowing this. And it certainly added something to our presence when, before the hearing
opened, I called at the Judge's chambers with the former Attorney
General of the United States. Judge Lambros gathered his staff to
meet Ramsey Clark. Looking up at his visitor, the Judge said: "Wel-
come to Cleveland, General."

Judge Lambros opened the hearing by saying that a trial of the
law suit was scheduled on March 17, but that U.S. Steel had informed
him by letter that it planned to shut down its Youngstown Works

prior to the trial date. The Judge then launched into the first of several extraordinary speeches which he delivered in the course of the litigation:

> I have reviewed the pleadings and the motions that are pending and, upon review of the file, sitting back and reflecting on this case, there is no question that more is at stake than the rights of the parties in this courtroom. In part, we are dealing with and deciding in this case the economic fate and survival of a large segment of this state, a large segment of our civilization.
>
> At first blush, when this case is reviewed by a trial judge, and applying the principles of law that we have learned from the textbooks in law school and our experience in dealing with the regular, routine business of the court, and when we instantly draw from that past experience and knowledge and attempt to apply those principles to this lawsuit, the first reaction is that there is no basis for this type of a lawsuit in American jurisprudence, that it is unheard of.[54]

Another judge might have stopped at this point and dismissed the case. Judge Lambros went on:

> But when one looks at the potential consequences of what is happening and the impact on the community, it compels a trial judge, in viewing the sufficiency of the complaint, to indulge in a greater degree of introspection as to whether or not a cause of action had been set forth.[55]

The Judge then said that he had difficulty comprehending how a contract could arise from the facts alleged by plaintiffs. Looking at Ramsey Clark and myself he continued:

> Are you suggesting that, absent a written contract, a written commitment negotiated at the bargaining table, the union members can compel United States Steel, a private corporation engaged in the free enterprise system, to keep operating its plants under a contract?[56]

Is There a Community Property Right? Judge Lambros digressed to speak (as he would do in almost every subsequent hearing) of the virtues of free enterprise. We all had a great admiration for the free enterprise system, he observed. Because of it this same courtroom was often filled by persons "who seek to raise their hands to become American citizens."

> We abhor government dictating to us and telling us what to do
> and what not to do. . . . [W]e do pride ourselves in the United
> States on the preservation of property rights. . . .[57]

Yet—and this was the Judge's contribution to the case—was there
involved a *property right of the community* as well as a property right
of U.S. Steel?

> We are not talking now about a local bakery shop, grocery
> store, tool and die shop or a body shop in Youngstown that is
> planning to close and move out. . . .
> It's not just a steel company making steel. . . .[S]teel has
> become an institution in the Mahoning Valley. . . .
> [T]hat city . . . built around this industry. Everything that
> has happened in the Mahoning Valley has been happening for
> many years because of steel. Schools have been built, roads have
> been built. Expansion that has taken place is because of steel.
> And to accomodate that industry lives and destinies of the in-
> habitants of that community were based and planned on the
> basis of that institution: Steel.[58]

The free enterprise system can no longer be viewed "albeit we desire
to view it, in terms of rugged individualism." The free enterprise
system has developed into and has required "an interdependence, a
greater interdependence than ever before." One might, the Judge
suggested, draw a comparison to the old English feudal system. The
lord provided the work and the vassal provided the labor, but the
vassals

> were taken care of, provided for and given assurances, didn't
> have to worry.[59]

Steel was virtually the reason for the existence of Youngstown,
stated Judge Lambros. Although courts do not desire to reach out
and seek power and authority, nor to make laws,

> we deal with human relationships and we try to deal with those
> human relationships so as to maintain stability and control those
> human relationships in a manner to maintain stability and tran-
> quillity. . . . And that is what is involved here.[60]

Once again the Judge paused to praise the right of a corporation to
pursue its self-interest.

> Now, no one, of course, can criticize United States Steel in
> making decisions which they feel are in their economic interest,

because we truly need today an economy that is responsive to changing world demands. And, truly, if it is less profitable to make steel in Youngstown, it is difficult to conceive that the company ought to be forced to remain in Youngstown and thereby hinder the United States position in the world market.

I think we have to be very cautious with respect to intruding on the free enterprise system and government dictating the decisions to be made, because this type of involvement could really upset the very foundation upon which our country is built, could have a profound effect on our competitive position in the world market. . . .[61]

No one sitting in the court room had ever heard anything like this before. Judge Lambros appeared to be thinking out loud, developing his argument dialectically by rebutting each successive point with the strongest thing to be said on the other side. Now, having set forth the case for the freedom to pursue profit maximization, he shifted back to the other foot:

But what has happened over the years between U.S. Steel, Youngstown and the inhabitants? Hasn't something come out of that relationship, something that out of which—not reaching for a case on property law or a series of cases but looking at the law as a whole, the Constitution, the whole body of law, not only contract law but tort, corporations, agency, negotiable instrument—taking a look at the whole body of American law and then sitting back and reflecting on what it seeks to do, and that is to adjust human relationships in keeping with the whole spirit and foundation of the American system of law, to preserve property rights. . . .

The judicial process cannot survive by adhering to the attitudes of the 1800's. My daily function cannot be regulated by those persons that reach into the dungeons of the past and attempt to stranglehold our present day thinking by 1800 concepts.

Were the framers of our Constitution or the judges of previous decades able to perceive the conditions that we find in America today and the reliance of a whole community and segment of our society on an institution such as the steel industry?

Well, the easy solution is: "Well, we haven't dealt with it in the past. There is no precedent. You have no case. The case is dismissed. Bailiff, call the next case."

Well, the law has to be more than mere mechanical acts. There has to be more than just form. There has to be substance.[62]

Judge Lambros did not dismiss our case. Instead he said:

> It would seem to me that when we take a look at the whole body of American law and the principles we attempt to come out with—and although a legislature has not pronounced any laws with respect to such a property right, that is not to suggest that there will not be a need for such a law in the future dealing with similar situations—*it seems to me that a property right has arisen from this lengthy, long-established relationship between United States Steel, the steel industry as an institution, the community in Youngstown, the people in Mahoning County and the Mahoning Valley in having given and devoted their lives to this industry.* Perhaps not a property right to the extent that can be remedied by compelling U.S. Steel to remain in Youngstown. I think the law could not possibly recognize that type of an obligation. But *I think the law can recognize the property right to the extent that U.S. Steel cannot leave that Mahoning Valley and the Youngstown area in a state of waste, that it cannot completely abandon its obligation to that community, because certain vested rights have arisen out of this long relationship and institution.*[63]

(Emphasis added.) It would seem to me, Judge Lambros elaborated, that the community has acquired a property right at least to the extent of "being permitted to preserve the institution of steel in that community" or in compelling the industry to figure into its costs of closing "the rehabilitation of that community and the workers."

There was one more step. If a property right was involved should the case not be in state rather than Federal court, Judge Lambros asked. He said that it was his view "that this court should abstain from recognizing this issue and that the relief that the plaintiffs seek ought to be addressed to the state courts." He also said that U.S. Steel should consider delaying the closing for 90 days so that the parties might seek a settlement. And then he asked that the parties take a ten-minute recess to assess his "preliminary views."[64]

Ramsey Clark, my colleagues Bob Clyde and Jim Callen, and I, retired to a conference room together with representatives of our clients, including Bob Vasquez and Chuck Rawlings. The lawyers were in a state of shock. Judge Lambros had gone further than any of us would have dared in suggesting that the very principles of justice and fairness required that a community devastated as Youngstown had been, possessed some rights. At the same time, he had followed that blockbuster with the equally sweeping suggestion that a case based on property rights belonged in state, not Federal, court. We were unsure what to think or what to say. All we could agree was that Ramsey Clark should go first.

Clark spoke, magnificently. I filled in some of the details. James Carney responded for U.S. Steel. There were good legal arguments on both sides. When we had finished everything still depended on Judge Lambros.

The Judge Says, Keep It Open. Judge Lambros suddenly referred to Harry Truman's statement, "The buck stops here."[65] Then he acted in the spirit of that famous quotation by doing the following:

1. He granted plaintiffs' motion to hold trial in Youngstown. This had the very important consequence that we could subpoena David Roderick and William Roesch, the chairman of the board and chief executive officer of U.S. Steel, to appear as witnesses. (A witness can only be compelled to travel 100 miles to testify. Cleveland is more than 100 miles from Pittsburgh. Youngstown is less than 100 miles from Pittsburgh.)

2. He reaffirmed his previous order that the trial should begin on March 17.

3. He issued an injunction restraining U.S. Steel "from terminating the operations of the steel plants which have been scheduled for shutdown . . . until further order of this Court." He also indicated that no bond would be required.

4. He denied a motion by U.S. Steel to prohibit the deposition of Mr. Roderick.

There was a flurry of post-hearing activity. Within two hours of Judge Lambros' statement that he would order the company not to close the mills, U.S. Steel had replaced the in-house attorney who had represented it thus far with the leading litigator of a Cleveland corporate law firm. The company filed a motion to "stay" (stop) Judge Lambros' injunction pending an appeal to the Sixth Circuit Court of Appeals, basing its motion, in part, on an affidavit by Mr. Kirwan that the mills would soon run out of iron ore.

Plaintiffs countered with the company's raw material inventory, resourcefully obtained by steelworkers at the plant, which showed that enough iron ore was on hand to keep the mills running the rest of the year. The company moved the Court to reconsider its decision to hold trial in Youngstown on the ground that Mr. Roderick's safety there could not be ensured! Both U.S. Steel motions were promptly denied.

The Trial

The trial began on March 17, 1980, one year to the day from the rally in downtown Youngstown organized by Local 1462. The court room was on the third floor of the old Federal court house. Presumably to ensure the safety of Mr. Roderick, Federal marshalls were present in force, and each entrant to the building was individually questioned. Media coverage was heavy. This being a trial before a judge without a jury, the jury box was not needed for the trial, and a number of the reporters were seated there. We felt we won the votes of that jury during the course of the week's trial. One television reporter who had covered the Youngstown shutdowns from the beginning told me later that during that week she found herself, for the first time, emotionally involved in a professional assignment. She said that initially this alarmed her, and she wondered if it compromised her objectivity; then she said, "To hell with it," and went on rooting for the plaintiffs. Another reporter who had been close to the story was unpersuaded until closing arguments that we were right about the plant's profitability. Then, he said, all at once he saw it and began to wonder how we could lose.

The Tri-State Conference had planned a second annual meeting that spring on the problem of plant shutdowns. When it became clear that the trial would go forward in March, it was decided that the trial would take the place of the meeting.

The Methodist church across the street from the court-house functioned as our headquarters. Each noon, and each afternoon after the close of court, we gathered in the church to eat, drink, and exchange impressions. The Ironclad Agreement theater group put on performances at the church of "Father K," a play, based on the life of a parish priest in Homestead, which centered on the 1919 steel strike. At noon on the last day of trial, Friday, March 21, just before the Court gave its judgment, plans were made to ring the church bells of Youngstown if plaintiffs were successful.

Ramsey Clark flew into Youngstown by chartered plane on the evening of the 16th and made an opening statement for plaintiffs the next day. At the close of the first day of trial he told us that he was going back to New York. In the first place, he said, he had other pressing commitments; in the second place we didn't need him; and thirdly, he liked the idea of Legal Services attorneys questioning the top executives of U.S. Steel.

When Court convened on the morning of the 17th, plaintiffs filed a Second Amended Complaint. We had previously stated the facts concerning Kirwan's promise on January 29 to offer the Works to the steelworkers, and Roderick's statement on the 31st that the company would not, after all, do so. We had presented these events as a breach of *contract* because we did not know enough about antitrust law to say that U.S. Steel might have violated the Sherman Act. In the interim, friends had looked into this issue. They assured us that a company could unilaterally violate section 2 of the Sherman Act if its "refusal to deal" with a would-be-purchaser was for illegal reasons. In this instance, Mr. Roderick had stated the company's reason: it declined to do business with a government-subsidized competitor. Believing that this motivation might be illegal the new Complaint stated a Third Cause of Action in antitrust. Finally, Judge Lambros' remarks on February 28 practically invited plaintiffs to claim a violation of a community property right. We did so, although in the briefest terms, having had little opportunity to research this area of the law.

The trial lasted for five days, from March 17 to 21. When it was over, it seemed to me that its most profound aspect was to have been a kind of morality play, obliging the individuals who had decided to close the mills to come to the community they had damaged and answer the question, Why? They came, flying to Youngstown in separate helicopters the morning of March 18. (Like the president and vice president of the United States, the chairman of the board and chief executive officer of U.S. Steel never fly in the same plane.) The most important testimony was not Mr. Roderick's or Mr. Roesch's, however, but that of William Kirwan, superintendent of the mills.

The Superintendent's Testimony. Mr. Kirwan testified that in August 1977 U.S. Steel had drafted letters to its hourly and managerial employees at the Youngstown Works informing them that most of the operations at the Works were to be phased out in coming months.[66] The letters were never sent, however, because Kirwan (then assistant superintendent) and the then-superintendent William

Ashton went to Pittsburgh and asked for another chance to keep the mills alive. They were given that chance.[67]

Mr. Kirwan then testified about what he did to try to keep the mills alive after becoming superintendent in 1978. He identified the "hot line" messages in which he exhorted the workers to do their part, including the message at Christmastime 1978: "[W]e have attained our 1978 goal, which was survival; and now we embark on the 1979 goal, which is revival."[68] He told how an article appeared in April 1979 in the *Wall Street Journal*, intimating that the Youngstown Works might be scheduled for shutdown, and how he and two other supervisors at the Works had written the *Journal* as follows:

> A complete turn-around has been achieved at Youngstown in the past year due to an aggressive management effort, streamlining of operations, and hard work on the part of all employees.
>
> Youngstown Works is creating a tremendously favorable impact that is sorely needed in the Mahoning Valley by keeping 3500 people working. . . .
>
> As long as a plant can generate an acceptable return, and the facilities are being properly maintained, facility age need not be a significant factor.[69]

Mr. Kirwan went on to describe his efforts to get U.S. Steel to commit some significant investment to its Youngstown mills. At a "budget meeting" in spring 1979 with executives of the company's Eastern Division Mr. Kirwan had delivered some opening remarks, beginning: "I want to take this opportunity to sow a seed—and I don't think we need a sprinkling of holy water from the Ecumenical Coalition to bring it to flower."[70] He noted that the Youngstown Works had just turned in its fourth best profit quarter since 1969, and that two of the four best earning quarters in that ten-year period had been in the past twelve months.[71] Then he told his executive audience what kind of "seed" he wished to sow:

> The seed I want to sow is a "Greenfield" plant on a "Brownfield" site complete with customers. . . . The plant can be built independent of interference with present production and, when complete, you can push the Stop button on one and the Start button on the other and achieve a tremendous saving in cost, an improvement in quality and a vastly improved profit contribution.[72]

Kirwan added that "[t]he favorable free publicity to be gained from a move of this kind in the Mahoning Valley should be worth a point in the stock price alone"; that Republic Steel, Sharon Steel, and Copperweld Steel were all operating profitably in the Valley; and that environmental requirements would require a decision about Youngstown in the near future. He concluded:

> All that is required is some "Positive Thinking" and one helluva lot less dollars than a Conneaut would require to retain a million tons of profitable participation for United States Steel.[73]

As I read these last words to Kirwan, the courtroom broke into cheers.

Kirwan explained how he had developed his seed into what became known as the "Kirwan Plan." At the budget meeting the head of the company's Eastern Division, Robert W. Smith, suggested that electric furnaces might make more sense than a Basic Oxygen shop.[74] In July 1979 Smith asked Kirwan to draw up a specific modernization plan,[75] and by the fall it was ready. "Youngstown Works: A Fresh Look" began with many of the same thoughts Kirwan had stressed in his speech half a year earlier. Modernization at Youngstown, he argued, "is a far more desirable short- and long-range alternative to the tremendous cost and the socio-economic impact involved in phasing out the plant."[76] Then the plan turned to specifics. "The proposal involves two 165-ton electric furnaces, a six-strand bloom caster, and a sizing mill, on acreage available adjacent to the 18 strip mill at the McDonald Mills."[77] The idea was that electric furnaces would be built adjacent to the finishing mills at the McDonald Works; that during construction, steel would continue to be made at the open hearths of the Ohio Works; and that when the new steel-making facilities at McDonald were ready to go, you could press the "stop" button on the Ohio Works, because you would be ready to press the "start" button on the McDonald electric furnaces. The estimated cost was $208 million.

Kirwan testified that he presented this plan on November 9 to company executives in Pittsburgh. The meeting lasted about an hour, and during it he was told for the first time that U.S. Steel was thinking of shutting down the Youngstown Works.[78]

Kirwan had a second chance to present his proposal at a subsequent meeting on November 26. At that time he was told that a couple of years from now the idea might look good, but that right now there wasn't a nickel to spend on it.[79]

The next day, November 27, the company announced the closing of the Youngstown Works. *Neither David Roderick, chairman of the board, nor William Roesch, chief executive officer, had heard of the Kirwan Plan when they made this decision, so they testified.*[80]

How Do You Measure Profit? Kirwan also testified about the Youngstown Works' profitability. We considered profitability the hardest part of our case to prove. Even if the company's promise, and the workers' sacrifices in reliance on that promise, were found to have created a contract, shutting the Works did not violate the contract unless the mills were profitable at the time.

When U.S. Steel made its profit data for the Works available, they showed the following:

Table 4

	Sales	Variable Costs*	Gross Profit Margin	Own Fixed Expense	Profit on Own Fixed Expense	Profit Before Taxes
1977	$227 mil.	$195 mil.	$25 mil.	$33 mil.	($8 mil.)	($24 mil.)
1978	227 mil.	188 mil.	42 mil.	32 mil.	10 mil.	(3 mil.)
1979**	220 mil.	191 mil.	33 mil.	24 mil.	9 mil.	(.3 mil.)

What did these figures mean? If profit were measured after deduction from sales of all costs and expenses except taxes, then the Youngstown Works lost $.3 million or $300,000 in the first ten months of 1979. Such a loss is hardly significant to a company like U.S. Steel. Indeed, when I asked Mr. Roderick at his deposition how the Youngstown Works were performing when he made the decision to close them, he said they were about breaking even. But the law likes Yes or No answers, and that $300,000 loss meant that the answer to the question, were the Works profitable when they were closed?, was likely to be No.

Then, at Mr. Kirwan's deposition (on February 27), a dramatic thing happened. I asked him:

> Q. Now, when you became General Superintendent February 1st, 1978, what was your understanding of what you had to do to keep the Youngstown Works operating?

*In this simplified presentation, "costs" equal standard (or predicted) costs, which are somewhat different from actual costs incurred. That is why "sales" minus "costs" does not exactly equal "gross profit margin."

**These figures are for the first ten months of 1979, through the end of October, since U.S. Steel made its decision to close the Works in November.

A. My understanding was that I had to at least pay my own
fixed expense.

Q. And from whom did you derive that understanding?

A. From my boss, R. W. Smith.

. . .

Q. Would it be fair to say that he communicated this orally to
you some time between September '77 and February '78?

A. Yes.[81]

I almost fell off the chair. In assessing the profitability of the
Youngstown Works, U.S. Steel considered three kinds of costs and
expenses. "Variable costs" signified money paid out by the Works
for factors of production such as wages, raw materials, and electric
power. "Own fixed expenses" included expenses incurred by the
Youngstown Works even if (in the short run) the Works were not
operating, such as management salaries, the cost of vacations and
holidays for hourly employees, equipment rental, local property
taxes, and depreciation. Finally there were other fixed expenses
which were incurred at U.S. Steel's Pittsburgh headquarters and in
part allocated to Youngstown, including sales and advertising. After
the deduction from revenue of *all* costs and expenses, including
Youngstown's portion of the "other fixed expenses," the Youngstown Works lost $300,000 in the first ten months of 1979. But if
profits were measured after the deduction from revenue only of
"own fixed expenses" Youngstown Works made $8,000,000 through
October 1979. *And Mr. Kirwan had just told me that top management told him that if he covered his own fixed expenses he would stay
open.*

It turned out that Mr. Kirwan had said the same thing to the
workers. Bob Vasquez, president of Local 1330, testified under oath:

Q. Did any representative of Youngstown Works ever tell you
exactly what was meant by the word "profitable"?

A. Mr. Kirwan did.

. . .

Q. As best you can recollect, exactly what words did he use?

A. We talked about paying our fixed expenses. . . .[82]

Mr. Kirwan's testimony enabled us to present the following
argument about profitability: In the law of contracts, the meaning of
the words in a contract is determined by the parties who make the
contract. In using the word "profit" with reference to whether the
Youngstown Works would be kept open, U.S. Steel's own executives

had used the term to mean "profit on own fixed expense," and had conveyed this same understanding to the other party to the contract, the workers. Therefore, in determining whether the Works were profitable at the time they closed, the Court should look to "profit on own fixed expense."

A final piece of the puzzle fell into place at the close of the fourth day of testimony, Thursday, March 20. U.S. Steel called as its own witness Dean Goldnetz, Comptroller of the Eastern Steel Division. Something which had puzzled us in preparing for trial and throughout the week of testimony was that U.S. Steel had used two different forms to record the profitability of the Youngstown Works. For each of the relevant years—1977, 1978, and 1979—there was one form which recorded only "profit before taxes," and another form which set forth both "profit on own fixed expense" and "profit before taxes." The second form had a heavy black line to the right of "profit on own fixed expense." Out of the blue Mr. Goldnetz explained, in response to a question by his own attorney, how this second form had come to be.

> A. . . . I was part of a group of Pittsburgh management people who met with the Youngstown management people at various times during 1977, when things were pretty dark around here, and a lot of the plans were laid to try to improve the profit situation.
>
> . . .
>
> What we really did was try to get people to walk before they could run. So the first objective was to get them to demonstrate enough improvement that they could say they were at least covering their own incurred fixed expense. That would demonstrate to the people in Pittsburgh that progress was being made.
>
> Q. So the "profit on own fixed expense" means what?
>
> A. It means they have covered the incurred costs here at Youngstown, as directly incurred here.[83]

Here was the top accountant of the company's Eastern Steel Division confirming Kirwan's testimony. Pittsburgh had given Youngstown the objective of covering own fixed expense, and had even devised a special accounting form to record Youngstown's progress toward that objective!

We Lose. There was another important patch of testimony from Mr. Kirwan. Counsel for U.S. Steel wished to attack the idea that

Kirwan had made a real promise to his employees, and chose the following way to do it.

> Q. You used the phrase several times, "Positive reinforce-ment"; and I asked you during recess what that meant, and you gave me an example. I wish you would give that to the Court, please?
>
> A. Well, your Honor, I have five children, and that's a task in itself. You learn, as you go on, and I learned after the first one, that there wasn't much acomplished if a report card or a test came home with 40 per cent on it and you banged the kid on the head and said, "You're a dummy."
>
> So I tried with the rest of them that, "Well, 40 per cent, at least you got 40 per cent; right? Why don't we try to, the next time, get 60."
>
> That's positive reinforcement. . . .[84]

As he said these words I looked at the local union presidents sitting at plaintiffs' table: Reno DePietro, a man of about Mr. Kirwan's age; Ed Mann, whose fiftieth birthday I had helped to celebrate not long before. The youngest appeared to be Bob Vasquez, who was in his thirties. Mr. Kirwan was comparing them to children.

On the morning of Friday, March 21 Charles Clarke, the U.S. Steel attorney, and I, gave closing arguments. I stayed up late the night before to type mine. It was good, and when I finished the union presidents clasped my hand; even Judge Lambros, whom I met in the hall during a recess just after I had finished, muttered "great argu-ment" as he walked past.

But I might just as well have gotten a good night's sleep. Not more than two hours after Mr. Clarke and I concluded Judge Lambros read a decision of more than twenty pages. He must have written his decision before either Mr. Clarke or I began to speak that Friday morning.

The Judge "dismissed" (denied) plaintiffs' contract and property law claims, and reserved judgment on plaintiffs' antitrust claim.

Judge Lambros dismissed plaintiffs' contract claim because 1) U.S. Steel had not really promised to stay open if the mills were made profitable, 2) if Mr. Kirwan had made such a promise he lacked the authority to do so, 3) if Kirwan had the authority and made the promise the mills were not profitable when they were closed. The Judge did not mention "profit on own fixed expense."

Plaintiffs' property claim seemed to cause the Judge some embarrassment. After all, it was he who had suggested it. Judge Lambros dealt with the Fourth Cause of Action as follows:

> This Court has spent many hours searching for a way to cut to the heart of the economic reality—that obsolescence and market forces demand the close of the Mahoning Valley plants, and yet the lives of 3500 workers and their families and the supporting Youngstown community cannot be dismissed as inconsequential. United States Steel should not be permitted to leave the Youngstown area devastated after drawing the lifeblood of the community for so many years.
>
> Unfortunately, the mechanism to reach this ideal settlement, to recognize this new property right, is not now in existence in the code of laws of our nation. At this moment, proposals for legislative redress of economic relocation like the situation before us are pending on Capitol Hill. Perhaps labor unions, now more aware of the importance of this problem, will begin to bargain for relocation adjustment funds and mechanisms and will make such measures part of the written labor contract. However, this Court is not a legislative body and cannot make laws where none exist—only those remedies prescribed in the statute or by virtue of precedent of prior case law can be given cognizance. In these terms this Court can determine no legal basis for the finding of a property right.[85]

The property claim was dismissed along with the contract claim.

The Judge then dissolved the injunction of February 28 which had directed U.S. Steel to keep the plants open. However, he did order U.S. Steel to keep the mills operable until the steelworkers had an opportunity to explore purchase possibilities by themselves or others. He did this because he felt that the antitrust claim might have merit, and that a trial of the antitrust claim should be had in sixty days. During those sixty days the company was to keep the mills in mothballs, so that, if plaintiffs were successful at trial of the antitrust claim, there would still be a Youngstown Works for them to buy.

But on April 14, 1979, after considering a posttrial motion by U.S. Steel, Judge Lambros also dismissed the antitrust claim, and dissolved as well the March 21 injunction directing the company to keep the plant in mothballs.

The reason given by the Judge was that plaintiffs' antitrust claim was not "ripe": that is, plaintiffs did not have the money to make a meaningful offer to buy the Works.

Appeal and Settlement

As *Local 1330 v. U.S. Steel* made its way through the courts, certain images kept appearing in my mind. "How do you feel?," a reporter would ask. For a while I answered: "We are like kids in Hungary in 1956, throwing bricks at Soviet tanks."

Then, during the summer and fall of 1980, the images were of boxing. "How do you feel?," came the question. And I would answer: "I feel like a boxer between the 13th and 14th rounds of a 15 rounder. The seconds are holding the sponge under the nose, holding up a finger to see if the eyes still focus. But you answer the bell."

Although it took a long time happening, the story of the case's ending can be quickly told.

"A Cry For Help." My associate Bob Clyde feels in hindsight that we may have made a mistake to appeal Judge Lambros' decision. Judge Lambros dismissed our antitrust claim only after we had angered him by appealing his decision. Had we not appealed, Judge Lambros might not have dismissed the antitrust claim. Had he not dismissed the antitrust claim, there would have been an injunction requiring U.S. Steel to keep the machinery and property of the Works intact. There would also have been a pending antitrust trial, which no doubt could have been postponed for a considerable time, during which we could have tried to get money from the Federal government. There is evidence that the Judge felt he was trying to help us all he could and that, as he saw it, we had kicked the help away. Encountering Bob Clyde and Chuck Rawlings in the corridor of the Federal court house in Cleveland shortly after we had filed our appeal, Judge Lambros snapped: "You blew it."

In any case, we did appeal, and the Sixth Circuit Court of Appeals reinstated, until the appeal was decided, the injunction requiring U.S. Steel "to maintain the plants and machinery intact and in place" although not prohibiting "negotiations for sale of the plants for operation by any prospective purchasers."

An effort was made to bring to the appeal court's attention the many unions and municipalities who, in one way or another, felt their interests to be bound up in the case of the Youngstown steelworkers. The Mahoning County Commissioners filed a brief *amicus curiae*. "Amicus curiae" is Latin for "friend of the court." A brief may be filed *amicus curiae* by someone who isn't directly affected by a law suit, but has a contribution which may help to resolve the case.

A second and more imposing *amicus* brief was filed by the Center for Constitutional Rights in New York City.[86]

The United Steelworkers of America declined to file an *amicus* brief or to join as one of the sponsors of the brief of the Center for Constitutional Rights.

In response, *amicus* briefs on behalf of U.S. Steel were filed by the United States Chamber of Commerce and the "New England Legal Foundation," a group apparently devoted to the principles of free enterprise.

For the most part the briefs expanded on arguments already presented to the trial court. The one sustained effort to break new ground was in the brief of the Center for Constitutional Rights. It was wholly devoted to the claim set forth in Plaintiffs' Second Amended Complaint, that a community has a "property right" not to be victimized by a unilateral decision to close a plant such as the Youngstown Works. The trial court itself had found as a fact that Youngstown would be "devastated" by the shutdown, the brief observed. Nor could it be disputed that the Youngstown Works had benefited over the years from tax breaks, price supports, waivers of EPA requirements, and other public assistance. Accordingly this was private property "affected with a public interest" the use of which could be regulated for the public good. The brief relied on a line of Supreme Court cases stemming from *Munn v. Illinois*, 94 U.S. 113 (1877), and including such Depression-era cases as *Nebbia v. New York*, 291 U.S. 502 (1934). The principal weakness of the argument was that these cases had upheld the right of a *legislature* to take emergency action affecting private property when the public interest demanded it. Here we were asking a *court* to do the same thing when the legislature had not yet acted.

Meantime, an effort proceeded to induce the Economic Development Administration to fund a feasibility study of plaintiffs' plan for modernizing the Youngstown Works. This was a study that should not have been necessary, since plaintiffs' plan was essentially that developed by the Works' own superintendent, William Kirwan. Like him, we envisioned that the open hearths at the Ohio Works would be shut down; that electric furnaces would be built adjacent to the finishing mills at the McDonald Works; and that this modern steel-making process would enable the bar and shape, and sheet mills at the McDonald Works to compete effectively.

EDA was not about to provide loan guarantees without feasibility studies to justify them, however. At the same time, Chuck Rawlings' persistent airing of the bias and unfairness in EDA's treatment of the Coalition had produced a somewhat chastened mood in EDA offices, and the steelworkers were therefore promised that this time EDA would provide rapid and impartial evaluation of a Youngstown proposal. After what seemed interminable negotiations among a variety of actors, EDA announced on the eve of the hearing before the appeals court that the agency would fund a feasibility study to be performed by Trundle Consultants of Cleveland. I filed an affidavit to this effect the morning we appeared in Cincinnati to argue our case.

The hearing was held on June 18, once again in a packed courtroom. In an unusual decision the court permitted counsel for *amici* as well as counsel for the principal parties to argue. Ramsey Clark had at the time barely returned from a controversial trip to Iran connected with the hostage crisis. The local union presidents involved in our case unanimously agreed that they would like Clark to continue to represent them, controversy or no controversy. However, Clark had had no time to read the appeal briefs and had his hands full responding to government threats to jail him for his trip to Iran. Accordingly I argued on behalf of plaintiffs, and Professor Arthur Kinoy of Rutgers University Law School on behalf of plaintiffs' *amici*.

The decision came down a month later, on July 25. The opinion began: "This appeal represents a cry for help from steelworkers and townspeople in the City of Youngstown, Ohio. . . ." The trial court's dismissal of the contract claim was upheld because it was not "reasonable" for plaintiffs to have relied on a promise that the mills would be kept open if they covered their fixed expenses. The dismissal of the property claim was upheld because of the absence of precedent. But the dismissal of the antitrust claim was reversed, and this claim alone was remanded for trial.

No Money From Washington. One paragraph of the appeals court's discussion of the antitrust claim had considerable interest. The Court's opinion stated:

> United States Steel's implied claim that it can, consistent with the antitrust laws, refuse to do business with a corporation which has been aided, directly or indirectly by the United States government through the operations of duly adopted law, is unique in this court's experience. Nor has our research served to date to disclose any legal precedent for such a position. The

ramifications of this refusal would be far-reaching. Could United States Steel, in the event the Chrysler Corporation sought to manufacture some portion of its own steel needs, refuse to sell steel to that corporation because of the massive aid which the federal government has seen fit to supply to Chrysler?

A note at this point added:

> As to this issue, we note that in *Nebbia v. New York*, 291 U.S. 502 (1934), the Supreme Court held: "Moreover, the state or a municipality may itself enter into business in competition with private proprietors. . . ."[87]

This paragraph strongly suggested that *if* we could get some assurance of help from the Federal government so that we could make a bona fide offer for the plant to U.S. Steel, the company would be poorly advised to refuse the offer, as before, on the ground that Community Steel was subsidized by the government.

But the "if" remained as big as ever. The rapid processing promised by EDA somehow endlessly eluded completion. Early in August the Trundle Consultants expert, Donald Meckstroth, was finally permitted to set foot on the property of the Youngstown Works. By the end of the month his study was essentially completed. Disturbingly, however, EDA now began to refer to his project as a "pre-feasibility study," and as serious preparation for trial of the antitrust claim began we seemed as far as ever from having Federal monies actually in hand.

U.S. Steel Leases Part of the Mill. The status of the injunction was our most immediate concern. From February 28 to March 21 U.S. Steel had been enjoined from closing the mills. From March 21 to July 25—more than four months—the company had been directed to maintain the plants and machinery intact and in place. At the June 18 hearing before the court of appeals, U.S. Steel's lawyers indicated that Republic Steel wanted to buy the sinter plant at the Ohio Works. (A sinter plant processes iron before it is put in a blast furnace.) Just before the court of appeals' decision on July 25, a story appeared in the press that U.S. Steel was planning to lease the 14 mill at the McDonald Works to a group of Youngstown entrepreneurs organized as Toro Enterprises. It was perfectly legal for U.S. Steel to have entered negotiations as to these properties. If, however, these deals were completed, our hopes for modernizing a still intact steel mill would be destroyed.

Yet the decision of the Sixth Circuit Court of Appeals said nothing about the continuing status of that court's own injunction. Phone calls to the Clerk's office in Cincinnati produced no further light. The judges were all out of town at the "judicial conference of the Sixth Circuit" in White Sulphur Springs, West Virginia.

At length we decided that I should simply go to White Sulphur Springs and ask the judges to resolve the issue. In making this decision, we were worried that U.S. Steel would cry foul if I appeared without giving them an opportunity to be present. I telephoned an associate of the company's lead counsel. It was no problem, he assured me: the company attorney was already at the same resort.

I got up at four in the morning, drove to Pittsburgh, flew to Roanoke, North Carolina, and rented a car to drive to White Sulphur Springs. I arrived somewhat the worse for wear about mid-morning.

White Sulphur Springs later came to the attention of the country when it was made available to the returned American hostages from Iran. It is a palatial affair, complete with black servants.

Court was convened amid potted palms on the mezzanine. I explained why failure to continue the injunction might, in the opinion of plaintiffs, make trial of the antitrust claim useless. There would be no steel mill left to buy even if plaintiffs were ultimately allowed to do so. U.S. Steel responded that its hands were being tied at the very moment that it sought to put parts of its Youngstown property back into productive use. The judges said that they would be in touch with us.

We heard from the Clerk's office late the following day. The Sixth Circuit would make no decision about the injunction but would immediately return the case to the District Court so that Judge Lambros could deal with the matter.

The next week Judge Lambros refused to reinstate his injunction restraining U.S. Steel from selling or leasing the mills. The court case thus was turned into a race. We were racing to get the Trundle study completed, then, assuming the study to be favorable, to get the EDA to commit the $100,000,000 in loan guarantees still promised for Youngstown, then to make an offer to U.S. Steel. U.S. Steel was racing to complete its sale of the sinter plant to Republic, and the lease of its 14 mill to Toro.

The Trundle study was favorable. Its recommended business strategy for Community Steel was the creation of a "multi-mini" mill which concentrates on special small hot-rolled carbon shapes and sections in a market radius up to 200 miles. In the jargon of steel industry specialists, a "mini mill" is a mill where steel is made by an electric furnace and production is limited to one finished item. The McDonald Works as envisioned by Trundle, as by Kirwan, would be a "multi-mini" mill in that its steel, made by electric furnace, would be used to produce several different shapes as well as sheets. In order to bring the multi-mini mill into being it was necessary to install a new electric furnace and continuous casting facility at the McDonald Works. The 18 mill which had made sheet (rather than shapes) at the McDonald Works should be mothballed and reopened in a second stage of development.

EDA asked the investment bankers Lehman Brothers Kuhn Loeb (yes, the same Lehman Brothers who recommended the closing of the Campbell Works, and the merger of Lykes and LTV) to comment on the Trundle study. Lehman Brothers took an incredibly long time to put its conclusions on paper. When the conclusions appeared they, too, were favorable:

> Lehman Brothers Kuhn Loeb Incorporated believes that with appropriate Federal government support, all of which appears authorized by current legislation, it should be possible to put together a financing structure which will be sufficient to fund Community Steel Corporation. We also believe that all required capital charges for the project can be adequately serviced, provided the earnings forecast contained in the Trundle Report is met and the trend continued.[88]

While these reports were being painfully brought to birth (it is impossible adequately to describe the daily crises, the emergency conference calls, the great mass of government indecision), U.S. Steel and Toro Enterprises entered into a lease. The lease concerned 12 acres of the McDonald Works including the 13, 14, and 15 mills. Toro agreed to incorporate a new entity to be called "McDonald Steel" and to cause McDonald to raise a certain amount of capital. Upon this capital being raised, U.S. Steel agreed to make certain improvements, notably the installation of a substation and conversion from 60-cycle to 25-cycle electric power. During the interim period, while McDonald was raising the capital necessary to trigger the improvements, Toro's rent would be "compliance with all of the terms and conditions of the Lease": in other words, nothing. The lease for the 13, 14 and 15 mills was to run for five years, with an option to renew the lease for three successive five-year terms. Toro was also given a "right of first refusal" to lease or purchase two other facilities at the McDonald Works, the 16 and 17 mills. This meant that if someone else were interested in purchasing or leasing these properties U.S. Steel had first to offer them to Toro on the same terms.

Plaintiffs obtained the Toro lease under restrictions imposed by Judge Lambros which allowed U.S. Steel to delete from the lease all numbers as to the agreed terms. But Agis Salpukas of the *New York Times* obtained some of this information by talking to one of the Toro principals, David Tod (the same David Tod who in 1977 advised Gerald Dickey to buy Wisconsin Steel). Not only had Toro entered into the lease without any money changing hands, there being no rent required during the interim period; Salpukas also learned that U.S. Steel would receive 30 per cent of McDonald Steel's profits and would at least initially supply the semi-finished steel which McDonald Steel would process.[89]

If the lease between U.S. Steel and Toro was valid, Community Steel was dead. The 14 mill which Toro/McDonald was to lease made tire rims, had few competitors, and was generally agreed to be the most profitable part of the McDonald Works. That was why Toro proposed to reopen it. That was also why Community could not succeed unless it, rather than Toro, obtained the 14 mill. Thus the long legal battle in the end came down to the issue: Was the agreement between Toro and U.S. Steel in itself a violation of the antitrust laws, and therefore invalid?

To help us evaluate this issue, Community Steel retained an antitrust specialist, Professor Thomas Kerr of Pittsburgh. (The word "retained" is used euphemistically. Like Ramsey Clark and Arthur Kinoy, Kerr served for expenses only.) Under his guidance we sought to amend the Complaint for a last time. In addition to asserting that U.S. Steel had violated Section 2 of the Sherman Act by refusing to deal with Community Steel, plaintiffs now alleged that U.S. Steel also violated Section 1 of the Sherman Act by entering into a conspiracy with Toro.

The conspiracy allegation rested on more than the remarkably generous and intimate terms of the lease between U.S. Steel and Toro. There was also the role of David Houck. Mr. Houck had been the manager of the bar and shape mills at the McDonald Works, including the 14 mill, before the facility closed. According to his sworn testimony at deposition and the documents which he and Toro produced, late in 1979 or early in 1980 superintendent Kirwan suggested to Mr. Houck that he consider reopening the 14 mill. Through the late winter and early spring of 1980 Houck contacted various possible sources of financing. At length he came to an understanding with David Tod, a Youngstown investment banker, and Daniel Roth, a Youngstown attorney. Both were longtime business associates in an enterprise named from the first two letters of each of their names, Toro ("To-Ro") Enterprises. This understanding was set forth in an agreement dated May 30, 1980. The agreement provided among other things that Tod, Roth, and Houck were to be directors of McDonald Steel, the entity that would be formed to operate the 14 mill.

At the time Mr. Houck signed this agreement the 14 mill was still in operation as a U.S. Steel facility, and Mr. Houck was still running it. (Whereas steelmaking at the Ohio Works stopped immediately after Judge Lambros' decision on March 17, steel finishing at the McDonald Works continued into July.) Mr. Houck was also still working for U.S. Steel when on July 18, 1980, he signed, together with Tod and Roth and on behalf of Toro, a "letter of intent" wherein U.S. Steel and Toro tentatively agreed on the lease of the 14 mill to the smaller firm by the larger.

Finally, there was reason to believe that Toro/McDonald Steel would try to operate non-union for as long as possible. On June 12, 1980, J. A. Hollister of U.S. Steel's realty subsidiary met with Tod, Roth, and a Toro director named Charles O. Smith. Hollister wrote of the meeting:

> The principals [Tod, Roth and Smith] are hopeful that unionization of the Corporation can be avoided for at least the first year of operations. Recognizing that Youngstown is a union town, they are not optimistic but they do expect to be able to set their crew sizes and establish operating practices prior to unionization of the company. We [U.S. Steel] commented, that in our experience, this was a reasonable expectation.[90]

The result could very well be similar to the experience at U.S. Steel's Joliet, Ill. plant, where the entire Works closed in 1979 only to have one of the component mills (the wire and nail facility) reopened at entry-level wages of $8.35 an hour rather than the previous $9.57 an hour.[91]

The Logic of the Settlement. In the end we settled the antitrust case out of court rather than going to trial. There were three reasons.

First, despite frantic efforts by Chuck Rawlings in particular on the eve of the 1980 elections, the Carter administration failed to make any financial commitment to Community Steel. We had been told that if our plan were feasible the $100,000,000 in loan guarantees still reserved for the Mahoning Valley by EDA would be available. The consultants, Trundle Consultants, and then Lehman Brothers, pronounced the plan feasible. EDA, however, refused to come through with the money. Instead they talked vaguely about a second, more detailed feasibility study. This meant that in November 1980, Community Steel had not a penny more than it possessed the previous April, and was no more in a position to buy the Youngstown Works, or any part of it, in the fall than it had been in the spring. It seemed certain we would be thrown out of court for lack of "standing," that is, for lacking the capability to buy the mill which would allow us to claim we were a genuine potential buyer. I was also concerned that Bob Vasquez and other steelworkers would be exposed to humiliating cross examination. (For instance: "You call yourself the chairman of the board of a corporation? Well, how much money does the corporation have? Not a *penny*?")

Second, Judge Lambros refused to let us amend the Complaint to include the conspiracy charge. This refusal would have made it much more difficult to introduce the evidence about the U.S. Steel-Toro relationship, even if we were able, somehow, to surmount the problem of "standing."

Third, even if the "standing" and refusal-to-permit-us-to-amend issues could have been appealed, we were under heavy pressure from our Youngstown constituency to step aside and let Toro recreate at least a few of the lost jobs rather than continue to pursue a vain hope. At least three persons wrote letters to the *Vindicator* stating, as one of them put it, that a bird in the hand was better than two in the bush.[92] Reverend Ed Weisheimer, probably the Coalition's most persistent Youngstown member, privately appealed to Community Steel to try to bargain with Toro for the inclusion of steelworkers in its project rather than continue the law suit.[93] John Greenman, former staff director of the Coalition, now a reporter for the *Warren Tribune*, argued editorially that a "steel deal [was] needed now."[94] Had we pursued a strategy involving lengthy further appeals during which Toro was unable to go forward, we would have represented nobody but ourselves.

And so we made the best deal that we could. U.S. Steel agreed to amend its lease with Toro to give Toro/McDonald a right of first refusal to the 12 as well as to the 16 and 17 mills. U.S. Steel further agreed to keep the 12, 16, and 17 mills intact for five years in case Toro/McDonald should wish to acquire them. Toro agreed not to oppose further efforts to obtain money from EDA for a second feasibility study, which might lead to loan guarantees for the construction of electric furnaces, and so more jobs. A six-person committee, three from Toro/McDonald and three from Community Steel, was created to oversee these arrangements.

Judge Lambros called the settlement "a valuable lesson across the United States,"[95] and the *Vindicator* editorialized: "It seems to be one of those rare cases where everybody won. Certainly the valley did."[96] Reporter Greg Garland of the *Warren Tribune* paid tribute to Vasquez, De Pietro and myself for keeping alive the idea of reopening the entire McDonald Works.[97]

The evening of the settlement I tried to describe my feelings to David Moberg, a friend and a reporter for *In These Times*.

> "It's like a wave coming into the beach: there's just so far up the beach that wave can go," Lynd said. "I think we've probably done as much as can be done in this valley as far as recreating the steel industry. It's not my utopia. It took the form of a capitalist enterprise, but one shouldn't be surprised at that, and it's better than nothing."

I also felt at the time that the EDA application might be enhanced now that the project involved some local businessmen.[98]

But we had reckoned without President Reagan. In January 1981, the further study required by EDA seemed all but assured. The Mahoning Valley Economic Development Committee (MVEDC) endorsed it. The United Steelworkers of America and Toro/McDonald each pledged $10,000 in matching funds. A coalition of persons and groups which had fought the Community Steel effort was on the verge of moving forward toward the goal of a new McDonald Works, producing its own steel with electric furnaces, and reemploying a substantial portion of those who had lost their jobs.

Then the President recommended the abolition of EDA. Although EDA was later restored to the budget, the loan guarantees first dangled before the Valley in September 1978 were not. Therefore, when in August 1981 EDA finally offered the money for the McDonald Works study, MVEDC, the Steelworkers, and Toro/McDonald turned it down, for the understandable reason that the study without the loan guarantees made no sense at all.

The most that the Mahoning Valley can hope for from its battle with United States Steel is a reopened 14 mill which would initially create only about 75 jobs and eventually perhaps 160.[99]

The Legal Strategy Evaluated. About a year after U.S. Steel's shutdown announcement I took a long drive with Bob Vasquez and had a chance to ask him what he felt he had learned in that time.

Vasquez said that what he had learned was not to expect fairness. He had always counted on being able to communicate what was fair to other people. As a grievance committeeman, he often confronted a person who had a strong grievance the winning of which would only hurt another union member. Vasquez's practice was to say, in effect: "It looks like you've got a winner. But I want to be sure you realize that, if you win, Brother So-and-So will be bumped back to Job Class 2"—or whatever the effect on a fellow worker would be. Usually the grievant himself would suggest a compromise fair to both workers involved, for instance that the grievant should be first in line for the next job opening but that the incumbent should not be displaced.

In dealing with U.S. Steel's local managers, Vasquez went on, he had generally been able to get them to do the fair thing even when the grievant had no case at all under the letter of the contract.

But the shutdown struggle had been different. U.S. Steel's headquarters people didn't seem to care about fairness. For them it was a question of what would be most profitable. In court, too, everything was either one thing or the other, either black or white. Vasquez concluded that courts were not for working people. Workers should do what they had to do outside of court and let the company go to court for an injunction.

I would express the idea a little differently.

At the time, it was an act of resistance to go to court against U.S. Steel. The reader will recall that in the Campbell Works struggle the Ecumenical Coalition decided not to file suit to try to block the merger between Lykes and LTV because it feared the political reaction in the Valley. The U.S. Steel locals, together with the local Congressman, sued U.S. Steel although they knew there would be criticism in the community. I think this was healthy.

Moreover, in the beginning the law suit was only one front in a campaign being waged on many fronts: in negotiations with U.S. Steel, in appearances before Congressional committees, and in direct action, as well as in court. The negative side of the law suit came to the fore when these other forms of struggle dropped away, and the law suit remained as the only visible resistance.

The negative side of a law suit is that it takes the action out of the hands of workers, and tends to make them passive spectators. There are several aspects of this. First, the very existence of lawyers and courts encourages people to believe that "if only we get into court" things will, somehow, turn out differently. This faith is misplaced. Law in the United States protects the interests of private property, and is administered by persons who themselves are well-to-do. Changes in the way U.S. Steel invests its capital are unlikely to come about as the result of judges' decisions. Second, the ordinary person has little opportunity to express himself or herself in the legal process. Litigation is conducted by experts with extensive legal training. The area in and around a court house is off limits for spontaneous popular expression. Picketing near a court house is felt to be an improper effort to influence a neutral decisionmaking process. Clapping or hissing in court may be found in contempt. Despite the best efforts of myself and others to include our clients in working out the strategy and tactics of our legal battle, the law suit did not do much to build a popular movement.

On the other hand, the legal process, if viewed not as a cure-all but as one among many means of struggle, can yield important benefits. Almost by definition a law suit tends to sharpen issues and provide opportunities to stimulate debate in the community. It was important to have compelled the top executives of U.S. Steel to come to Youngstown and to confront the community they had wronged. Even in a law suit which does not get to trial it may be possible to obtain essential information. The reason for this is that a party to a law suit has a right to "discover" information relevant to the suit from an opposing party, by asking questions of the opposite party under oath (as in our depositions of Mr. Roderick, Mr. Roesch, and Mr. Kirwan), or by requesting documents.

Finally, legal activity can sometimes create a breathing space in which other forms of dispute resolution have the time to become effective. A classic example is when General Motors during the sitdown strike in Flint, Michigan in 1937 got a court injunction ordering the workers to leave the occupied plants. The UAW held a press conference and exploded the fact that the judge who issued the injunction owned 3,665 shares of GM stock worth $219,900 at the market price, thus violating a state law which prohibited a judge from sitting in any proceeding "in which he is interested." GM was so embarrassed that it did not press to have the injunction enforced.[100] This may have bought the time which ensured the success of the strike.

In conclusion, this complex question can be summarized in a sentence: Legal activity can be very useful when it is one part of a larger struggle, but should not be relied on alone. The heart of resistance to a shutdown must be the struggle of workers, not of lawyers.

Chapter Five. Encore in Pittsburgh

The story of U.S. Steel's promises to its workers in Youngstown is not unusual. In Pittsburgh, Jones & Laughlin Steel and U.S. Steel itself seem intent on reenacting the Youngstown story.

Consider first Jones & Laughlin.

In 1970, roughly at the same time that the Lykes conglomerate acquired Youngstown Sheet & Tube, the Ling Temco Vought (LTV) conglomerate acquired Jones & Laughlin Steel (J & L). There was acute concern among steelworkers employed by J & L that this would lead to cutbacks and shutdowns. When the Justice Department brought suit to try to prevent the merger, Frank O'Brien, president of Local 1843 (J & L Pittsburgh Works), intervened in the litigation, and wrote a letter to the judge explaining the fears of his members. James Ling, then chairman of the board of LTV, flew to Pittsburgh and met with O'Brien at the Carlton House on May 31, 1970. Ling then wrote the following letter to O'Brien, on the strength of which Local 1843 dropped its objection to the merger:

> Dear Mr. O'Brien:
>   This will confirm the points made at our meeting in the Carlton House today. . . . In the event that I am in a position to have any participation in the management of Jones & Laughlin Steel Corporation, the following is a statement of my policy and intentions:
>
>   . . .
>   J & L has always been domiciled in Pittsburgh, and the Pittsburgh works have been an integral part of its operation. I assure you that LTV desires only to work with the management in making J & L a profitable enterprise. You have my personal

assurance that LTV has no plans to close the Pittsburgh works, or any other facility, or to decrease the hourly-paid work force. In that connection, it is my definite intention to obtain an independent study of ways and means by which the efficiency and viability of the entire J & L operation—including the Pittsburgh works—can be improved.[101]

LTV, however, at once began to phase out J & L's Pittsburgh facilities. According to *Business Week*, when steel profits zoomed in 1973 and 1974 an internal dispute arose over whether to plow those funds back into J & L or invest them elsewhere.

> J & L's Pittsburgh Works became the main issue. The company had spent $200 million in 1974 on its facilities at Aliquippa on the theory that the added capacity might enable it to close down the Pittsburgh plant.

In 1974, the J & L camp within the conglomerate succeeded in obtaining another $200 million for Pittsburgh.[102]

The reprieve was short-lived. When LTV proposed in 1977 to merge with Lykes (thus also merging, as will be recalled, J & L with Youngstown Sheet & Tube), internal discussion documents made available to the Justice Department assumed that after the merger the new J & L would close down Brier Hill and the hot strip mill in Pittsburgh.[103] Representatives of LTV and Lykes told the Justice Department that merger of J & L and Sheet & Tube would permit J & L's finishing mill at Hennepin, Illinois to obtain hot strip product from Sheet & Tube's mill at Indiana Harbor, Indiana. This, they said, would permit J & L's Cleveland Works, presently shipping hot mill product to Hennepin, "to concentrate its efforts towards competing more effectively in nearby areas"[104]—the same market served by J & L's Pittsburgh Works. When on May 18, 1978 Justice Department personnel met with LTV and Lykes representatives, James Paulos, Senior Vice President and Chief Financial Officer of LTV, stated that "the old (1902) strip mill at the Pittsburgh plant would be closed as soon as possible."[105] Nevertheless, in a memorandum to Attorney General Griffin Bell in June 1978 which urged that the proposed merger be approved, LTV representatives did *not* list J & L's hot strip mill in Pittsburgh among "the major properties which may be shut down" as a result of the merger, instead representing that

> job opportunities in the Greater Pittsburgh area would be enhanced because of increased utilization of steelmaking at the Aliquippa and Pittsburgh Works.[106]

In the fall of 1980 J & L informed the United Steelworkers of America that the Pittsburgh Works hot strip mill would be closed the following spring, terminating about 1,000 jobs.

In May 1979, the EPA negotiated a "consent decree" with U.S. Steel concerning nine of the company's western Pennsylvania plants. These plants include the Homestead Works, where steel is still made by open hearths; the Edgar Thomson-Irvin Works, whose modern BOF shop will reach full efficiency only if complemented by a continuous caster and modern hot strip mill; and the world's largest coke plant, the Clairton Works. Chairman of the Board Roderick's comments on the consent decree seemed to hold out a bright future for these mills:

> Although this is a demanding package, it clearly demonstrates that U.S. Steel is committed to remaining in the steel business in the Monongahela Valley. . . . U.S. Steel can now act aggressively to revitalize our Pittsburgh area operations, moving ahead to develop further the Valley's economic potential and that of its people.[107]

But paragraph 40 of the consent decree stated that U.S. Steel could achieve compliance either by installing pollution controls *or* by closing its plants. And in its 1980 Annual Report the company admitted: "The economics of the required investment may dictate that certain facilities be closed instead of modified to comply with the requirements."[108]

Two and a half years after the Consent Decree was signed, U.S. Steel had announced only one major new investment in its Pittsburgh mills—and withdrew that commitment soon after it was made. In December 1980 U.S. Steel announced that it would build a continuous caster by mid-1983 at the Edgar Thomson Works.[109] In its 1980 annual report the company repeated: "At Edgar Thomson Works, a 1.3 million tons per year continuous caster is being added."[110] But at the annual shareholders meeting on May 4, 1981 Mr. Roderick, under questioning by local steelworkers and community activists, contradicted this by stating:

> [The company] is reviewing the outlook for the entire flat-rolled market. He said the review may result in changes in U.S. Steel's previously-announced plan to install a continuous casting machine in its Edgar Thomson Works in Pittsburgh.[111]

The struggle in Pittsburgh differs from that in Youngstown precisely because Youngstown happened. In Youngstown, no one could really believe that any of the giant mills would close until the company made a formal announcement. Contract after contract, company negotiators had "rattled the tin cup" and threatened to leave town unless their demands were met. Union activists had grown accustomed to regard this rhetoric as crying wolf. But with the example of Youngstown before their eyes, local unions in Pittsburgh know that a shutdown is possible. They know that a failure to modernize amounts to a death sentence. They are asking for a voice in the decision.

Part IV. Some Conclusions From What Happened in Youngstown

Chapter One. Modernize Industry in "Brownfield" Communities Where It Already Exists

What the Companies Say

The steel industry says that plant closings are unpleasant but necessary, just like surgery.

The basic idea put forward by the industry is that capital must be free to go wherever the rate of profit is highest. The industry argues that only if businesses are free to shut down, and free to move elsewhere, will American industry be modernized so as to compete effectively with European and Japanese imports.

As the steel industry sees things, maximizing profit means closing down old facilities and building from the ground up in new ("greenfield") locations.

As the steel industry sees things, maximizing profit may even mean investing outside the steel industry entirely, so as to earn the money which *then* can be invested in steel. (We should ask industry spokesmen: If it is more profitable today to invest in real estate, or chemicals, or oil, rather than in steel, won't the same thing be true five years from now?)

Many people in public life agree with the steel industry. Mayor Caliguiri of Pittsburgh admits that Pittsburgh has no specific plans for retraining unemployed blue-collar workers. He suggests, in fact, that it might be a good idea if the city's unemployed moved somewhere else. "I'd rather have less people with high incomes than more people with relatively low earning and spending power," he has said.[1]

Similarly, in closing argument at the end of the United States Steel trial in Youngstown, the company attorney claimed that workers

who had lost their jobs could transfer to other United States Steel
plants if they desired. He said:

> They don't know what being out in the street really means,
> not like some lawyers do. They are not out of jobs. They only
> have an inconvenience of moving.
> Millions and millions of Americans every year move for better
> jobs and move from one city to another city but these Plaintiffs
> insist they have a contractual right not to move. . . .[2]

Three Arguments Against Industrial Flight

Youngstown workers have struggled to find words to express a
different point of view. Ed Mann said in meeting after meeting:
"We're not gypsies." John Barbero recalled how British labor leader
Aneurin Bevan told about the uprooting of his family from the coal
mining country of Wales. "When do we stop running?," Barbero
asked. It was common in Youngstown to meet steelworkers who had
lost one or more other jobs in shutdowns before the mill closed. And
after the Youngstown mills closed, there were many experiences like
Meldon Morgan's. He was laid off at U.S. Steel's Youngstown
Works, moved to U.S. Steel's Ambridge (Pennsylvania) Works as a
laborer, then was laid off there and transferred to Lorain. In February
1982 he was laid off at Lorain. "Maybe Texas is next for me," he
told the *Vindicator*.[3]

Out of the meetings, the kitchen-table arguments, the leaflet writing, and the law suits, workers in Youngstown spelled out an argument for modernizing industry in existing communities ("brownfield" modernization). The argument makes the following points:

1. Even from the standpoint of the single firm, greenfield modernization is more expensive than brownfield modernization.

2. When costs to the community as well as costs to the firm are
considered, the case for brownfield modernization becomes overwhelming.

3. In the last analysis, the question of brownfield versus greenfield
modernization is a question of what kind of society we want. There is
no economic necessity for the reindustrialization of America in new
towns rather than in old ones. The strongest motivation for industrial flight from the cities in which plants presently exist appears to be
anti-unionism. Management grows tired of labor troubles, and ima-

gines that new hires in a community which lacks a history of struggle will solve its problems. A second motive for industrial flight appears to be simply the American habit of scrapping last year's car, last year's community, and last year's spouse, and moving on. The concern for family and community so much talked about nowadays should express itself in a program for modernizing industry in existing sites because it is better for human beings.

Federal Studies Show Brownfield Modernization More Profitable

Two comprehensive Federal studies of the steel industry[4] have reached the conclusion that it is cheaper for a steel company to modernize in existing, brownfield sites than in new, greenfield locations.

In October 1977, the Council on Wage and Price Stability concluded that "replacement of existing plants by efficient, new greenfield operations is simply uneconomic at today's capital costs." What the Council termed "rounding out"—that is, adding some new facilities to existing plants—is a more profitable modernization strategy, the study found. Greenfield modernization results in steel production at a somewhat lower *operating cost* than results from roundout (brownfield) modernization. But the *capital cost* (cost of construction, interest on borrowed money, etc.) of greenfield modernization is so much greater than the capital cost of brownfield modernization that, adding operating and capital cost together, roundout or brownfield modernization is about *$60 cheaper per ton of finished steel.* The Council set out its results in the following table:

Table 5

	Average Existing Carbon Steel Plant	Rounding Out of Existing Plant	New Greenfield Carbon Steel Plant
Operating Costs	300	260	240
Additional Capital Charges (including Equity Returns)	—	100	177
Total Additional Costs per Ton	—	60	117

All figures in 1976 U.S. $/net ton.

A report by the Office of Technology Assessment released in the spring of 1980 came to similar conclusions. The report states:

> It is accepted that greenfield expansion provides the greatest opportunities for installing optimum new technology and plant layout and offers maximum production cost savings. These advantages, however, usually will not offset the large capital costs. . . . There is agreement that greenfield expansion cannot be justified, either on the basis of the price necessary to obtain an acceptable level of profitability or in terms of the *net* increase in costs.

The study gives the example of energy conservation. By spending $11 per metric ton of steel for brownfield modernization, a steel company could save 1.1 million British thermal units per metric ton. Greenfield replacement of the same facilities could save *8* times as much energy, but would cost *120* times as much!

This conclusion is supported by data from government, university, industry, and consulting firm studies.

Table 6

Integrated Carbon Steel
Plant Capital Cost Estimates for New Shipments Capacity

(1978 dollars/tonne of capacity)

Source	Year	Roundout	Greenfield
A. D. Little	1975	$628	$1,296
Fordham	1975	880	1,474
COWPS	1976	710	1,502
U.S. Steel	1976	NA	1,220
Marcus	1976	630	1,514
Inland Steel	1977	520	956
Mueller	1978	715	1,210
Republic Steel	1979	372–636	1,367–1,317
American Iron & Steel Institute	1980	743	1,287

The comparison can be made more concrete by considering U.S. Steel's Youngstown Works. William Kirwan, superintendent of the mills, proposed a plan to his corporate superiors for modernization of the Works by building electric furnaces and a continuous caster. The estimated cost was $208 million. The capacity of the reindustrialized facilities was estimated at 7– 800,000 tons a year, so that the cost of modernization via the Kirwan Plan was to be $350 to $400 per ton of capacity. By way of contrast, U.S. Steel's proposed greenfield mill at Conneaut, Ohio would have a capacity of about 4,000,000 tons a year and would cost about $4 billion. The cost per ton of capacity of modernization at Conneaut would be about $1,000 per ton. (This is a minimum figure. Edgar B. Speer, then Chairman of the Board of U.S. Steel, estimated the cost of building the Conneaut facility at $4 billion in 1976. See *Industry Week*, April 15, 1976. By 1979, when Mr. Kirwan developed his plan for the Youngstown Works, internal U.S. Steel documents obtained in the course of the Conneaut litigation put the cost of the Conneaut plant at $6.72 billion.[5] In Mr. Kirwan's words, his plan recommended that "a greenfield plant be built on a brownfield site" which would cost "one helluva lot less dollars than a Conneaut" and be "a far more desirable short and long range alternative to the tremendous cost and the socio-economic impact involved in phasing out the [Youngstown] plant."[6]

There is no reason to suppose that the comparative figures for the cost of brownfield and greenfield modernization will change significantly in the future. They have been relatively constant for the past quarter century. In 1958, Bethlehem Steel estimated that an entirely new fully integrated plant in the Chicago area of 2,500,000 tons ingot capacity would cost $300 per ton ingot capacity as compared to $135 per ton ingot capacity for expansion of Youngstown Sheet & Tube's existing plant in the area.[7]

The question may arise, Why then should a U.S. Steel prefer "greenfield" expansion? The answer appears to be that *once a greenfield plant is built* it can produce steel more cheaply than a modernized brownfield facility. Hence, if the company can induce the government (that is, the taxpayer) to build the plant for it, that is the desirable option for the firm.

Company Decisions Ignore Human Costs

A comparison of the cost to the company of "greenfield" modernization with the cost to the company of "brownfield" modernization is only the first step in an adequate analysis.

One must also consider human costs. Even if greenfield modernization were cheaper than brownfield for the company, it might be more expensive for society as a whole.

Late in 1978 an analysis was conducted of the socio-economic effects of the Campbell Works shutdown. It found that in addition to the employees at the Works who were terminated, at least another 3,600 jobs would be lost through the secondary multiplier effect on suppliers, retail businesses, and others. Loss of wages to the former Campbell Works employees during the first three years after the shutdown was estimated at $50–70 million, and loss of wages to those in other businesses during the same period at $63.5 million. The study projected costs to the public sector during the same three years of $60–70 million. About half of these public costs were expected to take the form of local, county, state, and Federal tax losses. In the city of Campbell, for example, the Campbell Works had provided about 65 per cent of the city's property tax revenues. The other $35 million in projected public costs was expected to come from various benefit programs, particularly the Trade Readjustment Assistance Act which provides benefits to workers held to have lost their jobs because of imports.[8]

City after city in the Mahoning Valley has experienced a budgetary crisis followed by wage cuts and layoffs for public employees, and cutbacks in social services. Frank Fasline, treasurer of the Campbell school board, told Carol Greenwald and Dorie Krauss:

> This thing is wrecking the school system here in Campbell. It is really a drastic situation. We're down to the state minimums in every area. We've had layoffs; we've curtailed purchasing supplies; we're down to the bare necessities. We've reduced all the extra-curricular activities. We have to make kids pay for some of their own football equipment. We're borrowing every year to pay the deficit from the previous year.

In May 1980, nearly all of Youngstown's municipal employees, including firefighters and police officers, went on strike for pay increases the city said it could not provide because of revenue lost in the shutdown of the Valley's steel mills.

By January 1981, unemployment in the Youngstown-Warren Metropolitan Statistical Area had reached 15.4 per cent, the highest level since the Depression. A year later, adjoining stories on one front page of the *Vindicator* told of the following: 3,400 more workers to be indefinitely laid off at General Motors' Lordstown plant; an unemployment rate in Trumbull County (where the Lordstown plant is located) of 17.8 per cent; and 10,000 people seeking 180 five-pound boxes of free government surplus cheese distributed by the Youngstown office of the Salvation Army. In February 1982, the unemployment rate in Trumbull and Mahoning counties reached 19.9 per cent.[9]

Statistics cannot convey the full human costs of the Youngstown shutdowns. This was a community in which the generations of a family cared for one another, in which grandparents did babysitting, and were themselves cared for by families rather than institutions. Now, as a result of the shutdowns, young people feel compelled to leave town. One graduating high school senior wrote to the local paper that the mills had been closed for two years as of June 1981, but little had been done to revitalize Youngstown. Population was going down, unemployment lines were increasing. With Youngstown's economic state to look forward to, wrote Tina Stryffeler, "who wants to graduate?"[10]

And what balance sheet can adequately reflect these lines by a son about his unemployed father?

> He's losing his mind with nothing to do,
> because he got laid off from the Sheet & Tube. . . .
>
> Dad sits around the house, all worried and sick,
> with nothing to do the dog he does kick.
> It's all Lykes fault and dad knows it by now,
> he just wants to go and blow his brains out.
>
> Yet he sits in his chair, impatient and worried,
> I guess he'll be there until the day he is buried. . . .[11]

In Great Britain, because the steel industry is largely owned by the government, it is possible to compare the savings to the government from closing old steel mills with the costs to the government of providing social services to the workers laid off. Cambridge University made such a calculation of the costs and benefits over five years of a shutdown program undertaken by the British Steel Corporation in December 1979. The calculation was as follows:

Table 7

	British Steel Corporation (million pounds)	Other nationalized industries (million pounds)	Total (million pounds)
Annual savings to industry	231	77	308
Annual cost to industry in unemployment benefits, etc.	57	19	76
Net annual savings to industry	174	58	232
Tax loss to national government			408
Additional welfare payments			134
Total lost to Exchequer			542

Therefore, the effect of the shutdowns on the national government considered both as mill owner *and* as provider of social services is estimated at 542 minus 232 equals 310 million pounds (about $600 million) *lost* per year.[12]

Fully to take into account the social costs of brownfield versus greenfield modernization one must also consider the increased social costs of modernization at the new, greenfield site. For example, Conneaut, Ohio presently has a population of about 15,000. U.S. Steel estimates that construction of its proposed mill in Conneaut would cause the population of the three counties nearest to Conneaut to increase by 15,800. Planners associated with local governments in the area estimate a population increase in the range of 37,187 to 58,500.[13] Such an influx of new residents would require heavy investment in new social services of all kinds. James Williams, a partner in Philadelphia's Murphy-Williams Urban Planning and Housing Consultants, estimates that the development of the mill could cost each resident of Erie, Crawford, and Ashtabula counties $6,500 a year over a period of 25 years. This is his estimate of what it would cost the community to develop services like sewer plants, water plants, fire and police protection, school operations including busing, roads, government administration, utilities, libraries, health care, and recreation.

Felix Rohatyn, the financier who engineered New York City's "survival," echoes the analysis developed by Youngstown steelworkers in the following ways:

> In a world where capital will be in shorter supply than energy, is it really a valid use of resources to have to build anew in the Sun Belt the existing schoolhouses, firehouses, transit systems, etc., of the North for the benefit of the new immigrants in the South, instead of maintaining and improving what we already have in place here? Is it rational to think that northern cities teeming with the unemployed and unemployable will not be permanent wards of the federal government at vast financial and social cost? . . . Doesn't the notion of "taking the people to the jobs" completely ignore that many of those people, in large parts of this country, are unwilling and unable to move?[14]

What Kind of a World Do We Want to Live In?

To include human costs in an analysis of the greenfield and brownfield alternatives is not enough. The value of some things simply cannot be put in terms of money. The challenge to advocates of brownfield modernization is to find a precise way to talk about values that cannot be measured.

The greenfield model of modernization reminds one of how the rebuilding of cities was envisioned 25 years ago. At that time it was supposed that the best way to rebuild a city was to bulldoze areas several square blocks in size, disperse the residents to the four winds, and completely replace the housing. Only gradually did it become clear that this was a crude, and in the long run self-defeating, approach, which tended to replace old slums with new ones. The newer vision of how to remake a city is to rebuild the structures gradually without relocating the people or destroying the social fabric of neighborhoods. Let the churches, settlements, and traditional meeting places of the community remain. Begin to rebuild in the least densely populated parts of an area. As new housing becomes available on the first small sites, relocate residents *within* the neighborhood. Proceeding in this fashion with a scalpel rather than a sledge-hammer, cities can be rebuilt without losing their social identity.

Sweden Provides One Alternative

Twenty-five years from now, no doubt too late for many, many Youngstowns, this is how every civilized nation will modernize its industry. Several of us in Youngstown had a glimpse of that future when we met at the Local 1462 union hall with Per Ahlström, editor of the weekly magazine of the Swedish Metal Workers Federation. Ahlström began by emphasizing that Sweden, like the United States, is a capitalist economy. Then he went on to describe the Swedish steel crisis and how it was resolved. Several years ago, he said, Sweden faced the same problems of overcapacity and low profitability which now exist in the United States. There were three Swedish steel companies, two privately owned, and one owned by the government. Each was trying to carry on the whole steelmaking process from blast furnace to rolling mill, and all were losing money. Accordingly, the Swedish government insisted that the three enterprises coordinate their activities. At the same time, however, it was decided as a matter of principle that rather than concentrate all steelmaking in a single location it would be socially preferable to preserve each of the three, traditional steel towns if a way could be found to do so. The resolution was that each company remained where it was, but each henceforth was responsible for a single phase of steelmaking. The mill closest to sources of iron ore in northern Sweden did the initial processing. The mill located on the seacoast did most of the finishing. Meantime, since all modernization and rationalization tends to eliminate jobs, imaginative programs were designed to help people leave the steel industry, not in shock and defeat, but with a sense of moving forward in their lives. All Swedish employers were required to list all job openings, and a computerized printout of currently available jobs was posted each day in the mill itself. Persons who wanted to visit other communities where there were job openings were paid to do so, as were their spouses. Every steel worker was guaranteed two years' pay during the period of transition. The social objective, our visitor stated, was that no one ever be compelled unwillingly to leave a job.

Sweden does what it does for essentially "political" reasons. Helen

Ginsburg says this well in an article in *The Nation*. She quotes an unnamed Swedish official: "Swedes are not particularly religious but one thing we do hold almost sacred is everybody's right to work." The result, she continues, is that the unemployment rate in Sweden was 1.7 percent from 1960 to 1970, and 2.1 percent from 1971 to 1979. This is not because the Swedish economy in general or its steel industry in particular are immune to the shocks affecting other capitalist economies. On the contrary, Sweden is more dependent than the United States on exports, and has no coal or oil of its own.

> The answer is that the Swedish commitment to full employment is politically unassailable. Even though it has traditionally been regarded as an important means of raising the output of goods and services, and hence living standards, it is not viewed solely in economic terms. It is also linked to other vital social goals. . . .[T]he concept of "normalization" is fundamental to the Swedish social welfare system; that is, the goal is to enable everyone to live as normal a life as possible and "to reduce the risk of isolation, loneliness and alienation." And work is considered the key to a normal life. In short, a job is considered a basic right.[15]

Listening to Per Ahlström in Youngstown, Ohio was like hearing a fairy tale. For instance, early retirement, which is the *objective* of the United Steelworkers of America in its collective bargaining about shutdowns, is, according to Ahlström, considered a *defeat* in Sweden because it deprives a person of years of contribution to society as a worker.

The principle is not that industry should always be modernized where it presently exists. A company might carry out "brownfield" industrialization in such a way as to sacrifice social values to profit. Thus General Motors is locating new plants in or near the existing cities of Baltimore, Flint, Pontiac, Detroit, and St. Louis. But the new Cadillac assembly plant proposed by General Motors in Detroit would destroy 1,021 homes and apartment buildings, 155 other businesses, churches, and one hospital, and displace 3,500 people, thereby wiping out a traditional and racially integrated neighborhood. Karl Greimel, dean of the Lawrence Institute of Technology school of architecture and an experienced industrial architect, testified in court that the plant could be built in a much smaller space so as to save most of the "Poletown" neighborhood. For instance, instead of placing a mammoth parking lot next to the plant, General Motors could build a multi-level parking structure or provide parking on the plant roof. General Motors has refused to make such changes.[16] Moreover, after all the land was cleared except for a wooden cross where the Immaculate Conception Church once stood, GM announced that it would delay construction for at least one year.[17]

The principle, in the words of one Youngstown picket sign is: People First, Profits Second. As long as a company is making *some* profit it should not have the right to make the *highest possible* profit if to do so is destructive to workers and the community. Ordinarily this will mean that it is better to rebuild in one place, rather than scrapping and moving on.

Brownfield versus Oil Field: The Problem of Disinvestment

Ultimately, the choice may not be between "brownfield" and "greenfield" modernization of the American steel industry. The choice may be between brownfield modernization and no modernization at all.

Under cover of arguments about the obsolescence and non-competitiveness of particular mills and particular locations, the American steel industry is giving up the steel business altogether. The United States is losing the ability to supply its steel needs because steel companies are investing outside the steel industry. Investment in steel is profitable; indeed, it appears that the American steel industry may be the most profitable in the world. In 1977 the Federal Trade Commission found that for the period 1961–1971 the United States had the highest profit rate, Japan the second highest, and the European Community the lowest, when profit was measured by net income as a percentage of sales. When profit was measured by net income as a percentage of equity, the profit rates of the United States and of Japan were approximately equal, and that of the European Community again the lowest.[18] In 1980 the Office of Technology Assessment of the Federal government reported that in the period 1969–1977 net income as a percentage of net fixed assets in five major steel-producing countries was:

United States 6.7
Japan 1.7
West Germany 2.9
United Kingdom . . . . −5.3
France (1972–1976) . . . . −8.3[19]

But investment in steel is not *as profitable* as investment in, say, the chemical industry or downtown real estate, and therefore United States Steel and other steel companies have been putting their new investment dollars elsewhere.

In the case of United States Steel, from 1976 to 1979 the company's non-steel assets grew 80 per cent to $4.7 billion, while steel assets increased only 13 per cent to $5.9 billion and steelmaking capacity actually decreased.[20] Consider the year 1979 in which the shutdown of the Youngstown Works and other steel facilities was announced. That year the company opened a new joint venture shopping center near Pittsburgh containing the largest enclosed mall in Pennsylvania. A few weeks after the Youngstown shutdown announcement, it signed a letter of intent with Tenneco Chemicals, Inc. to build world-scale chemical facilities in Houston.[21] Of the mills which U.S. Steel decided to close in 1979, at least the New Haven wire mill appears to have consistently turned a modest profit of about $500,000 a year.[22] It fell victim to the philosophy reaffirmed by David Roderick, chairman of the board of U.S. Steel, in February 1981, that new spending will go to those businesses that provide the highest rate of return.[23]

U.S. Steel's strategy of disinvestment in steel climaxed in November 1981 when the company used a painfully accumulated war chest of $6.3 billion in cash and credit not to modernize its steel mills but to offer to buy the Marathon Oil Company. This $6.3 billion would have constructed the proposed new integrated steel mill at Conneaut. Alternatively, $6.3 billion could have paid for the modernization of U.S. Steel's existing "brownfield" facilities. For example, the cost of replacing the open hearths at Homestead with new Basic Oxygen or electric furnaces has been estimated by U.S. Steel at $150 million.[24]

Publicly, Mr. Roderick laments the possibility that the United States may become dependent on steel imports as it has become dependent on foreign oil.[25] Meantime the company continues to cut back its steel capacity. There is at least the possibility that the industry, led by its largest company, is deliberately *restricting* steel output so as to be able to charge higher prices.[26] Certain financial analysts recommended this strategy just before the wave of shutdowns began in 1977. Charles Bradford, steel analyst for Merrill Lynch, advised: "The announced expansion plans of the United States steel industry do not make any sense to us unless an equal amount of antiquated facilities are closed."[27] Argus Research Corporation of New York City was more blunt:

By contracting their capacity base, American steel producers will concede a still larger share of the U.S. market to foreign suppliers, but along with this will go increased power to set pricing patterns. This is not unlike the situation that developed in the domestic oil industry earlier in this decade, after which petroleum prices soon began to rise sharply. We expect the same pattern to occur in steel prices.[28]

Congress has attempted to stop disinvestment in steel by giving the steel companies tax breaks and other incentives. In 1981, the Tax Reform Act included a provision sought by the steel industry which permits new investment to be depreciated more rapidly, thus permitting the companies to retain cash they would otherwise have had to pay in taxes.[29] There is no assurance that these incentives will bring about modernization of the steel industry because nothing in the law requires the money saved to be invested in steel. Joel Hirschhorn, project director of the Office of Technology Assessment steel study, commented before the new law was enacted:

Federal policies toward the steel industry mostly benefit the large integrated companies. Nevertheless, these producers are likely to continue to diversify and get out of steelmaking. . . . Measures such as refundable tax credits may only hasten non-steel investments by large steelmakers who have decided to diversify. . . .[30]

After the new incentives became law, a New York Times survey found that U.S. Steel was "looking for an acquisition outside the steel industry" (which proved, three months later, to be the Marathon Oil Company); that Armco was closing a steel plant in Marion, Ohio and trying to add Ladish, which makes aircraft forgings; that National Steel had paid $241 million in 1980 for a savings and loan company; that Inland and Bethlehem Steel were considering non-steel acquisitions; and that, in general,

the $60 billion steel industry stands at a crossroads, trying to decide whether to spend its new wealth in rebuilding its steel-making plants or to try to improve profitability by expanding into more promising sectors.[31]

As a piece of social planning the new tax incentives are like throwing paint at a wall and hoping for a picture.

Brownfield modernization, therefore, may serve more than the parochial objectives of a Youngstown: it may be the means necessary to preserve a steel industry in the United States. There are increasing indications that government, labor, and even the steel industry have begun to accept a brownfield perspective.

In September 1980, a Steel Tripartite Advisory Committee made up of top level representatives of the government, the Steelworkers union, and the major steel companies including U.S. Steel, endorsed an amendment to the Clean Air Act which would permit a company to postpone compliance with the Act provided, among other things, that

> [f]unds which would have been spent to comply with the dead-line will be expended in the same time period for modernization *and in existing steelmaking communities.*

(Emphasis added.) The amendment, this requirement included, was enacted in summer 1981 as the Steel Industry Compliance Extension Act.[32] U.S. Steel reported to its stockholders in May 1981 that "[the] massive expenditures required to keep our existing capability efficient and competitive . . . preclude consideration of a greenfield site steel plant in Conneaut, Ohio for the time being." Instead U.S. Steel announced construction of continuous casters at a number of existing mills.[33]

The choice seems to be: Minimum brownfield modernization of only the most efficient and profitable plants, with an overall reduction in the nation's ability to make steel; or more ample brownfield modernization, sufficient to preserve both steelmakers' jobs and America's capacity to meet its own steel needs.

Chapter Two. New Choices Needed When Private Enterprise Fails

It remains to be seen whether tax breaks and other subsidies, granted on condition that the money provided be reinvested in steel, would induce U.S. Steel and other steel companies to rebuild aging mills in places like Pittsburgh, Gary, Indiana and Lackawanna, New York. If not, the people of the United States will have to consider doing the job themselves. In the 1930s, the government created the Tennessee Valley Authority to provide electric power to areas that private utilities could not profitably serve. Frank O'Brien, former president of Local 1843, USWA, representing production and maintenance employees at J & L's plant in Pittsburgh, has suggested formation of a "Monongahela Valley Authority" that could acquire and operate steel mills that the industry did not wish to modernize.

Are Employee-Community Ownership Plans Workable?

Employee or community ownership of a single firm presents many familiar problems. Some of them are as follows: Will the present owner sell you the plant? (This, of course, was a difficulty at U.S. Steel's Youngstown Works.) If you acquire the plant can you sell the product? Will banks, suppliers, and customers boycott an institution challenging their basis of existence? Won't a worker-owned company be tempted to take wage cuts in order to survive? (An example of this is the General Motors Hyatt bearing plant in Clark, New Jersey where UAW workers have agreed to cut wages by 25 per cent and buy the plant through an Employee Stock Ownership Plan.)[34] If employees are encouraged to buy stock, can the company also afford a pension, and if there is no pension are workers not being asked to bet their security in old age on the fortunes of a single firm? (This is what happened at the South Bend Lathe Company.)[35] If employees own stock, can stock ownership be kept equal, and if not, will not the inequalities that prevented democratic decisions when the firm was privately owned be reproduced? (This was the sequence of events at a worker-owned Vermont asbestos mine.)[36] Even if the distribution of stock is equal, will stock ownership lead to worker participation in decisionmaking, or will the stock be managed by a conventional trustee who votes the workers' shares?

A critical problem in every major experiment in employee ownership in the United States is the lack of democracy in day to day decisions on the shop floor. This is a problem even at Rath Packing Company in Waterloo, Iowa, where employees name 11 of the 17 members of the Board of Directors. A *Wall Street Journal* reporter found dissatisfaction with the way decisions are made about the work. And Lyle Taylor, president of the local union, has commented:

> I'd have done some things differently if I'd known what I know now. I'd have set it up so we'd have more input into the management of the company as far as day to day control.[37]

Our experience in Youngstown showed that besides all the problems just listed, there is another problem when the plant you want to buy is very *capital-intensive* (that is, uses a great deal of expensive machinery). The problem is that buying and modernizing something like a steel mill requires so much money that it is only possible with help from the Federal government.

Massive Federal Aid a Must in Capital-Intensive Industries

The strategy of the Youngstown struggle was to seek Federal government aid to assist an employee-community coalition in buying and modernizing the mill.

Once the decision was made to try to buy the mills and to operate them again under employee-community ownership, there was no alternative to seeking Federal help. The steel industry is unimaginably capital-intensive. The feasibility study of the Campbell Works, and later, independent studies of the Brier Hill and Youngstown Works, estimated the cost of replacing open hearths with electric furnaces and a continuous caster at $150–250 million. There was no point in acquiring any one of these facilities without such modernization. It was the presence of high-cost open hearths in the mills of the Mahoning Valley which caused them to be closed in the first place.

We could not, in the case of the Campbell Works, raise the needed amount of capital by calling a union meeting and asking that those whose jobs were endangered pool their savings. Suppose each of the 5,000 workers terminated at the Campbell Works had $5,000 to contribute (an unlikely assumption). That would have generated only $25 million, barely enough to buy the Campbell Works, without provision for modernization or working capital.

Other efforts at employee-community ownership in the United States teach the same lesson: workers cannot buy their plant unaided when the technology is capital-intensive. Steffi Domike, who works at U.S. Steel's Clairton Works, has studied the producers' cooperatives in the Pacific Northwest plywood industry. These enterprises represent by far the strongest example of worker ownership in the United States: between 1942 and 1956 they produced about one-fourth of the industry's product. Ms. Domike found that during the first half of the century the plywood industry was characterized by unchanging technology, relatively skilled labor, and low capital requirements.[38] When E. E. Westman organized the first cooperative in 1921 he sold 125 shares for $500 down, $500 due, mostly to or through his Scandinavian friends.[39] By 1964, however, the cost of a new plywood plant had risen to over $5 million.[40] As a result, the cooperatives' role in the industry has been declining and it is unlikely that any new cooperatives will be formed.

A successful experiment in employee-community ownership in Youngstown, which succeeded at about the time that the Ecumenical Coalition's effort failed, offers further proof that when capital requirements are high, worker ownership is possible only with massive Federal help.

The Republic Rubber plant on Albert Street in Youngstown was operated in the 1970s by Aeroquip, in turn a subsidiary of the Libby-Owens-Ford conglomerate.[41] The plant made rubber hoses. In August 1978, the parent conglomerate shut the plant.

A joint committee of former managers and hourly employees asked Aeroquip whether it would be willing to sell the plant to them.

The company said yes, gave the committee an option to buy, and set a price of $2 million.

Six former supervisors invested $100,000 in stock of the new company. The Dollar Bank of Youngstown loaned $1,350,000, guaranteed by the Economic Development Administration of the U.S. Department of Commerce (the same EDA from which the steel struggle sought much larger guarantees). The Urban Development Action Grant program of the U.S. Department of Housing and Urban *UDAG* Development provided $750,000 outright, and the Small Business Administration another $500,000. The new enterprise was thereby enabled to pay $2 million for the plant while reserving $600,000 for working capital.

Apart from the much smaller purchase price, the critical difference between the Republic Rubber situation and the situation at the Campbell, Brier Hill, and Youngstown Works was that at Republic Rubber no modernization was required. The machinery consists of 23 or 24 braiding machines, which cost about $250,000 apiece new but are in good condition. The company estimated in February 1981 that it would need to invest no more than $100,000 per year in each of the next five years.

Republic Rubber was successful in putting together a financial package whose components were the same as those proposed by Youngstown steelworkers: employee purchase of stock in the new company; Federal grants; and Federal loan guarantees. Republic Rubber was successful because it needed capital only for purchase of the plant, not for modernization. Yet even Republic Rubber's requirements for $2.6 million—roughly 1 per cent of the sum involved in buying and modernizing any one of the Mahoning Valley steel mills—could be met only with Federal government assistance.

Thus buying, operating, and especially modernizing a major capitalist enterprise is possible only when workers have the Federal government behind them.

The Need for Democratic and Decentralized Workers' Control

Many Americans, including many American workers, feel that anything which requires Federal aid is going to be bureaucratically managed from Washington, and should be opposed for this reason.

People who feel this way would turn their backs on the idea of worker ownership once they realized that it would require massive Federal money.

I think this is mistaken. The Federal financing required to make employee-community ownership a reality is not in contradiction to management of such an enterprise in a democratic, decentralized way, with workers making most of the decisions.

We should get out of our heads the notion that Federal government involvement means that a plant must be bureaucratically managed from Washington. It is possible to take Federal tax money and place it in the hands of enterprises which are both locally-managed and nationally-supervised. One example is the Tennessee Valley Authority, at least as it was originally envisioned. Another is the National Legal Services Corporation for which I work. Congress appropriates money for the National Legal Services Corporation. The Corporation allocates more than 95 per cent of this sum to offices in the field. Each office in the field is managed by a combination of local lawyers and local clients. The work of the field offices is supervised by the national Corporation, which puts out regulations, and monitors the work of offices in the field to make sure the regulations are being followed. In the case of Legal Services, the "product" provided is free legal service for those too poor to afford private attorneys. But the same management model would work for another kind of product or service.

The Tennessee Valley Authority Model

Frank O'Brien's idea of a Monongahela Valley Authority is another example of how employee-community ownership could be *locally* managed.

O'Brien has described his idea this way:[42]

> When you work in a mill, and you see all these guys with the know-how, all together right there, then you see that you have the ability to operate the mill no matter what top management does.
>
> The company says, "Hey, it's not profitable for us any more to produce steel here." But *we* still need jobs. Companies like J & L are making money. They are moving because they don't

make *enough* money to suit them. They've let their plants run down like an old automobile: you run it into the ground, and then you take the license plate off and walk away from it.

So we should think about forming an Industrial Development Authority and running the mills ourselves. . . .

The companies have used this . . . for their own purposes. In the 1950's J & L used it to evict people from their homes in Scotch Bottom in Hazelwood. They said they needed the land to expand, but when they had evicted the people and gotten the land they didn't expand. They just let the land sit there and stored raw materials on it.

So I'm thinking the law can be used in reverse.

I think back to the time when the Port Authority was born. Pittsburgh Railways was the big operator transporting people in the City of Pittsburgh. They ran into a financial bind. So the Port Authority was formed, taking in all the bus companies in Allegheny County as well. It bought up the railway and the bus companies because people still had to be transported.

Recently they decided to close down the J & L hot strip mill. A thousand people lost their jobs.

A couple of Sundays later the Mayor was out to our father-and-son communion breakfast at St. Stephens in Hazelwood. He made a little speech and then he opened it up for questions.

So I got up. I said the Mayor had better start worrying now about the U.S. Steel mills, that when they build that plant in Conneaut they're going to shut down every plant up and down the river.

He said, "Well, what would you do?" I told him: "You, and the County Commissioners, sit down and form an authority, like the Port Authority. We can run the plants ourselves."

The Need for Big Changes in American Society

We found in Youngstown that seeking to buy and manage steel mills which had been closed by absentee corporate bureaucrats made us dependent on absentee government bureaucrats who were no more helpful. We should have expected this. It should not have surprised us that, under the Carter administration, the Economic Development Administration of the Department of Commerce was on intimate terms with steel industry executives and hostile to the proposal for employee-community ownership of the Campbell Works even before the final Alperovitz report. We were naive to have imagined that anything else was possible.

The Coalition's failure does not diminish the need for social control of investment decisions in the steel industry. Nor does it weaken the argument that the most effective form of social control is some kind of public ownership. The lesson to be drawn is that so capital-intensive an industry as steel requires national government financing, and that this financing will be forthcoming only when the political complexion of the national government has changed.

In my view, worker ownership or something like it will be necessary in the steel industry in the long run. Private industry is not going to give American society the modernized steel mills we need. The only long range solution will be for the government and workers, joining together, to do the job.

But worker ownership only makes sense in the long run, as part of a broader change in American society that will change what the Federal government is willing to do. In the short run, workers will have to look elsewhere for a strategy to fight plant shutdowns.

Chapter Three. In the Short Run, the Best Way to Influence Investment Decisions is by Direct Action

One day in the summer of 1980 I happened to be at the hall of Local 1330. It was from here that workers had marched to the occupation of the company's administration building, six months before.

Defeat was visibly evident. With the mill down, dues income had ceased. Secretary Terri Cannon had been laid off. The now-empty building with its big glass windows was a natural target for neighborhood kids, and several windows, the glass door, and the window of the secretary's office had been smashed.

When I came in Bob Vasquez, president of the local, was alone in the building sorting out papers. He looked up and said, "I understand you're a historian," and gave me some typewritten pages.

The papers consisted of several drafts of the first contract of March 1937 between the United States Steel Corporation and the Steel Workers Organizing Committee. The drafts reflected management and union approaches to such matters as seniority, adjustment of grievances, and health and safety. One clause, however, was the same in all drafts, by whomever presented, and indeed remains essentially unchanged in the current Basic Steel Contract. Then the clause stated:

> The management of the works and the direction of the working forces, including the right to hire, suspend or discharge for proper cause, or transfer, and the right to relieve employees from duty because of lack of work or for other legitimate reasons, is vested exclusively in the Corporation. . . .[43]

Today it reads:

> The Company retains the exclusive rights to manage the business and plants and to direct the working forces. . . . The rights to manage the business and plants and to direct the working forces include the right to hire, suspend or discharge for proper cause, or transfer, and the right to relieve employees from duty because of lack of work or for other legitimate reasons.[44]

This is the heart of economic decisionmaking in the United States. Workers may take part in deciding wages, hours, and some working conditions. Management reserves to itself the right unilaterally to make the big decisions about investment, plant location, and plant closings. And since this one-sided power is, in form, a part of a collective bargaining agreement to which rank and file workers have —in theory—voluntarily consented, filing a grievance or an NLRB charge will almost always be unsuccessful. It may be possible to obtain an injunction freezing the status quo until an arbitrator, a Regional Director of the Board, or, as in our Youngstown law suit, a Federal judge, reaches the merits of the case. But when that time comes, the decisionmaker will look to the management rights clause in the contract and affirm, however reluctantly, management's freedom to close a plant if it so chooses.[45]

The main thing to be learned from the Youngstown experience is that workers *must* seek to take part in decisions about what products to make, where capital should be invested, when a new plant should be built or an old plant shut down (investment decisions). As Bob Vasquez has said:

> Don't wait till they shut down. Look at the trade manuals. Watch what the competition is using. The best job security is a competitive factory. When they tell you [what they invest in] is none of your business, say, "What do you mean, none of our business? You've seen what happened in Youngstown."[46]

But how is the ordinary worker or local union to go about getting a voice in investment decisions? It's not easy.

The Limitations of Collective Bargaining

The most obvious strategy would be for national unions to insist on contract language providing job security or directly controlling investments.

There are a few examples. The United Shoe Workers negotiated, and an arbitrator and Federal court enforced, a clause which stated: "It is agreed by the Employer that the shop or factory shall not be removed from the County of Philadelphia during the life of this Agreement."[47] Clothing workers obtained and enforced the following contract language:

> A. During the term of this Agreement the Employer agrees that he shall not, without the consent of the New York Joint Board, remove or cause to be removed his present plant or plants from the city or cities in which such plant or plants are located.
> B. During the term of this Agreement the Employer shall not, without the consent of the New York Joint Board, manufacture garments or cause them to be manufactured in a factory other than his present factory or factories.[48]

Despite these promising precedents, American unions have been slow to demand contract language restraining management's freedom to close plants at will. The Steelworkers union is a case in point. After the shutdown epidemic of 1977–1979 there was strong pressure from the rank and file to put new language about shutdowns in the 1980 Basic Steel Contract. The Basic Steel Industry Conference, a gathering of local union presidents which sets bargaining objectives, resolved that the following protections "must" be negotiated:

> 1. No plant or major operating department should be closed permanently during the life of a three-year agreement.
> 2. A minimum of one year's advance notice of intent to shut down a plant or major operating department should be given to the union and to affected workers. Failure to comply should be penalized by substantial payments to affected workers, in addition to other benefits provided by law or contract.
> 3. All information necessary to evaluate the decision to shut down must be supplied to the union. Reasonable proposals by the union, affected workers, or economic development agencies of the community or the government to avert the shutdown or preserve the jobs involved must be considered. The company must provide the detailed information necessary to develop these proposals. If such proposals are rejected an explanation of the reasons for such rejection must be provided, in writing.
> 4. The company must cooperate in intensive efforts to create alternative employment opportunities, if the shutdown cannot be averted, utilizing existing facilities to the maximum possible

extent. Such cooperation should include retraining of affected workers where necessary, provision of income maintenance payments and social insurance until workers are re-employed, and job search and relocation allowances for those who cannot be re-employed locally.

5. Workers affected by a plant or departmental shutdown should be provided preferential employment opportunities at plants of other companies in the industry, particularly those in the same geographical area or serving the same market. In such cases pensions should be "portable" between companies.

6. When a company opens a new plant, workers at its existing plants should have preferential rights to be hired in the new plant.[49]

But what was actually negotiated in the 1980 Basic Steel Contract was a clause stating:

Before the Company shall finally decide to close permanently a plant or discontinue permanently a department of a plant it shall give the Union, when practicable, advance written notification of its intention. Such notification shall be given at least 90 days prior to the proposed closure date, and the Company will thereafter meet with appropriate Union representatives in order to provide them with an opportunity to discuss the Company's proposed course of action. Upon conclusion of such meetings, which in no event shall be less than 30 days prior to the proposed closure or partial closure date, the Company shall advise the Union of its final decision. The final closure decision shall be the exclusive function of the Company. This notification provision shall not be interpreted to offset the Company's right to lay off or in any other way reduce or increase the working force in accordance with its presently existing rights as set forth in Section III of this Agreement.[50]

This language leaves the rank and file member worse off than before. The company's only obligation is to give 90-day notice "when practicable." The union for the first time expressly recognizes management's right unilaterally to close a department or plant.

The Supreme Court Makes Bargaining More Difficult

In June 1981, the Supreme Court made it even more difficult for a union to bargain effectively over a company's investment decisions.

The Supreme Court held that an employer is not required by the National Labor Relations Act to bargain with its workers over a decision to close part of its business.[51]

At the time the Supreme Court ruled in the First National Maintenance case, the courts of appeal in the Second (New York and Connecticut), Third (Pennsylvania, New Jersey and Delaware), Sixth (Michigan, Ohio, Kentucky and Tennessee) and Seventh (Wisconsin, Illinois and Indiana) Circuits, had held that an employer has a duty to bargain over a partial shutdown. They reasoned that Sections 8(d) and 8(a)(5) require an employer to bargain in good faith with the representatives of its employees "with respect to wages, hours, and other terms and conditions of employment," and that whether a plant stays open or shuts down is a "condition of employment." All these courts were in the Midwest and Northeast where plant closings have devastated communities like Youngstown.

The Eighth, Ninth and Tenth circuit courts of appeal, all located west of the Mississippi, disagreed. They said that management didn't have to bargain over decisions involving "a major commitment of capital investment" or a "basic operational change." It was this conflict among the courts of appeal which brought the case to the Supreme Court.

The Supreme Court went with the Sunbelt. The most revealing sentence of its decision, written by Justice Blackmun, is: "Congress had no expectation [when it passed the National Labor Relations Act] that the elected union representative would become an equal partner in the running of the business enterprise in which the union's members are employed."

For all of the reasons set out above—the timidity of national union leadership, the hostility of the courts to union participation in decisions about investment—it will be difficult to do much about the shutdown problem at the bargaining table. But it would be wrong to give up. International unions at contract time should be swamped with resolutions dealing with plant shutdowns. Local unions should do their best to make the question of what will happen to particular plants a subject of local bargaining. Rank-and-file workers and their friends should ceaselessly expose the folly of giving up something real and concrete, like the Cost Of Living Adjustment or a wage increase, in return for vague company promises about what management *might* do. Any concession should be in exchange for a written, legally-enforcible promise by the company.

Direct Action Can Work

Is a strike any use in a plant which management wants to close anyway? The answer is emphatically Yes, for two reasons.

First, a decision to stop operations in one place can be challenged by *national* strike action at *all* the plants of the company. This tactic would be ineffective only where the plant to be closed was the company's only operation. A dramatic illustration of the effectiveness of this strategy was the strike of 26,000 Welsh coal miners in February 1981 to protest the planned closing of as many as 50 mines by the government-owned coal board. They were immediately joined by 3,000 miners in Kent. When by the second day more than 50,000 miners were on strike, the government withdrew its plan.[52]

Second, aggressive direct action can be effective even if limited to the locality where management proposes to discontinue production. Where the plant contains valuable machinery or an inventory of bulky products, management has capital invested in the facility it plans to abandon. In 1981 the newsletter *Labor Notes* reported an instance of successful direct action against a shutdown where the victory was due precisely to "the valuable dies and machinery in the plant."[53]

> Gulf & Western employs around 150 workers at Windsor Bumper, in Windsor, Ontario. . . .
>
> G&W claimed they could economize by moving production to their plant in Grand Rapids, Michigan if they didn't get their way.
>
> The workers at Windsor Bumper voted the offer down 118 to 4, and on June 12 they walked out on strike. On June 17 G&W sent a letter to local members saying that the plant would be permanently closed and all the workers fired. . . .
>
> At 9 pm on June 17, 18 union members went into the plant and began a sit-in in the plant cafeteria. They were supported by 300 people demonstrating outside. As soon as word of the occupation spread in Windsor, workers in other UAW locals, a grocery store local, Steelworkers, and others pledged support, including possible walk-outs if the sit-in strikers were forcibly removed by the police.
>
> Danny Flynn, plant chairman and organizer of the sit-in, told Labor Notes, "It wasn't so much the sit-in that reversed the closing as the support we got. Had they pulled out the dies and pulled us out of the plant, the plants in the city would have all stopped working and come to bolster the line. There were people

waiting at phones for that call. That was organized through the UAW movement."

At stake for G&W were the valuable dies and machinery in the plant. One striker said, "If the police would have gone in, we would have leveled the plant. We were ready. Our jobs and ability to support our families was at stake. . . ."

G&W backed off. They did not bring in the police. Supporters passed food and supplies over the factory fence.

On Father's Day, the strikers' wives brought their children to the plant. "We had planned that the kids and families would sing the Solidarity song and we would sing along with them, but we couldn't do it," Flynn said. "Nobody could finish it. It was a pretty moving day."

After seven and a half days, UAW Local 195 signed a three-year agreement with the "newly" opened G&W Windsor Bumper. . . .

This was the first time a plant had been re-opened by such action, with workers using tactics that haven't been seen since the 1930s.

Moreover, in the typical shutdown situation there is intense management concern to transfer orders smoothly to other facilities, and generally, to have an "orderly" shutdown. This is the real reason companies are so reluctant to notify their workers in advance of a shutdown.[54]

It is the considered opinion of the steelworkers most active in the Youngstown struggle that what little they accomplished was by direct action: by demonstrations, confrontations, and sit-ins. In particular, they feel that their single biggest mistake was calling off the occupation of the U.S. Steel administration building in Youngstown on January 28, 1980.

Bob Vasquez, the man who called off the occupation, agrees. If he had to do it over again, feeling as he now does that fairness doesn't matter to a company like U.S. Steel, he would keep the occupation going forever. Ed Mann concurs. He feels that if energy had been directed to controlling the drinking, rather than to the question of whether to leave, the occupation could have been successfully continued.

I asked Bob Vasquez about the responsibility I knew Vasquez had felt about the likelihood that if any one were arrested he would also be fired, and thereby lose unemployment compensation, Supplementary Unemployment Benefits (SUB), and the possibility of transfer to another U.S. Steel plant. If Bob were to plan another sit-in would he try to have only young single men with relatively little to lose exposed to arrest and discharge?

No, Bob Vasquez said at once. He had thought too much in that way the first time. Another time he would ask all 3,500 workers and their families to join in, and see if the company was prepared to fire them all. Once people began comparing who had most to lose, Bob said with conviction, you were beaten. Instead, there has to be a spirit of one for all, and all for one.

Introduction

1. "Another Youngstown First," *Warren Tribune*, Nov. 9, 1981.
2. John Barbero, Ed Mann, and others, "A Common Bond," in Alice and Staughton Lynd, ed., *Rank and File: Personal Histories by Working-Class Organizers* (second revised edition; Princeton University Press, 1981), page 268.
3. Mann and Barbero describe their histories more fully in *Rank and File*, pages 265–284. The other biographical sketches are based in part on interviews by Carol Greenwald and Dorie Krauss.

Part I. The Ecumenical Coalition's Campaign to Reopen the Campbell Works

1. Booz, Allen & Hamilton, "Economic Impact of Pollution Control Regulations on Steel Plants in the Mahoning River Valley" (Mar. 3, 1976).
2. Youngstown Sheet & Tube Company, *1973 Annual Report*, page 5.
3. Youngstown Sheet & Tube Company, 1976 S-1 *Registration Statement*, page 3.
4. Youngstown Sheet & Tube Company, *1975 Annual Report*, pages 2–3.
5. Robert H. Schnorbus, John J. Erceg, and Roger H. Hinderliter, "Cleveland and Northeast Ohio: An Economic Perspective," prepared for the Economic Stabilization Subcommittee, House Committee on Banking, Finance and Urban Affairs by the Federal Reserve Bank of Cleveland (Aug. 28, 1981). Profitability is measured as the percentage of net income to total assets over a three year period.
6. As of December 1981, a company called Youngstown Steel had re-opened a portion of the Struthers bar mill (a part of the Campbell Works), and was said to be installing electric furnaces; McDonald Steel, more fully described in Part III, had begun production at the 14 mill of the former McDonald Works with about 75 employees; and the newly-formed Hunt Steel company, owned in part by Quanex Corporation of Houston, had announced plans to construct at the site of the former Brier Hill Works two electric furnaces, secondary refining capabilities, a vertical continuous caster, piercer, rolling mill and sizing mill, as well as a quench and temper unit. Hunt Steel was expected to begin production in September 1982 and eventually to employ as many as 1,500 workers, the same number who used

to work at Brier Hill. The products of the three new enterprises are steel bars (Youngstown Steel), tire rims and other special shapes (McDonald Steel), and seamless pipe (Hunt Steel).

7. The article was summarized in the *Youngstown Vindicator*, June 13, 1976.

8. The National Labor Relations Board statements relied on were taken under oath, in the presence of the author, by an NLRB investigator about one month after the announcement of the Campbell Works shutdown. The NLRB charge which prompted the investigation was filed on October 5, 1977 and is described in Part II.

9. Interview with Duane Irving by Carol Greenwald and Dorie Krauss.

10. *Niles Times*, Sept. 20, 1977.

11. Interview with Gerald Dickey, Mar. 23, 1981.

12. Tom Scoville, "Steelworkers March on Washington," *Brier Hill Unionist*, Oct.-Nov. 1977.

13. *Forbes Magazine*, Sept. 15, 1973.

14. Edward Kelly and Mark Shutes, "Lykes' Responsibility for Closing the Youngstown Campbell Works," summarized in "The Youngstown Sheet & Tube Closing," *OPIC Monthly Report*, Oct.-Nov. 1977.

15. George H. Schueller, Anti-Trust Division, United States Department of Justice, "Report on Merger between Lykes Corporation and Youngstown Sheet & Tube Company" (Apr. 30, 1969).

16. This prophecy was uncovered as the result of a suit filed by Eugene Green and myself on behalf of Charles J. Carney, then the incumbent Congressman for the 19th District of Ohio. Carney v. Anti-Trust Division, Civ. 77–209–Y (N.D. Ohio, filed Oct. 11, 1977).

17. This summary is based on notes I took at the time.

18. The following paragraphs are based on an interview with Gerald Dickey, March 23, 1981, except where other sources are indicated. Direct quotations are from this interview.

19. The minutes of the Lykes Board of Directors show that Cleary was the only director who did not vote to close the Campbell Works. He abstained.

20. I first set down my recollections of this conversation less than a year after the events in a talk to a group of friends in West Virginia. An edited version of the talk appeared as "Worker-Community Ownership in Youngstown?," *WIN*, Jan. 25, 1979.

21. *Brier Hill Unionist*, Oct.-Nov. 1977.

22. This paragraph is based on notes I took at the time.

23. Gar Alperovitz and Jeff Faux, "Youngstown Lessons," *New York Times*, Nov. 3, 1977.

24. Gar Alperovitz and Jeff Faux, " 'Full Employment,' With a Different Focus," *New York Times*, Apr. 15, 1978.

25. *Seven Days*, Aug. 1978 (asbestos mine); *United Mine Workers Journal*, Dec. 16–31, 1976 (Rushton mine); *WIN*, Nov. 24, 1977 (plywood plants and International Group Plans); *New Hampshire Times*, Oct. 5, 1977 (Bates Manufacturing Company); *The Progressive*, Aug. 1978 (Herkimer furniture factory); *Working Papers*, May-June 1979 (Saratoga Springs knitting mill); *In These Times*, Oct. 8–14, 1980 and *Wall Street Journal*, Dec. 8, 1980 (South Bend Lathe Company).

26. *Congressional Record*, Mar. 1, 1978. Congressman Lundine, formerly mayor of Jamestown, New York, mentions four additional firms in the state of New York owned by workers in the course of his speech.

27. George Beetle to William A. Sullivan, Dec. 15, 1977, letter of transmittal accompanying the WREDA study.

28. National Center for Economic Alternatives, "Youngstown Demonstration Action Project: Summary of Preliminary Findings" (Apr. 11, 1978), page 4; Western Reserve Economic Development Agency, *New Steel at Campbell: A Study of the Feasibility of Reopening the Campbell Works* (Dec. 16, 1977), pages 53–54.

29. NCEA, "Youngstown," page 4; WREDA, *New Steel*, page 38.

30. NCEA, "Youngstown," page 4; WREDA, *New Steel*, page 39.

31. NCEA, "Youngstown," page 7 ($473 million); WREDA, *New Steel*, pages 42–58 ($535 million). In the final report released in September 1978, NCEA projected the capital needed for the "electric furnace alternative" as $525 million, a figure almost identical to Beetle's initial forecast. NCEA, *Youngstown Demonstration Planning Project: Final Report—Summary* (Sept. 1978), page 21.

32. WREDA, *New Steel*, page 61, projected the following losses and profits at a Campbell Works reopened in fourth quarter 1978:

1978 ($63 million)
1979 ($141 million)
1980 ($119 million)
1981 ($85 million)
1982 ($16 million)
1983 $24 million
1984 $59 million
1985 $117 million

33. Brad Dewan and Karl Frieden, "Preliminary Recommendations of Worker/Community Ownership Structure for Reopened Campbell Works" (May 10, 1978).

34. Dewan and Frieden, page 13.

35. Dewan and Frieden, page 13.

36. Dewan and Frieden, page 16.

37. Dewan and Frieden, page 11.

38. Staughton Lynd to Executive Committee, Steering Committee, the

Youngstown Community, Dec. 8, 1978. Karl Frieden wrote another contribution to the Alperovitz feasibility study entitled "Worker Democracy and Productivity." He surveyed American instances of worker participation in management and found increases in productivity up to 20 per cent and more.

39. Statement before the Subcommittee on Trade, House Ways and Means Committee, Sept. 20, 1977. Also *Steelworkers Legislative Newsletter*, Sept. 20, 1977.

40. For example, *The Yield*, the newspaper produced by Youngstown Sheet & Tube for its employees, stated in its issue of Sept.-Oct. 1977, pages 4–5: "Imports, red tape, inflation, de facto price controls plague the American Steel Industry."

41. United Steelworkers of America, *The Foreign Competition Hoax: Industry's Newest Excuse for Not Resolving Steelworker Problems* (1959). Thanks to Los Angeles steelworker Carl Kessler for providing a copy of this pamphlet.

42. The resolution adopted by the District 31 conference was reprinted in *Steelworker Rights*, a rank-and-file newspaper put out at the Republic Steel mill in Cleveland.

43. The following history of the Experimental Negotiating Agreement was compiled in preparation for trial of a law suit challenging the ENA, *Aikens v. Abel*, 373 F. Supp. 425 (W.D. Pa. 1974).

44. United Steelworkers of America, *A New Era: Installation of I. W. Abel*, page 18 (emphasis added).

45. *Business Week*, Nov. 18, 1967.

46. *Steel Labor,* Dec. 1967 (emphasis added).

47. *Wall Street Journal*, July 24, 1972.

48. Testimony of Bernard Kleiman, Transcript, pages 215, 216, 256, 267, 274–75, *Aikens v. Abel*.

49. *Steel Labor*, Apr. 1973.

50. Mann's statement occurs in an affidavit dated December 17, 1973 and executed in preparation for trial of *Aikens v. Abel*.

51. Philip Shabecoff, "No-Strike Steel Accord Periled," *New York Times*, Sept. 14, 1973.

52. Bureau of Labor Statistics, *Employment and Earnings: United States, 1907–1970*, pages 11, 97, 235, 432, 439.

53. Leaflet, "Steelworkers at the Crossroads in 1976."

54. *Youngstown Vindicator*, Sept. 28, 1976.

55. *Pittsburgh Post-Gazette*, Feb. 25, 1982.

56. "USW May Sue S & T Over Cuts," *Youngstown Vindicator*, Oct. 14, 1977.

57. Frank Leseganich to local union presidents, Oct. 25, 1977.

58. Frank Leseganich to Staughton Lynd, Dec. 5, 1977.

59. James W. Smith, "Effects of the Proposed Merger of LTV and Lykes on USWA Members," pages 37–38.

60. Interview with Duane Irving by Carol Greenwald and Dorie Krauss.

61. James W. Smith to Frank Leseganich and others, "National Center for Economic Alternatives Summary of Preliminary Findings" (May 3, 1978).

62. In 1973 Beacon Press published a book by Alperovitz and myself entitled *Strategy and Program: Two Essays Toward A New American Socialism.* Never a best seller, the book enjoyed lively sales in 1977–79 after the steel industry and the international union learned of its existence. It has a bright red cover.

63. This summary is based on a hand-written summary of Mann's remarks provided by Gerald Dickey.

64. *Brier Hill Unionist*, Sept.-Oct. 1978.

65. Id.

66. "And Now, the McBride Plan . . . ," *Youngstown Vindicator*, Sept. 25, 1978.

67. Dale Peskin, "Steel Targets 3 Coalitionists," *Youngstown Vindicator*, May 28, 1978.

68. *Youngstown Vindicator*, June 6, 1978.

69. Executive Committee minutes, Aug. 29, 1978.

70. This may be as good a place as any to suggest the national interest in the Coalition by citing the following articles, which are by no means exhaustive: "An Alternative to Trade Restraints," *Washington Post*, Oct. 8, 1977; "U.S. Funds Available to Reopen Plants, Steel Group is Told," *New York Times*, Nov. 26, 1977; "Youngstown, Ohio Effort is Launched to Revive Mill," *Wall Street Journal*, Dec. 13, 1977; "Ohio city will try to run steel mill," *Baltimore Sun*, Dec. 16, 1977; "H.U.D. Rushing Study to Revive an Ohio Steel Works," *New York Times*, Dec. 31, 1977; "Youngstown: Recovery Model?," *Catholic Times*, Jan. 13, 1978; "Save Youngstown—Save America," *Grapevine* [of the Joint Strategy and Action Committee of the Methodist and Presbyterian Denominations], Jan. 1978; "Youngstown: Can It Work?," *Environmental Action*, Feb. 25, 1978; "Steelyard Blues" and "Making Nectar for Lemon Socialism," *Mother Jones*, Apr. 1978; "The Steel Crisis in Youngstown," *America*, Apr. 29, 1979; "Desperate Jobless City Seeks to Buy Failing Steel Plant," *Washington Post*, May 9, 1978; "Does Youngstown Have A Prayer? The Clergy's Gamble to Save Steel," *Akron Beacon*, May 21, 1978; "The Drama of Youngstown," *National Catholic Reporter*, June 2, 1978; "Youngstown Seeks a Grasp on its Fading Steel Industry," *New York Times*, June 20, 1978; "Youngstown—Fire and Hope," *United Presbyterian*, Aug. 1978; "Youngstown Group Presses to Reopen Steel Mill," *Washington Post*, Sept. 19, 1978; "Still Crusading in Youngstown," *Business Week*, Sept. 25,

1978; "Will Youngstown Point the Way?," *The Progressive*, Oct. 1978; "Two Views on the Youngstown Project," *Alternatives*, Winter 1978–79; "Youngstown Fights Back," *New Republic*, Jan. 6, 1979; "Worker/Community Ownership in Youngstown?," *WIN*, Jan. 25, 1979; "Roulette at the Casino-on-the-Potomac, or: Will Youngstown win its biggest prize?," *Metal Producing*, April 1979; "The Fight to Save the Steel Mills," *New York Review of Books*, Apr. 19, 1979; "Going Bust in Youngstown," *New Republic*, May 1979.

71. This memorandum was obtained by reporter Dale Peskin through a Freedom of Information Act suit and made public by him in an article published on the third anniversary of the Campbell Works shutdown announcement, "Memo suggests Carter duped Coalition," *Warren Tribune*, Sept. 19, 1980.

72. "$100 Million U.S. Aid is Pledged to Valley," *Youngstown Vindicator*, Sept. 28, 1978.

73. "Coalition Plan Leading In Bid for Federal Aid," *Youngstown Vindicator*, Sept. 29, 1978; "Religious Leaders Backed in Plan to Reopen Steel Mill," *Washington Post*, Sept. 29, 1978.

74. *Youngstown Vindicator*, Oct. 15, 1978.

75. Jack Watson to James W. Malone and others, Oct. 18, 1978.

76. This memorandum was written before September 15, 1978, when the NCEA Final Report was released, because it refers to that report as something NCEA "will recommend." This and the two memoranda from Williams to Hall summarized in the same paragraph were obtained by the Ecumenical Coalition through a Freedom of Information Act suit.

77. Dale Peskin, "Memo suggests Carter duped Coalition," *Warren Tribune*, Sept. 19, 1980.

78. Thomas C. Graham to James W. Malone, Aug. 11, 1978.

79. *Cleveland Plain Dealer*, Nov. 8, 1978.

80. R. G. Allen to Edward Stanton, Nov. 17, 1978.

81. Thomas Petzinger, "Bouncing Back: A Year After Closing of Youngstown Steel Plant, Economy, Employment Are Surprisingly Bright," *Wall Street Journal*, Oct. 18, 1978.

82. Linda Snyder Hayes, "Youngstown Bounces Back," *Fortune*, Dec. 17, 1979.

83. James H. Burt to Richard P. Gray, Dec. 6, 1978. Bishop Burt and Mr. Gray were both members of the Episcopal Church. Gray sent a copy of his remarks to Burt.

84. Certificate of Inspectors of Election, Lykes Corporation shareholders meeting, Dec. 5, 1978.

85. Executive Committee minutes, Jan. 23, 1979.

86. "Steel Union, Making Concession, Backs Plant's Reopening in Ohio," *New York Times*, Mar. 30, 1979; James W. Smith, "Comments on

the Rosenbloom Analysis of the Youngstown Report, and the Revised Application for Urban Development Action Grant, City of Youngstown, for the Ecumenical Coalition of the Mahoning Valley," Mar. 21, 1979.

87. *Cleveland Plain Dealer*, Mar. 30, 1979.

88. On families at work, see William Kornblum, "Mill Work and Primary Groups," Chapter 2 of *Blue Collar Community* (University of Chicago Press, 1974), pages 36–67.

89. Linda Snyder Hayes, "Youngstown Bounces Back," *Fortune*, Dec. 17, 1979.

90. *Youngstown Vindicator*, Mar. 20, 1979.

91. According to "Reassessing Loan Aid for Steel," *New York Times*, Jan. 2, 1981, the following loan guarantees were made by EDA to steel companies seeking help from the steel industry loan guarantee fund:

Table 8

Company	Date	Amount and Purpose
Korf Industries	June 1978	$19.1 million to sustain operations
Phoenix Steel	May 1979	$38 million to sustain operations, install pollution abatement equipment and improve steel finishing capacity
Wheeling-Pittsburgh Steel	Aug. 1979	$90 million to install pollution abatement equipment and to construct a rail mill
Jones & Laughlin Steel	Sept. 1979	$99.9 million to install pollution control equipment and to improve capacity
Wisconsin Steel	Nov. 1979	$90 million to sustain operations and to improve capacity

92. Quoted in National Center for Economic Alternatives, *Youngstown Demonstration Planning Project: Final Report—Summary*, page 70.

93. Id.

94. Executive Committee minutes, Apr. 5, 1979.

Part II. The Struggle For Brier Hill

1. The Final Judgment in U.S. v. Ling-Temco-Vought, Inc, et al., Civ. 69-638 (W.D.Pa.), entered June 10, 1970, provided: "LTV is enjoined and restrained, and J&L is enjoined and restrained, if not divested, for ten (10) years from the date of entry of this Final Judgment (1) from acquiring one percent (1%) or more of the voting securities in any company the assets of which [are] in excess of One Hundred Million Dollars ($100,000,000) . . .

without first obtaining the consent of the plaintiff [United States Department of Justice]. . . .''

2. Executive Committee minutes, June 26, 1978.

3. Ecumenical Coalition of the Mahoning Valley, et al. v. U.S. Department of Justice, Civ. 79–484–Y (N.D. Ohio). The suit was settled in the summer of 1979 when the Department agreed to provide substantially all the documents requested.

4. G. S. Kimmel to J. T. Lykes, Jr. and F. A. Nemec, Nov. 30, 1976.

5. Id.

6. "Outline of Preliminary Approach to Studying Alternatives to Steel Division Problems, as defined at the January 13, 1977 [Board of Directors] Meeting."

7. "Preliminary Report presented to Executive Committee on sale of Indiana Harbor—February 11, 1977."

8. Eric F. Kaplan, Anti-Trust Division, United States Department of Justice, "Memorandum to Files: LTV-Lykes—Interview with Officers of Lykes," Mar. 27, 1978.

9. Gary L. Swenson, First Boston Corporation to George S. Kimmel, Lykes Corporation, June 13, 1978.

10. Eric F. Kaplan, "Memorandum to Files: Lykes-LTV Merger—Meeting with First Boston," Mar. 27, 1978.

11. Eric F. Kaplan, "Memorandum to Files: Lykes-LTV Merger—Meeting with Lehman Brothers Kuhn Loeb," Mar. 27, 1978.

12. Lykes Corporation, "J & L Strategies" [1975], pages 23–24.

13. Lehman Brothers, "Confidential Memorandum to the LTV Corporation concerning Potential Acquisitions," Aug. 1977.

14. "Melding Lykes and LTV Steel," Business Week, Dec. 18, 1978.

15. Lehman Brothers, "Confidential Memorandum to the LTV Corporation concerning Potential Acquisitions," Aug. 1977.

16. John [Lawrence], J. Lawrence, Inc. to Raymond A. Hay, LTV Corporation, Sept. 9, 1977.

17. Deposition of William R. Roesch, pages 6–7, and Transcript of the trial of March 17–21, 1980, pages 142–147 (testimony of William R. Roesch), in the case of Local 1330, et al. v. U.S. Steel, 492 F. Supp. 1 (N.D. Ohio 1980), aff'd in part and rev'd in part, 631 F.2d 1264 (6th Cir. 1980).

18. Department of Industry, Government of Great Britain, "British Steel Corporation Chairman Appointed," May 1, 1980. Thanks to the Rev. Ray Taylor of Wales for providing this document.

19. Many of the facts in the foregoing paragraph are derived from reporter John Greenman's dramatic investigative reporting of the merger decision in the Warren Tribune, Dec. 9–14, 1979.

20. John Greenman, "Bell ignored 'messianic' staff," Warren Tribune, Dec. 12, 1979.

21. John Greenman, "LTV bought merger influence," *Warren Tribune*, Dec. 14, 1979.

22. Ecumenical Coalition of the Mahoning Valley, "Memorandum to the United States Department of Justice Regarding the Proposed Merger of the Lykes Corporation and the LTV Corporation," pages 7, 8–16.

23. Lykes and LTV Corporations, "Memorandum to the Department of Justice in Support of the Proposed Merger of the LTV Corporation and Lykes Corporation," Jan. 13, 1978, page 38.

24. *Brier Hill Unionist*, Jan. 1979, quoting "Melding Lykes and LTV Steel," *Business Week*, Dec. 18, 1978.

25. *Brier Hill Unionist*, Jan. 1978.

26. Ed Mann, President and Gerald Dickey, Recording Secretary to Eric F. Kaplan, Anti-Trust Division, United States Department of Justice, Dec. 29, 1977.

27. "Memorandum to the Department of Justice . . . ," Jan. 13, 1978, page 41.

28. Gerald Dickey, Minutes of meeting at Justice Department, Anti-Trust Division, Old Star Building, Washington, D.C., Jan. 23, 1978.

29. *Youngstown Vindicator*, Feb. 3, 1978. See also Agis Salpukas, "Steel Union Offers a Lykes-LTV Merger Conditional Support," *New York Times*, Apr. 11, 1978.

30. Rene A. Torrado, Memorandum to Files, June 16, 1978.

31. Alex George, President, Local 1211, to Rene Torrado, May 18, 1978, and to the same effect, Paul Piccirilli, General Griever, to Eric Kaplan, Mar. 6, 1978. Samuel Myers, Recording Secretary, Local 1418, to Patricia Harris, Secretary, Dept. of Housing and Urban Development, Mar. 27, 1978. Norman Purdue, President, Bob Rospierski, Chairman of the Grievance Committee, and Henry Rowsey, Vice President, Local 1011, to Donald Baker, Asst. Attorney General, May 31, 1978, and to the same effect, Norman Purdue to Griffin Bell, June 12, 1978.

32. Ed Mann, President, and Gerald Dickey, Recording Secretary, Local 1462, to Patricia Harris, Secretary, Dept. of Housing and Urban Development, Mar. 30, 1978.

33. Press release, United States Department of Justice, June 21, 1978.

34. "Melding Lykes and LTV Steel," *Business Week*, Dec. 18, 1978.

35. *Youngstown Vindicator*, Dec. 10, 1978.

36. "Joint Proxy Statement for Annual Meeting of Stockholders of the LTV Corporation . . . and Special Meeting of Stockholders of Lykes Corporation," Oct. 27, 1978, page 10.

37. Ed Mann, President, and Gerald Dickey, Recording Secretary, to Gordon Allen, Nov. 20, 1978.

38. R. G. Allen to Ed Mann, Nov. 28, 1978.

39. Ed Mann, President, to Frank Leseganich, Nov. 30, 1978.

40. *Brier Hill Unionist*, Jan. 1979.

41. Telegram, Ed Mann, President and Gerald Dickey, Recording Secretary, to Frank Valenta, Director, Dec. 19, 1978.

42. *Brier Hill Unionist*, Nov. 1978.

43. In Alice and Staughton Lynd, ed., *Rank and File: Personal Histories by Working-Class Organizers* (second revised edition; Princeton University Press, 1981), Ed and John tell at pages 281–83 of a wildcat at Brier Hill in the late 1960s. The wildcat was caused when a fellow worker named Tony, with seven days to go to retirement, was killed by a truck backing up. The local had previously filed a grievance asking that trucks backing up have a warning system.

44. *Youngstown Vindicator*, Dec. 20, 1978.

45. William Shuzman, Field Attorney, National Labor Relations Board, Region 8, to Lloyd McBride, International President, United Steelworkers of America, Jan. 16, 1979. The international subsequently made a pro forma request that the NLRB consider the unfair labor practice charge. The Board did so, and decided not to issue a complaint.

46. Frank Leseganich to Frank Valenta, Dec. 20, 1978.

47. Mr. McBride's citation to the constitution of the United Steelworkers of America was selective.

The USWA constitution states, "The International Union shall be the contracting party in all collective bargaining agreements and all such agreements shall be signed by the International Officers," Article XVII, Section 1, but also, "The International Union *and the Local Union to which the member belongs* shall act exclusively as the member's agent to represent the member in . . . grievances and other matters relating to terms and conditions of employment or arising out of the employer-employee relationship," Article XVII, Section 3 (emphasis added).

48. *Youngstown Vindicator*, Jan. 7, 1979.

49. *Brier Hill Unionist*, Feb. 1979.

50. *Youngstown Vindicator*, Jan. 19, 1979.

51. *Youngstown Vindicator*, Jan. 20, 1979.

52. *Brier Hill Unionist*, Feb. 1979.

53. Local 1462, "How Long Will Your Job Last?" [Mar. 1979].

54. R. G. Allen to "Dear Youngstown District Employee," Mar. 30, 1979. Later, the company extended the period during which the Works was "idled but not permanently shutdown" for two more months.

55. "The Conflict: New Forms of Action," an account of the struggle at Longwy kindly made available by Professor Olivier Kourchid, Group de Sociologie du Travail, Université de Paris, and translated by Steve Greenhouse of N.Y.U. Law School.

56. Id.

57. *Brier Hill Unionist*, Nov. 1978.
58. *Brier Hill Unionist*, Mar.-Apr. 1979.
59. *1397 Rank and File*, Apr. 1980.
60. *Youngstown Vindicator*, Sept. 26, 1980.

Part III. The Battle for U.S. Steel's Youngstown Works

1. *Ohio Works Organizer*, Sept. 1979.
2. Lake Erie Alliance, et al. v. U.S. Army Corps of Engineers, Civ. 79-110 (W.D. Pa.). This suit is described in Tri-State Conference on the Impact of Steel, "Environmental Impact of New Industrial Plants: The Case of Conneaut," 1980 *Utah L. Rev.* 331. The suit was dismissed by the District Court on November 23, 1981, and as this is being written is on appeal.
3. *New York Times*, Dec. 1, 1979.
4. *Youngstown Vindicator*, Dec. 28 and 31, 1979.
5. Transcript of the trial of March 17-21, 1980, in the case of *Local 1330, et al. v. U.S. Steel,* 492 F. Supp. 1 (N.D. Ohio 1980), aff'd in part and rev'd in part, 631 F.2d 1264 (6th Cir. 1980)(hereafter Transcript), pages 317-319 (testimony of William Kirwan), and interviews with union participants.
6. Interview with Michael Mignogna, grievance committeeman at Local 1307. According to Mr. Mignogna this meeting took place on June 18, 1979, and the supervisor was Robert Griffith.
7. Transcript, pages 320-321 (testimony of William Kirwan), and interviews with union participants.
8. According to Vasquez, Kirwan told him this at a scheduled meeting about a grievance. Perhaps the superintendent was indirectly asking the union's help to save the mill.
9. "Tri-State Conference Calls For Emergency Action To Save Ohio Works," Oct. 31, 1979. The story was carried on the front page of the *Warren Tribune*, Nov. 2, 1979 ("Ohio Works facing end, group says") and on an inside page of the *Youngstown Vindicator*, Nov. 2, 1979 ("Steel Group Joins in Efforts To 'Save' U.S. Steel Facilities").
10. Robert Appleyard to David Roderick, Nov. 5, 1979.
11. *Warren Tribune*, Nov. 2, 1979. Greg Garland, the reporter who wrote the story, testified at trial as to what Foote had told him, Transcript, pages 57-62. Bob Vasquez testified that Foote had made the same statement at the November 1 forum, Transcript, pages 464-465.
12. *Youngstown Vindicator*, Nov. 25, 1979.
13. U.S. Steel public announcement, Nov. 27, 1979.
14. I have been unable to identify the author of this memorandum.

15. "Hot Strip Mill Loadings—New Lake Plant Location" in U.S. Steel Engineering Services, Design and Construction, "Lake Front Plant," Apr. 22, 1975.

16. Douglas R. Sease, "Testing Mettle: At Three Steelmakers, New Chief Executives Try for Turnarounds," *Wall Street Journal*, July 22, 1980.

17. Transcript, pages 248–250.

18. Transcript, pages 654–663.

19. *Youngstown Vindicator*, Dec. 28, 1979.

20. *Warren Tribune*, Nov. 30, 1979.

21. *New York Times*, Dec. 1, 1979.

22. *Youngstown Vindicator*, Dec. 1, 1979.

23. *Warren Tribune*, Nov. 30, 1979.

24. *Warren Tribune*, Nov. 30, 1979.

25. *Warren Tribune*, Nov. 30, 1979.

26. *Warren Tribune*, Dec. 1, 1979. *Pittsburgh Post-Gazette*, Dec. 1, 1979.

27. Press release, December 11, 1979.

28. "Will Ask Court Bar Steel Closings," *Youngstown Vindicator*, Dec. 11, 1979.

29. "USW Official Is Dubious On Effort to Save Two Mills," *Youngstown Vindicator*, Dec. 12, 1979.

30. "Cruel deception: Mill opening efforts described as fruitless," *Warren Tribune*, Dec. 19, 1979.

31. *Youngstown Vindicator*, Dec. 21, 1979.

32. *Warren Tribune*, Dec. 23, 1979.

33. "Steel panel backs suit," *Warren Tribune*, Dec. 23, 1979; "Steel Suit Support Pledged by Carney," *Youngstown Vindicator*, Dec. 23, 1979.

34. *Warren Tribune*, Dec. 28, 1979. *Youngstown Vindicator*, Dec. 28, 1979.

35. *Youngstown Vindicator*, Dec. 28, 1979.

36. *Youngstown Vindicator*, Dec. 28, 1979.

37. *Warren Tribune*, Jan. 29, 1980.

38. Transcript, pages 469–471.

39. Transcipt, page 472.

40. *Youngstown Vindicator*, Dec. 29, 1979. *Wall Street Journal*, Dec. 31, 1979.

41. *Youngstown Vindicator*, Jan. 22, 1980.

42. Eric Leif Davin, "Workers occupy U.S. Steel, protest Youngstown closings," *In These Times*, Feb. 6–12, 1980. The following direct quotations from Ed Mann and Bob Vasquez are from a tape recording made by Mr. Davin.

43. *Warren Tribune*, Feb. 3, 1980.

44. *Youngstown Vindicator*, Jan. 28, 1980. *In These Times*, Feb. 6–12, 1980.

45. Interview with Arlene Denney by Carol Greenwald and Dorie Krauss.

46. *Warren Tribune*, Jan. 30, 1980.

47. Transcript, page 374.

48. *Warren Tribune*, January 31, 1980.

49. *Cleveland Plain Dealer*, Jan. 30, 1980.

50. Ms. Hopkins tape recorded the exchange. The recording was played at the trial. Transcript, pages 78–79.

51. *Youngstown Vindicator*, Feb. 2, 1980.

52. *Youngstown Vindicator*, Feb. 8, 1980.

53. *Youngstown Vindicator*, Feb. 2, 1980.

54. Proceedings Had Before the Honorable Thomas D. Lambros . . . On Thursday, February 28, 1980, pages 2–3.

55. Proceedings, page 3.

56. Proceedings, page 5.

57. Proceedings, pages 5–6.

58. Proceedings, pages 6–7.

59. Proceedings, page 7.

60. Proceedings, page 8.

61. Proceedings, page 9.

62. Proceedings, pages 9–11.

63. Proceedings, pages 11–12.

64. Proceedings, pages 13–15.

65. Proceedings, page 79.

66. Transcript, pages 282–283.

67. Transcript, pages 283–284.

68. Transcript, page 306.

69. Transcript, pages 307–308, quoting W. H. Kirwan, C. L. Richards, Jr., and R. M. Greer to Editor, *Wall Street Journal*, Apr. 26, 1979.

70. Transcript, page 311, quoting "1980 Facility Budget, Youngstown Works."

71. Transcript, page 312.

72. Transcript, page 322.

73. Transcript, page 323.

74. Transcript, pages 324–328.

75. Transcript, page 357.

76. Transcript, page 361, quoting "Youngstown Works: A Fresh Look."

77. Transcript, pages 361–362.

78. Transcript, pages 368–369.

79. Transcript, pages 369–370.

80. Transcript, pages 175 (Roesch), 240–241 (Roderick).

81. Deposition of William H. Kirwan, page 36.

82. Transcript, pages 427–428.

83. Transcript, pages 807–808.

84. Transcript, page 406.

85. 492 F.Supp. at 10.

86. This brief was filed on behalf of: the International Chemical Workers Union, AFL-CIO; the United Rubber, Chalk, and Linoleum, and Plastic Workers International Union, AFL-CIO; the Oil, Chemical and Atomic Workers International Union; the National Conference of Black Lawyers; the National Lawyers Guild; the Associacion Nacional de Empleados Publicos; Black Economic Survival; the Coalition for a People's Alternative in 1980; the Coalition of Black Trade Unionists; the Dayton Full Employment Committee; the Federacion de Musicos de Puerto Rico; the Grand Jury Project; the Interreligious Foundation for Community Organization; Local 455 of the International Association of Bridge, Structural and Ornamental Iron Workers; Congressman John Conyers, Jr.; Legal Services of New Jersey (concerned because of the closing of the Ford plant at Mahwah, New Jersey); the National Black Political Assembly; the Coordinating Committee for Trade Union Action and Democracy; the National Emergency Civil Liberties Committee; the National Employment Law Project; the National Labor Law Center; the National Organization for Legal Services Workers; the Teamsters for a Democratic Union; the Texas Farm Workers Union; the United Farm Workers, AFL-CIO; the Union Independiente de Trabajadores de Aeropuerto de Puerto Rico; the Union Independiente de Trabajadores de Servicios Legales de Puerto Rico; and the United Coalition.

87. 631 F.2d at 1283.

88. Neil A. Eisner to Mahoning Valley Economic Development Corporation, Oct. 22, 1980.

89. *New York Times*, Nov. 6, 1980.

90. This memorandum was obtained during pre-trial "discovery."

91. *Pittsburgh Press*, Aug. 3, 1981.

92. "Asks Firm To Drop Lawsuit," *Youngstown Vindicator*, Sept. 24, 1980; "Says Toro Can Reopen Mills," *Youngstown Vindicator*, Nov. 9, 1980; "Fears Report Kills Community Steel," *Youngstown Vindicator*, Nov. 14, 1980. The author of the first letter was a steelworker said to have been promised a job by Toro. The author of the third letter was the operator of a steelhauling trucking company.

93. Ed Weisheimer to "Dear Colleagues," [c. Aug. 5, 1980].

94. John Greenman, "Steel deal needed now," *Warren Tribune*, Sept. 27, 1980.

95. "Calls Steel Suit Lesson For Nation," *Youngstown Vindicator*, Nov. 14, 1980.

96. "Clouds Cleared over McDonald," *Youngstown Vindicator*, Nov. 14, 1980.

97. "Valley is winner in mill suit," *Warren Tribune*, Nov. 16, 1980.

98. *In These Times*, Nov. 26–Dec. 9, 1980.

99. This is Toro's own estimate. *Youngstown Vindicator*, July 24, 1980.

100. Sidney Fine, *Sit-Down: The General Motors Strike of 1936–1937* (University of Michigan Press, 1969), pages 193–195.

101. James J. Ling to Frank O'Brien, May 31, 1970.

102. *Business Week*, Jan. 9, 1978.

103. "Confidential—Assumptions for Cases," Sept. 29, 1977.

104. "Memorandum to the Department of Justice in Support of the Proposed Merger of the LTV Corporation and Lykes Corporation," Jan. 13, 1978, page 40.

105. J. Robert Kramer II, Memorandum to Files, "Meeting with Lykes-LTV Officials," May 23, 1978, page 4.

106. "The New LTV Corporation," attachment to Taggart Whipple to Hon. Griffin B. Bell, June 14, 1978.

107. EPA, *Environmental News*, May 22, 1979.

108. *1980 Annual Report*, page 29.

109. *New York Times*, Dec. 5, 1980.

110. *1980 Annual Report*, page 10.

111. *Wall Street Journal*, May 5, 1981.

Part IV. Some Conclusions From What Happened in Youngstown

1. Los Angeles Times News Service, *Pittsburgh Press*, Nov. 7, 1980.

2. Transcript, page 939.

3. *Youngstown Vindicator*, Feb. 25, 1982.

4. Council on Wage and Price Stability, *Report on Economic Conditions within the American Steel Industry* (1977), page 82; and Office of Technology Assessment, *Technology and Steel Industry Competitiveness* (1980), pages 312, 315. A "tonne," or metric ton, weighs 2,204.6 pounds.

5. L. E. Malin, General Manager, Engineering Services, U.S. Steel to M. B. Lanier, II, Director—Facilities Plans, U.S. Steel, June 19, 1979.

6. "Youngstown Works: A Fresh Look" and "1980 Facility Budget, Youngstown Works," Plaintiffs' Exhibits 69 and 70 in the case of *Local 1330, et al. v. U.S. Steel*, 492 F.Supp. 1 (N.D. Ohio 1980), aff'd in part and rev'd in part, 631 F.2d 1264 (6th Cir. 1980).

7. *United States v. Bethlehem Steel Corporation*, 168 F.Supp. 576, 616 (S.D. N.Y. 1958).

8. Policy and Management Associates, Inc., "Socioeconomic Costs and Benefits of the Community-Worker Ownership Plan to the Youngstown-Warren SMSA" (1978).

9. *Youngstown Vindicator*, Mar. 5, 1981; Mar. 1, 1982; Mar. 28, 1982. In Bucks County, Pennsylvania, where United States Steel's Fairless Works is the largest employer, Chase Econometrics forecast that shutdown of the Works would cause a loss of 8,000 jobs at Fairless, 1,600 jobs in other manufacturing industries, and 11,000 non-manufacturing jobs. Don Wolf, "Fairless Works: What's on road ahead," *Bucks County Courier Times*, Dec. 2, 1980. In fact, by the end of 1981 there were already 4,500 Fairless Works employees laid off, according to the local union president there.

10. *Youngstown Vindicator*, June 2, 1981.

11. Stephen J. Kotis, "A Family Game." My thanks to Duane Irving for this poem.

12. Iron and Steel Trades Confederation, *New Deal for Steel* (1980), pages 76–79. At page 177 this study cites B. Rowthorn and T. Ward, "How to run a company and run down an economy: the effects of closing down steel-making in Corby," *Cambridge Journal of Economics* (Dec. 1979). The Iron and Steel Trades Confederation is the leading trade union in the British steel industry.

13. U.S. Army Corps of Engineers, *Final Environmental Impact Statement* (1979), volume 3, pages 4–104 and 105.

14. Felix Rohatyn, "Reconstructing America," *The New York Review of Books*, Mar. 5, 1981, page 20.

15. Helen Ginsburg, "A National Commitment: Full Employment The Swedish Way," *The Nation*, Dec. 6, 1980.

16. David Moberg, "Detroit: I Do Mind Moving," *In These Times*, Feb. 4–10, 1981; William Serrin, "Huge New G.M. Plant, Like Many, to Get Subsidies," *New York Times*, Feb. 25, 1981.

17. "More Moving Violations," *In These Times*, Nov. 18–24, 1981.

18. Federal Trade Commission, *The United States Steel Industry and its International Competitors: Trends and Factors Determining International Competitiveness* (1977), pages 504–505.

19. Office of Technology Assessment, *Technology and Steel Industry Competitiveness* (1980), page 126.

20. "Big Steel's Liquidation," *Business Week*, Sept. 17, 1979; OTA, *Technology and Steel Industry Competitiveness* (1980), page 80.

21. *1979 Annual Report*, page 11.

22. "U.S. Steel Closing Down," *N. Haven Advocate*, Dec. 5, 1979.

23. "The Turnaround at U.S. Steel," *New York Times*, Feb. 19, 1981.

24. Defendant United States Steel Corporation's Motion to Modify Consent Decree of July 10, 1979, United States of America, et al. v. United States Steel Corporation, Civ. 79–709 (W.D.Pa.), page 12.

25. David Roderick, "Is There An OSEC In Our Future?," a speech before the Purchasing Management Assocation, Houston, Texas, Sept. 11, 1979.

26. U.S. Steel's express commitment to *reduction* of its steelmaking capacity is documented in such articles as Helen Shapiro and David Volk, "Steelyard Blues: New Structures in Steel" (North American Congress on Latin America pamphlet, Jan.-Feb. 1979), page 15; "Big Steel's Liquidation," *Business Week*, Sept. 17, 1979; "U.S. Steel: Shrinking to Survive," *New York Times*, July 20, 1980; "Steel Girds: Industry Moves to Scrap Excess Capacity, Diversify," *Barron's*, Sept. 1, 1980; "Big Steel Recasts Itself," *Fortune*, Apr. 6, 1981.

27. Charles A. Bradford, "Japanese Steel Industry: A Comparison With Its United States Counterpart," June 24, 1977, page 26.

28. Argus Research Corporation, "Steel: An Industry In Flux," Aug. 31, 1977, page 2.

29. Previously investment was depreciated over an estimated useful life of about 15 years. The new law permits depreciation of new investment over 10 years in the case of buildings, and 5 years in the case of machinery.

30. Joel Hirschhorn, "Putting Steel into Steel," *New York Times*, Dec. 17, 1980.

31. *New York Times*, Aug. 17, 1981.

32. Section 113(e)(1)(B) of the Clean Air Act as amended by the Steel Industry Compliance Extension Act of 1981 permits a company to postpone compliance with the requirements of the Clean Air Act provided, *inter alia*, the company makes

> additional capital investments in the iron- and steel-producing operations owned or operated by such persons, *and located in communities which already contain iron- and steel-producing operations*, to improve their efficiency and productivity. . . . (Emphasis added)

33. *1980 Annual Report*, page 10.

34. Thomas C. Hayes, "Revival at Dying G.M. Factory: Workers Plan to Buy Plant and Cut Pay," *New York Times*, Oct. 26, 1981. Rube Singer, a former president of Local 376, UAW, points out that the heart of the plan is a commitment by General Motors to purchase $100 million a year of the plant's product for three years, and to buy 100,000 shares of preferred stock in the new corporation for $10 million. *In These Times*, Feb. 17-23, 1982.

35. *In These Times*, Oct. 8-14, 1980; *Wall Street Journal*, Dec. 8, 1980.

36. *Seven Days*, Aug. 1978.

37. Terri Minsky, "Workers Who Bought Iowa Slaughterhouse Regret That They Did," *Wall Street Journal*, Dec. 2, 1981. Union officers and others close to the Rath situation rebut that more than 1,000 workers at the plant signed a statement rejecting Ms. Minsky's conclusions. Taylor's comment is quoted in Jan Schaffer, "Rath workers go whole hog at owning firm," *Philadelphia Inquirer*, Mar. 14, 1982.

38. Steffi Ronder Domike, "Producer Co-operatives in the Pacific Northwest Plywood Industry" (1975), pages 122-123.

39. Id., page 74.

40. Id., page 52.

41. This account of events at Republic Rubber is based on an interview with Peter Broadwater, chief executive of Republic Rubber, Feb. 12, 1981.

42. Frank O'Brien, "Introduction" to Tri-State Conference on the Impact of Steel, *What Can We Do About Plant Closings?* (1981).

43. *Agreement Between Carnegie-Illinois Corporation and the Steel Workers Organizing Committee*, Mar. 17, 1937, Section 8.

44. *1977 Basic Steel Contract*, Section 3.

45. See my "Investment Decisions and the Quid Pro Quo Myth," 29 *Case Western Reserve L. Rev.* 396 (1979).

46. *In These Times*, Nov. 26-Dec. 9, 1980.

47. *United Shoe Workers v. Brooks Shoe Mfg. Co.*, 183 F.Supp. 568, 569 (E.D. Pa. 1961), aff'd, 298 F.2d 277 (3d Cir. 1962).

48. *Jack Meilman*, 34 *Lab. Arb.* 771, 773 (Gray 1960).

49. United Steelworkers of America, "Basic Steel Industry Conference: a Statement of Goals and Objectives" (1980), page 13.

50. *1980 Basic Steel Contract*, Section XVI A.

51. *First National Maintenance Corporation v. NLRB*, 49 U.S.L.W. 4769 (1981).

52. *New York Times*, Feb. 17, 18, 19, 1981.

53. "Sit-in Stops Plant Closing in Ontario; UAW Supports Action," *Labor Notes*, Sept. 29, 1981.

54. The view of management motivation stated is dramatically illustrated by the interviews with company decisionmakers in Alfred Slote, *Termination: The Closing at Baker Plant* (Bobbs-Merrill, 1969). See especially the reminiscences of the plant manager quoted and paraphrased at pages 15–18, 36–40, 44–46.

The question of *work* and how it could be made more fulfilling by the people who actually do it, has never become an issue of public discussion in America. In the last decade there has been a growth in the literature about work, but almost none of it has been written by those who spend over half their waking lives doing it.

We are all hungry for images of ourselves, for identity and for aids to communicate the condition of our lives and the good in them. But the millions who do the so-called "unskilled," "semi-skilled," "craft," and even "professional" jobs in American workplaces are seldom, if ever, represented fairly in the popular literature and media of our nation. Commonly they are shown as clowns and culprits, near-apes or gum-smacking hollow-heads. It is rare to find any one of these media and fiction characters involved in the actual work of their occupation. Thus, the value of the contribution made by a majority of the citizenry is robbed of visibility and recognition.

The Singlejack *Little Book* effort is primarily directed at the publication of writings about, or related to, work, written by the people who are doing it or who have done it; and further, to writings which are designed to provide ideas which working people will find of practical use. We know that in workplaces around the nation there are writers (some of whom have not yet written) who need to see evidence that there are places where they can publish before they come forth. As we find some of them—and prove our existence to more—it is hoped that our success will encourage similar publishing endeavors.

WATERFRONT SUPERCARGO, *by Tom Murray*. For more than 30 years on the San Francisco Bay-area waterfront, Murray "kept book" on what went on around him. Starting in the 1930's, he details the dockside procedures for the movement of cargo that have all but vanished today—and the men who helped move it: Paintlocker Charlie, Chips, The Turk, Tanglefoot. Authentic and often funny, Murray's Little Book describes a life that has largely disappeared. (10–6) 59 pages $1.95

STEELMILL BLUES, *by Steve Packard*. Describing his experiences in the basic steel industry, Packard's Little Book represents one of the mainly overlooked benefits of the 1960's. In their aftermath, hundreds of youths with already developed writing skills became industrial workers and Packard is one of them. He writes from the heart, without affectation and with a lot of humor. (03–3) 31 pages 95¢

Labor Law for the Rank & Filer, *by Staughton Lynd*. Every day we see new assaults upon the unions and working people of our nation. This small book has one goal: to help both be more effective when the law is against them and to get more accomplished when the law is on their side. This newly revised edition is enlarged to 72 pages and has been brought up to date with the latest high court decisions, including sexual harassment. It assesses the six major Federal labor laws and unravels the intricate web of law and National Labor Relations Board decisions which dominate every American's working life. Thousands of copies of the first edition have been sold to local unions and rank and filers as an aid in grievance procedures, negotiations and organizing. (0–917300–04–1) $2.50

The Grievance: Poems from the Shop Floor, *by Martin Glaberman*. Although the long title-poem has circulated from hand-to-hand for years in the Detroit area—and is certainly the best/funniest treatment ever done on Pursuing a Grievance—Glaberman's remaining poems in this short collection touch on many aspects of working in auto that are sure to be familiar to anyone who has ever worked in a factory or shop. (12–2) 31 pages 95¢

Night Shift in a Pickle Factory, *by Steve Turner*. Seasonal cannery work in the northeast corner of our country—but the clanking, rattling old factory could be located in any number of places in the U.S.A. Turner sees it, understands it, and gets it all on paper for one of the best pieces of reporting of its type ever written. (13–0) 61 pages $1.95

Longshoring on the San Francisco Waterfront, *by Reg Theriault*, describes what it means to be a member of an occupation which undergoes an automation/mechanization revolution. Spanning the period from the 1950's to the 1980's, Theriault compares hand-handling cargo with containerization, and not only provides remarkable insight, but not-a-few laughs as well. (02–5) 30 pages 95¢

Foundry Foreman, Foundrymen, *by Lloyd Zimpel*. Two exceptional short stories that not only put-you-through the long shifts working in a foundry core room, but also show what it means to both be foreman as well as work "beneath" him. Two fine stories that will not soon be forgotten. (11–4) 60 pages $1.95

[If ordering directly, please add for postage: 25¢ for each 32-page book and 45¢ for each of the others. Californians please add 6½% sales tax.]

In the late 1960's, Staughton Lynd left college teaching in order to focus his work as a historian on the lives of rank and file labor unionists, particularly in the steel industry. Less than a decade later he became an attorney and joined a labor law firm in Youngstown. Publication of *Labor Law for the Rank and Filer* (Singlejack Books, 1978) caused him to be fired, and he now works for Legal Services.

After the Youngstown Sheet and Tube Company closed the Campbell Works in September 1977, Lynd became general counsel for the coalition which sought to reopen the mill under employee ownership. He was also lead counsel in a lawsuit filed by six local unions in December 1979, which temporarily prevented U. S. Steel from shutting its Youngstown mills. He recently represented the Homestead Works (Pennsylvania) local of the Steelworkers' union as part of the overall effort of the workers in that mill to retain their jobs.

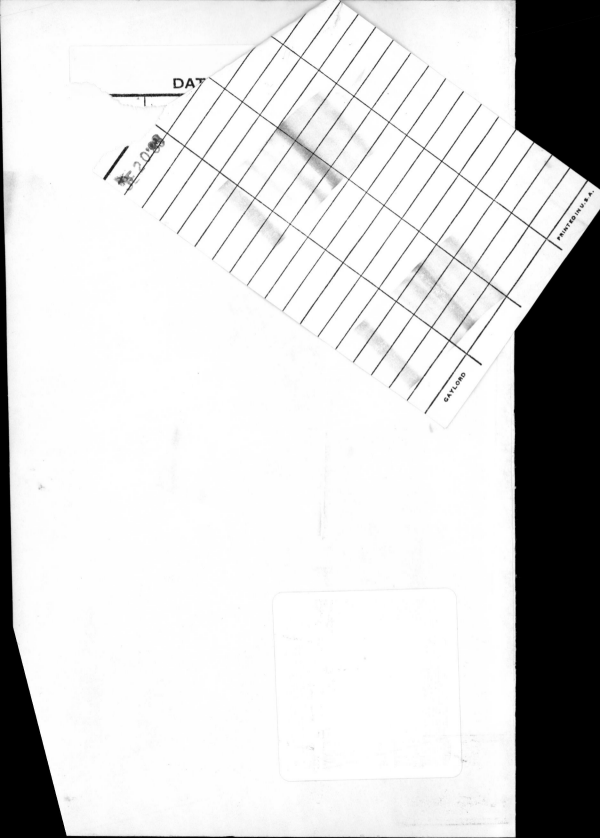

GAYLORD

PRINTED IN U.S.A.